Life-Study
of
The Psalms

Messages 1-23

Witness Lee

Living Stream Ministry
Anaheim, California

First Edition, June 1993.

ISBN 0-87083-726-5

Published by

Living Stream Ministry
1853 W. Ball Road, Anaheim, CA 92804 U.S.A.
P. O. Box 2121, Anaheim, CA 92814 U.S.A.

Printed in the United States of America

00 01 02 03 04 05 / 11 10 9 8 7 6 5 4 3 2

CONTENTS

vi

LIFE-STUDY OF THE PSALMS

MESSAGE ONE

AN INTRODUCTORY WORD

Scripture Reading: Psa. 1:2, 6; 2:6-7, 12; Luke 24:44

In a recent conference, there were four main points which I would like us to take note of in this introductory word to the Psalms:

1) The economy of God is to bring forth an organism for His Divine Trinity.

2) The law in the economy of God is to be used by God for exposing the sinful nature and evil deeds of the sinners.

3) The grace in the economy of God is God's embodiment for man to receive to be his enjoyment and supply.

4) The issue of the experience of grace in the economy of God is the organic Body of Christ, consummating in the New Jerusalem.

I praise the Lord for His sovereign arrangement in allowing us to have this conference with these four main points before we begin our life-study of the Psalms. In the Psalms we will see these four main points.

The first psalm is concerning the law. David did not know the real function of the law. He likened himself, as one who delighted in the law, to a tree growing beside streams of water and flourishing all the time (v. 3). But after Psalm 1, there is Psalm 2 concerning Christ. Then there is Psalm 3. The heading of Psalm 3 says, "A Psalm of David, when he fled from Absalom his son." The one who enjoyed the law as the streams of water by which he grew became a kind of exile due to the rebellion of his son. This happened to David because of his murder of Uriah and his taking of Uriah's wife (2 Sam. 12:10-12). The one who enjoyed the law so much in Psalm 1 became an intentional murderer. Does this show that the law works? The law does work, but not in David's way. The law works to expose us. The law exposed David to the uttermost as one who conspired to kill Uriah and rob Uriah of his wife. Does the law work or not? We have to say that the law works, not according to David's concept in Psalm 1, but according to the apostle Paul's teaching in the New Testament. Paul pointed out that the law was something added to the central line of the divine revelation to expose man's sinful nature and wicked deeds (Rom. 3:20b; 5:20a). We need this view of the law in order to understand the Psalms according to the divine concept in the New Testament. We are not in the Old Testament as David was, but we are in the New Testament.

I. THE PSALMS BEING:

A. Not a Book of Doctrines or Any Kind of Teachings

The book of Psalms is not of doctrines or of any kind of teachings. The writings of the Psalms are in the form of praises. These praises were not composed by doctrine or understanding of teachings.

B. But a Book of the Expressions of the Sentiments, Feelings, Impressions, and Experiences of Godly Men

The book of Psalms is composed of the expressions of the sentiments, feelings, impressions, and experiences of godly men. This is the very crucial key for us to understand the Psalms. If we do not pick up this key, we have no way to understand this book. Not seeing this key is a big mistake many Christians have made.

The book of Psalms is not a book of stories, but a book of divine revelation through the expressions of the sentiments, feelings, impressions, and experiences of godly men concerning eight things. We need to see what these eight things are; otherwise, we will not be able to understand the Psalms. These eight things are:

1) God and the way He is in His dealing with them.

2) The law of God as the holy Word with the divine revelation.

3) The house of God, the temple, and Mount Zion on which the temple was seated, as the center of God's dwelling place on the earth.

4) The holy city of God, Jerusalem, as the encompassing protection of the house of God.

5) The holy people of God, Israel, as God's beloved elect among the nations.

6) Their love toward God, their fellowship with God, their blessings received of God, their sufferings under God's dealing, and their environment.

7) Their captivity.

8) Their thanksgivings and praises to Jehovah their God, whom they tasted and enjoyed.

The psalmists, as godly men, loved the law, loved God, loved the temple, loved the holy city, and loved the holy people, but eventually, they were exiled. They were brought into captivity. The law, after being given, results in captivity. Jeremiah shows the pitiful captivity and exile which the people of Israel experienced. They experienced captivity upon captivity and exile upon exile. Many of them were killed by the Babylonians. A small remnant of them remained, but they would not take the word of God to remain in their holy land. Instead, they wanted to go to Egypt. They went there to be exiles (Jer. 42:1—43:7).

The Old Testament law given by God through Moses resulted altogether in captivity. Captivity came because of the failure of the carrying out of the first covenant. Because the old covenant was altogether a failure, Jeremiah said that God would make a new covenant (31:31-34). Even by the end of the time of the early apostles, the New Testament believers had entered into captivity due to the fact that they remained in the old covenant although they had been put into the new covenant. Today's Catholic Church is a mixture of the Old Testament and the New Testament. Their rituals, formalities, and even the clothing of their clergy are an Old Testament mixture. Today's Pentecostalism is also a mixture of the Old Testament with the New Testament. These are proofs that even today's New Testament believers have entered into captivity as a result of keeping the Old Testament practices with the law. Eventually, the psalmists turned from enjoying the law in which they delighted to enjoying their God whom they loved and sought after.

II. THE PSALMS WERE WRITTEN
ACCORDING TO TWO KINDS OF CONCEPTS

The Psalms were written according to two kinds of concepts. We also have to pick up this point. Otherwise, we cannot properly understand the Psalms.

A. The Human Concept of the Holy Writers

The first concept, according to which the Psalms were written, is the human concept of the holy writers. Their human concept was produced out of their good nature created by God, formed with the traditions of their holy race, constituted with the teachings of their holy Scriptures, promoted by their practice of a holy life, and uttered out of their holy sentiments and impressions. These are the constituents of the human concept of the holy writers of the Psalms. They were from a holy race, possessing the Pentateuch, the first five books of Moses. They were a greatly cultured people. The traditions of their holy race formed their human concept according to which many of the psalms were written.

B. The Divine Concept of God

The Psalms were also written according to the divine concept of God as the divine revelation. This divine concept of God as the divine revelation is concerning His eternal economy in Christ, taking Christ as its centrality and universality. It is also concerning Christ in His divinity, humanity, human living, all-inclusive death, life-imparting and seed-producing resurrection, glorification, ascension, appearing in glory, and reigning forever. All these points are clearly, and even in detail, revealed in the Psalms. The divine concept in the Psalms is also concerning God's heart's desire, His good pleasure in Christ as His centrality and universality, in the church as His fullness for His expression, in the kingdom for His eternal administration, and in the recovery of the earth for His eternal kingdom in eternity. This divine concept of God was uttered from the godly writers of the Psalms as a part of the utterance in their holy writings. The same writers uttered two kinds of concepts—the human concept and the divine concept.

We need to apply these two kinds of concepts to Psalm 1 and Psalm 2. Psalm 1 says:

1 Blessed is the man
　　Who does not walk
　　In the counsel of the wicked,
　Nor stand on the path of sinners,
　　Nor sit in the company of mockers;
2 Rather his delight is in the law of Jehovah,
　　And in His law he meditates by day and by night.
3 And he will be like a tree
　　Transplanted beside streams of water,
　Which yields its fruit in its season,
　　And whose foliage does not wither;
　　And everything he does prospers.
4 The wicked are not so,
　　But are like chaff,
　　Which the wind drives away.
5 Therefore the wicked will not stand in the judgment;
　　Nor the sinners, in the assembly of the righteous.
6 For Jehovah knows the way of the righteous,
　　But the way of the wicked will perish.

According to what concept was Psalm 1 written? Is Psalm 1 good or not? Surely it is a good psalm, yet it was written according to the human concept. In Psalm 1 the psalmist said that the one who delighted in the law of Jehovah would prosper in everything that he does, but eventually the psalmists were not prospering. They were suffering. In Psalm 73, the psalmist was bothered. He thought that he had cleansed his heart in vain because he was being plagued and chastened (vv. 13-14). On the other hand, he saw all the evil ones prospering (v. 3). He was bothered until he went into the sanctuary of God, the temple of God (v. 17). Then he received the revelation, and he was led to have nothing in the heavens nor anything on the earth but God (v. 25). So,

he declared that God was his living portion (v. 26); not the
law, but the very God Himself was his portion.

This shows us that Psalm 1 is good, but it was written
with a wrong concept. The law was not given for us to keep for
our prosperity. Instead, the law was given to expose us. The
writer of Psalm 1, David, was exposed by the law as being a
murderer and a robber of someone's wife. Because of what he
had done, the situation with his entire family became a mess.
Fornication and murder were among his children (2 Sam.
13:1-29), and rebellion came from his son, Absalom (15:7-12).
The third psalm was a psalm of David when he was fleeing
from his rebellious son. Thus, we should not highly appraise
Psalm 1. It was written wrongly with a wrong concept, a
human concept.

Now let us read Psalm 2:

1 Why are the nations in an uproar,
　　And why do the peoples contemplate a vain thing?
2 The kings of the earth take their stand,
　　And the rulers take counsel together,
　　Against Jehovah and against His Anointed:
3 Let us break apart their bonds
　　And cast their ropes away from us.
4 He who sits in the heavens laughs;
　　The Lord has them in derision.
5 Then He will speak to them in His anger,
　　And by His burning wrath He will terrify them:
6 But I have installed My King
　　Upon Zion, My holy mountain.
7 I will recount the decree of Jehovah;
　　He said to Me: You are My Son;
　　Today I have begotten You.
8 Ask of Me,
　　And I will give the nations as Your inheritance
　　And the limits of the earth as Your possession.
9 You will break them with an iron rod;
　　You will shatter them like a potter's vessel.
10 Now therefore, O kings, be prudent;
　　Take the admonition, O judges of the earth.

11 Serve Jehovah with fear,
    And rejoice with trembling.
12 Kiss the Son
      Lest He be angry and you perish from the way;
      For His anger may suddenly be kindled.
    Blessed are all those who take refuge in Him.

Jehovah's Anointed in verse 2 and the King in verse 6 are Christ. The Son in verse 7 is also Christ as the resurrected One. He was the only begotten Son of God from eternity (John 1:18; 3:16), but He needed to be begotten again in His resurrection to be the firstborn Son of God (Acts 13:33; Rom. 8:29). Psalm 2:8 says that the nations and the earth will be given to Christ. The nations will be His inheritance, and the earth will be His possession.

We need to consider why the Psalms are arranged with Psalm 1 as the first one and Psalm 2 as the second one. Psalm 1 is altogether not related to Psalm 2. David was saying that the one who delights in the law and meditates in the law will be blessed and will prosper in everything he does. While he was declaring this, God came in to make a declaration concerning Christ in Psalm 2, saying, "I have anointed Him and set Him up as the King. He will prosper because He will gain the whole earth as His possession, and He will gain all the nations as His inheritance. Blessed are those who take refuge in Him. You have to kiss Him."

These two psalms are two kinds of declarations. One is made by the psalmist according to his human concept, and the other declaration is made by God according to His divine concept, concerning Christ as His centrality and universality. We have to say amen to God's divine concept in Psalm 2. In God's eyes, it is not a matter of our keeping the law. In God's eyes, it is a matter of taking refuge in Christ and kissing Him. To take refuge in Christ means to believe in Him, and to kiss Him means to love Him. This is according to the divine concept of the New Testament. We need to believe in Christ and to love Christ. By doing this, we are blessed.

Have you seen the difference between the two concepts in the Psalms? Through one writer, David, two different declarations came out in Psalms 1 and 2. Psalm 1 was a declaration by David, and Psalm 2 was also a declaration by David. Psalm 1 was declared according to his human concept. Psalm 2 was also his declaration, but according to the divine concept. First, the human concept came out of this one speaker. But while he was speaking humanly, the tone changed! Another speaking came out according to the divine concept.

Many preachers have spoken on Psalm 1, exalting this psalm. But it is hard to find anyone who has spoken properly on Psalm 2. It seems that not many understand Psalm 2. When we read Psalms 1 and 2 in the past, we may have greatly appreciated Psalm 1. How good Psalm 1 was to us! But Psalm 2 may have been placed into the category of portions of Scripture which we did not understand. We all need to see the two kinds of concepts, human and divine, in the Psalms, as seen in Psalms 1 and 2.

C. The Human Concept of the Holy Writers Uplifting the Law as Their Central Emphasis

I hope that we would remember these points concerning the human and divine concepts in the book of Psalms. The human concept of the holy writers uplifts the law as their central emphasis to treasure the law and remain in it for their whole life.

D. The Divine Concept of the Unveiling God Exalting Christ as His Central Stress

The divine concept of the unveiling God exalts Christ as His central stress to turn the holy writers' human concept from the law to Christ according to the divine concept of the divine revelation.

III. THE CONTENTS OF THIS BOOK

A. The Book of Psalms, Composed of One Hundred Fifty Psalms, Being Divided into Five Books

The book of Psalms, composed of one hundred fifty psalms, is divided into five books. Psalms 1—41 are the first book;

Psalms 42—72 are the second book; Psalms 73—89 are the third book; Psalms 90—106 are the fourth book; and Psalms 107—150 are the fifth book. These five books can be likened to the five floors of a building. The first book is the ground floor, whereas the fifth book is the highest floor. Book Five is a book of praises with thanksgivings.

B. The Contents of the Psalms according to the Human Concept

Apparently, according to the human concept, all the Psalms are the expressions of the sentiments, feelings, and impressions of godly men who were intimately close to God.

C. The Contents of the Psalms according to the Divine Concept

Actually, according to the divine concept, the central thought of the book of Psalms is Christ, as revealed in plain words (Luke 24:44), and the church as the house of God and the city of God for His kingdom, as typified by the temple and the city of Jerusalem.

Thus, the book of Psalms is one book, but in two kinds of tones. One tone is uttered according to the human concept, and the other tone is uttered according to the divine concept. How could this be? No doubt, these holy writers were wrong in their understanding according to their human concept, but they were still godly men. They were very close to God. Therefore, while they were speaking wrongly, God came to speak through them. Because they were so intimate, so close, and even so one with God, while they were speaking, God came in to speak in their speaking. We should not separate Psalm 1 from Psalm 2. These two psalms were one speaking by David. The first psalm was uttered according to the human concept spoken by David directly. The second psalm was also David's speaking, but it was actually uttered by God.

Then in Psalms 3 through 7, there is David's tone again, but in Psalm 8 God's tone came. Psalms 3 through 7 show us how poor and full of trouble the situation on earth is. But Psalm 8 begins by saying, "O Jehovah our Lord, / How excellent is Your name / In all the earth" (v. 1). When His name is absent, the earth is a mess. When His name is here on the earth, the earth is excellent. This is the name of the One who became a human being, a little lower than the angels, and the name of the One who passed through human life and died, resurrected, and ascended to the heavens to be glorified and honored (vv. 5-6). When this One's name is on this earth, the earth becomes excellent.

Today in the newspapers murders are reported all the time. We have to warn the sisters that they should not walk home alone after the meetings in the evening. Can we say that it is excellent on the earth today? If we want to make the earth excellent, we need to preach the gospel and turn sinners into Christians. The day will come when the entire earth will be excellent because the Lord's name will eventually be excellent in all the earth. This is the divine concept. According to God's divine concept, the central thought in the five books of the Psalms is Christ and the church.

1. Book One

Book One indicates that God's intention is to turn the seeking saints from the law to Christ that they may enjoy the house of God—the church. In Book One there are forty-one psalms. In Psalm 1 the psalmist appreciated the law to the uttermost, but in Psalm 27 he no longer appreciated the law. Instead, he appreciated dwelling in the house of God to behold God's lovliness. He desired to dwell in the house of Jehovah all the days of his life (v. 4). This is to enjoy God, not the law, in God's house. Then in Psalm 36 the psalmist declared that they would be abundantly satisfied with the fatness of God's house. In God's house they could drink the river of His pleasures. The psalmist also said that with God is the fountain of life and in His light we can see light (vv. 8-9). What a difference we can see between Psalm 1 and Psalms 27 and 36. Psalm 1 begins from the ground floor, the basement. But in Psalms 27 and 36 the psalmists have gone up to the "fifth floor." They came up from the basement. If we still highly appreciate Psalm 1, we are remaining in the basement. We need to come out of the basement in our appreciation to the higher level of the divine concept.

2. Book Two

Book Two indicates that the saints experience God and His house and city through the suffering, exalted, and reigning Christ.

3. Book Three

Book Three indicates that the saints, in their experiences, realize that the house and the city of God with all the enjoyments thereof can be preserved and maintained only with Christ properly appreciated and exalted by God's people.

4. Book Four

Book Four indicates that the saints, being joined to Christ, are one with God so that He can recover His title over the earth through Christ in His house and city. Psalm 90 is the first psalm of Book Four. The title of Psalm 90 says that it is a prayer of Moses, the man of God. In the first verse, Moses says, "Lord, You have been our dwelling place / In all generations." The one who wrote the law declared that God was his eternal dwelling place. I was shocked when I read this psalm for the first time and saw that it was written by Moses. According to our thought, Moses only knew how to give the law, the Ten Commandments.

When we read the Ten Commandments, do we feel that they bring us close to God? After reading these commandments, a number of Christians would say that they cannot make it since they break the commandments all the time. People lie frequently and spontaneously. Someone may call on the telephone and ask, "Is your father home?" Then the person would say that he is not home, even though his father is there reading the newspaper. People lie to one another all the time. The children lie to their parents. The husbands lie to their wives and vice versa. People also break the commandment concerning not coveting again and again. When we see others with possessions better than ours, we covet what they have. A person covets another person's expensive car. A young boy in school covets another boy's expensive pen. The commandments of the law are impossible for fallen man to keep.

The law does not bring people close to God. However, the law does escort people to Christ. The law of God is the custodian and child-conductor of God's chosen people to bring them to Christ (Gal. 3:23-24).

When Moses, the one who wrote the Ten Commandments, became old, he declared, "O God, You are our dwelling place for eternity. I am not actually living on this earth. I am living in You. I am dwelling in You. You are my dwelling." This is the introductory word to Book Four of the Psalms.

5. Book Five

Book Five indicates that the house and the city of God become the praise, safety, and desire of the saints, and that Christ comes to reign over the whole earth through the house and the city of God—the church.

This is the content of the five books of the Psalms. We need to pick up all of these crucial points in this introductory word. Then we will be prepared and qualified to study the book of Psalms. We will be able to receive the real and genuine interpretation of all one hundred fifty psalms.

We need to see that, on the one hand, the book of Psalms was written according to the human concept, and on the other hand, it was written according to the divine concept. If we do not see this, our understanding will be natural, and the Psalms will be understood by us according to the human concept. In our understanding of the Psalms, we will not have anything of the divine concept. We all need to be brought into the divine concept of the unveiling God. We need to be turned from the law to Christ according to the divine concept.

LIFE-STUDY OF THE PSALMS

MESSAGE TWO

CHRIST IN GOD'S ECONOMY
VERSUS THE LAW IN MAN'S APPRECIATION

(1)

Scripture Reading: Psa. 1:1-6; Rom. 5:20; Gal. 4:24-25; Rom.
7:12, 14a; Psa. 119:103, 105, 130; 2 Tim. 3:16a; Exo. 20:3-17;
Psa. 78:5; 119:88b; Rom. 3:20b; 4:15b; 5:20b; 7:7b; Gal.
3:23-24; Rom. 3:19; Gal. 3:21b; Rom. 8:3a; 3:20a; Gal. 3:11a,
12b; Psa. 36:8; 1 Cor. 3:6; John 4:10, 14; Rev. 21:6; 22:1, 17b;
John 7:38-39; Psa. 73:1-7, 13-17, 23-26; Matt. 5:10; Psa. 1:5-6;
Rom. 2:12; Rom. 10:4a; 6:14b

In the previous message, we gave an introductory word
concerning the Psalms. In this message we want to see the
truth concerning Christ in God's economy versus the law in
man's appreciation.

I. THE LAW IN MAN'S APPRECIATION

Psalm 1 is concerning the law in man's appreciation (v. 2).
I hope that we will receive a clear view to see this Psalm. We
need to see the truth concerning the law in its position, its
nature, its content, its function, and its weakness. We need to
fight the battle against the wrong teachings concerning the
law which are not in the light of God's New Testament economy. Among Christians there are two schools concerning the
law. One school is positive and the other school is very negative. The top person in the negative school related to the law
is the apostle Paul. Concerning the law, he was negative to
the uttermost. I want to point out some of the points he
stressed in his teaching concerning the law.

In Romans and in Galatians, Paul stressed that no flesh,
no fallen human being, can be justified before God by the

works of the law (Rom. 3:20a; Gal. 2:16; 3:11a). To work to be justified by the law is to labor in vain. In Romans 7 Paul told us that the law, instead of giving us life, becomes the killing instrument by which sin deceives and kills us (v. 11). Do we like something that kills us? David was wrong to exalt and appreciate something by which we can be killed. This shows us how negative Paul was in his view concerning the law.

I want to raise up Paul's argument as my argument against the law. Some may say that Paul told us in Romans 7 that the law is holy, righteous, good (v. 12), and even spiritual (v. 14a). But this is only in its nature. In nature the law is holy, righteous, good, and spiritual, but we also need to see what Paul says concerning its position, its function, and its weakness.

A. Its Position

We need to consider what the position of the law is. In order to see the law's position, we have to take Paul's teaching.

1. Entering In alongside the Main Line of God's Economy

The first thing we need to see concerning the position of the law is that the law entered in alongside the main line of God's economy (Rom. 5:20a). Because of this, the law does not have an orthodox position. It was not orthodox because it entered in alongside the main line of God's economy.

Many today do not see this main line. Instead, they teach the Bible according to the natural way, without any governing principles. Over sixty years ago, I first heard that we have to interpret the Bible with the proper principles. When I heard that, I was asking myself, "What are the principles for us to understand the Bible?" At that time, I did not understand, but gradually I came into the proper realization of the governing principles of understanding and interpreting the Bible. In this message I am interpreting the Word according to these principles.

The principle we need to see concerning the law is this—Paul in Romans 5:20a told us that the law entered in alongside.

The Greek word here also means to "come in alongside." The law did not come in by itself. It came in alongside of something. This means that the main line of God's economy was there already.

After the creation of man, however, something happened. Satan came in, sin followed Satan, and man became fallen. Thus, man became a fallen man constituted with sin to be a sinner. God created man in His own image and after His own likeness (Gen. 1:26) with the intention that man could take in God, live God, and express God. The main line of God's economy began with man and was on the way when something happened. A "car accident" occurred. Therefore, the law needed to come in alongside the main line of God's economy. This should help us to understand Paul's word in Romans 5:20a.

The law was not originally ordained and arranged by God. In God's original economy, there was not such a thing. God in His economy planned to create and to have a man in His image and after His likeness that man one day could receive Him as life to live Him and to manifest Him so that He might have an organism to express His Divine Trinity. But Satan came in to deceive man, and Satan and man became one. The man created by God in His own image was constituted by Satan with Satan's nature to be a sinful man. Now God had to fix the situation. Would God keep man out of His plan, forgetting about man? Of course, God would never do that because He is the Alpha and also the Omega (Rev. 22:13). He cannot start anything without completing it.

In order to continue His purpose with man after man's fall, God added something to the main line of His economy. The Chinese version of the Bible says in Romans 5:20 that the law was added. It was something in addition to grace. The law was in addition to the orthodox line of grace in God's economy.

2. As a Concubine, Symbolized by Hagar

Second, the position of the law is that of a concubine, symbolized by Hagar (Gal. 4:24-25). Paul told us in Galatians 4 that Abraham had two wives. One was the orthodox

wife, Sarah, and the other was the concubine, Hagar
(vv. 22-31). We all know that a man's concubine does not have
an orthodox position. Paul indicated that Sarah signifies
the new covenant of grace, and he pointed out that Hagar
symbolizes the old covenant of the law. Thus, the law's position is that of a concubine.

In God's creation, He did not ordain man to have a concubine. He ordained that man should have one wife (Matt.
19:3-9). Anyone that has more than one wife enters into
corruption. We should not try to bring a concubine into God's
economy. If we are appreciating and uplifting the law, we are
bringing a concubine into God's economy. This is absolutely
against God's ordination.

The law as a concubine entered in alongside the main line
of God's economy. Whoever is of the law is a child of the
concubine, not a son of the free woman. The law does not have
an orthodox position. The followers of the law are not the
children of the orthodox wife. Ishmael, the son of the concubine, Hagar, was looked down on and was chased away. He
was chased away from the main line of God's economy,
the line of grace. We must remember this point in our interpretation of Psalm 1. The writer of Psalm 1 uplifted the law
according to the human concept, which is contradicting to the
main line of God's economy.

B. Its Nature

1. Holy, Righteous, and Good

Now we need to see the nature of the law. In its nature, the
law is holy, righteous, and good (Rom. 7:12).

2. Spiritual

The law is also spiritual (7:14a). This is because the law
was God's speaking. Since the Ten Commandments are God's
speaking, they are God's breathing. All Scripture is God-
breathed (2 Tim. 3:16a). The entire Pentateuch, the first five
books of the Bible considered as the law, is God's breathing.
God's breathing, of course, is altogether spiritual. Thus, in
this sense, the law is spiritual.

Although the position of the law is not right, the nature of the law is good. This is the point where troubles can arise in our understanding. The positive school stands on the nature of the law. They point out that Paul said that the law is holy, righteous, good, and even spiritual. Then they ask, "How could you say the law is negative?" It is true that the nature of the law is good and spiritual, but its position is wrong. A lady may be good and spiritual in her nature, yet still be a concubine. This lady may be a "golden" lady, a spiritual lady, but she does not have an orthodox position.

The nature of the law is good because the law is spiritual, being the word of God (Psa. 119:103, 105, 130) and the breath of God (2 Tim. 3:16a). This is why we may have a problem in our understanding of the law when we come to Psalm 119. We need to realize that Psalm 119 refers to the word again and again. No other psalm refers to the law as God's word so much. In verses 147-148, the psalmist said that he anticipated the morning dawn that he might meditate in the Lord's word. The psalmist said here that he meditated, not in the law but in the word. Psalm 119:103 does not say that the law is so sweet. Instead, the psalmist declares here how sweet the Lord's word is to his taste. Because the law is the word of God, it is good and spiritual in its nature.

C. Its Content

1. The Ten Commandments

Now we need to see the content of the law. The content of the law mainly is the Ten Commandments. We need to analyze the Ten Commandments in a proper way. The first three commandments require man to have only God and not have any idols (Exo. 20:3-7). The first commandment says that we should not have another god, the second is that we should not make idols, and the third is that we should not worship idols.

The fourth commandment is concerning keeping the Sabbath (vv. 8-11). To keep the Sabbath is to take God and all He has created for us as our satisfaction and rest. The fourth commandment requires man to have satisfaction and rest only in God and all that God has accomplished for man. God created the heavens and the earth with billions of items for us. On the sixth day, the last day of God's creating work, God created man. Man came out of the creating hand of God with everything ready. The universe was just like a wedding room. Before the bride comes, the wedding room is fully prepared. Man came out of God's creating hand, and everything was ready for man. God worked for six days, and the seventh day was the day of rest, the Sabbath, for man to enjoy God and God's work as his rest and satisfaction.

The fifth commandment requires man to honor his parents that man might trace back to man's source—God who created man (v. 12). If we trace our genealogy back to the beginning of creation, we come to the first pair of parents, Adam and Eve. Adam and Eve came from God. When we honor our parents, we trace back to God.

We should have a heart to honor our parents, but quite often, we fallen people do not honor our parents as we should. Today in this evil age many people want to put away their parents when their parents become old. To lose our parents, though, is a big loss. If we honor our parents, we realize something of God as our source. The fifth commandment concerning honoring our parents goes with the foregoing commandments. The Ten Commandments were written on two tablets. The first tablet covers the first five commandments, from having only God to honoring our parents.

The last five commandments were on another tablet as a group. These commandments are concerning the prohibition of murder, fornication, stealing, lying, and covetousness (vv. 13-17). These five commandments may not seem so sweet, but they are very good for mankind. The sixth through the tenth commandments require man to live out the virtues that express God according to God's attributes.

The law of most major countries today is based on Roman law, and Roman law was based upon and written according to the Mosaic law, the Ten Commandments. The Ten Commandments are so brief, yet they are so complete and all-embracing. They cover our relationship with God, our relationship with our parents, and our relationship with others. If a man did not kill people, did not commit fornication, did not steal and rob, did not tell lies, and did not covet, he would be the top ethical person.

However, we need to ask ourselves whether or not we have been successful in keeping these commandments. Actually, according to the Lord's word in Matthew, we have broken these commandments. The Lord said that everyone who is angry with his brother shall be liable to the judgment (5:21-22). Eventually, the Lord Jesus, in interpreting the Ten Commandments, did not deal merely with the act of murder, but with anger, the motive of murder. To be angry and to hate others is equal to killing in the Lord's higher law of the kingdom of the heavens. This is logical. If you are not angry and do not hate, you could never kill anyone. Killing comes out of anger and hating. The Lord Jesus also went deeper in His teaching concerning the outward act of adultery. Again, He dealt with the inward motive of the heart (Matt. 5:27-28). When Paul was in the Jewish religion, he endeavored to keep every item of the Ten Commandments, but later he testified that he had no way to keep the last commandment—"You shall not covet" (Rom. 7:7-8). This commandment is not related to outward conduct, but rather to the sin within man.

In order to illustrate this, I would like to relate a story about a missionary speaking to his cook about man's sinfulness. This Chinese cook was a proud, ethical person. He had the attitude that the foreigners who came to China did many things wrong, but he did not do anything wrong. The missionary knew this. One day he asked the cook if he was sinful. Then the missionary said, "Of course, I know you would say that you are not sinful. But, let me know what you are thinking about right now. Right now, tell me the truth. What are you thinking within?" This cook then confessed to the missionary that he was jealous of the missionary's having a big horse and that he was thinking about how he could get this horse. Then the missionary replied, "This is coveting. Are you not sinful?" The cook had to admit that he was sinful.

Even as you are reading this message, perhaps there is something in your heart right now which is violating the law.

If a certain sister were to tell me right now what is in her heart, she might say, "This morning a sister offended me, and I cannot forgive her. I am still thinking about how she offended me!" This is evil. The law exposes our sinful nature and evil deeds. The law is holy, righteous, good, and spiritual in its nature, but the function of the law is another matter.

2. A Portrait of God, Hence, the Testimony of God

In its content the law is also a portrait of God, hence, the testimony of God (Psa. 78:5; 119:88b). The law, the Ten Commandments, is a photo of God. Because it is a photo of God, it is a testimony. This is like saying that our picture is a testimony of ourselves. The psalmists referred to the law as the testimony of God.

D. Its Function

1. To Expose Men in Their Sinful Nature and Evil Deeds

The function of the law is to expose men in their sinful nature and evil deeds (Rom. 3:20b; 4:15b; 5:20b; 7:7b). In this sense, the law works as a mirror. If we do not look in a mirror, we cannot see how dirty our face is. But when we look at the mirror, the dirty condition of our face is exposed. The law works like a mirror to expose our sinful nature and evil deeds.

2. To Guard the Chosen People of God and Escort Them to Christ

Furthermore, in its function the law was used by God to guard His chosen people and escort them to Christ (Gal. 3:23-24). Paul told us in Galatians that before Christ came, God gave His chosen people the law as a guardian to guard them. Then when Christ came, this guardian was used by God to escort and bring them to Christ. By being exposed by the law, subdued by the law, and convinced by the law, God's chosen people would go through the law to Christ.

3. *To Subdue Men as Sinners under God's Judgment*

The law also functions to subdue men as sinners under God's judgment (Rom. 3:19). We need to see the law in this light. God's purpose in giving the law was to expose man, to subdue man, and to guard or keep God's chosen ones for Christ that they may be led to Christ. If we stayed only in the book of Psalms, we could not receive this kind of light. This light comes altogether from Paul's teaching.

E. Its Weakness

1. *Not Able to Give Life*

The law is good and spiritual, but it is weak. In its weakness, it is not able to give life (Gal. 3:21b). Regardless of how good, how holy, how righteous, and how spiritual the law is, the law cannot impart life to us. We sinners were not only evil but also dead (Eph. 2:1). The basic thing we need is life. The good law, the righteous law, the holy law, the spiritual law, is good, but it cannot impart life into us.

2. *Not Able to Do That Which God Wants Because It Is Weak through the Flesh*

Furthermore, the law is not able to do that which God wants because it is weak through the flesh (Rom. 8:3a). The law itself may not be that weak, but the law is given to the flesh, and the flesh is the law's companion. The law is not that weak, but its companion, the flesh, is weak to the uttermost. We need to consider how weak we are. Many of the sisters are easily offended. If you offend them, they will not forget it. To remember another person's faults is not good. The Bible tells us that forgiving means forgetting (Heb. 8:12). As long as we still remember another's fault, this indicates that we have not forgiven him. The proper forgiving is to forget. Forgiving and forgetting seem to be a small thing, but we cannot fully overcome in this matter. This shows that we are weak. Because we are weak, we are the instrument to the law, so the law becomes weak.

Out of the works of the law no flesh will be justified before

God (Rom. 3:20a; Gal. 3:11a). This is repeated by Paul in both Romans and Galatians.

F. Being the Center and Requirement of the Old Covenant

The law was the center and requirement of the old covenant. The law was for the old covenant in God's economy.

G. To Be Performed by Men's Work

The law, as the requirement of the old covenant, is to be performed by men's work (Gal. 3:12b). The law has to be performed. Without man's performance, the law means nothing.

H. Concerning the Personal Benefit of the Saints, Such as Being Blessed in Prosperity

Psalm 1, which is concerning the law in man's appreciation, is for the personal benefit of the saints, such as being blessed in prosperity (vv. 1-3). We need to compare this to Christ's attainments concerning the accomplishment of the economy of God in Psalm 2. Psalm 1 is for the personal benefit of the saints, and Psalm 2 is for the accomplishment of the economy of God. The concept in Psalm 1 is very low compared with the revelation in Psalm 2.

I. Appreciated and Uplifted by Godly Men according to Their Human, Ethical Concept

In Psalm 1 the law was appreciated and uplifted by godly men according to their human, ethical concept (vv. 2-3). Psalm 1 and a number of other psalms show the human, ethical concept of these godly men in uplifting the law. Psalm 1:2-3 says, "His delight is in the law of Jehovah, / And in His law he meditates by day and by night. / And he will be like a tree / Transplanted beside streams of water, / Which yields its fruit in its season, / And whose foliage does not wither; / And everything he does prospers." The human concept in Psalm 1 is one of appreciating and uplifting the law.

1. The Concept of a Tree Absorbing the Water of the Streams Not Being as High as the Concept of Drinking of the River of God's Pleasures in Psalm 36:8

One concept in Psalm 1:2-3 is that of a tree absorbing the nearby water, and the other concept in Psalm 36:8 is that of drinking of the river of God's pleasures in God's house. The concept of drinking is the highest. All of the one hundred fifty psalms, composed in five books, were arranged in a good sequence. They go progressively up and up, step by step, to the highest level of revelation. Also, the end of each book is higher than its beginning. Book One contains forty-one psalms. Psalm 36 is much higher than Psalm 1. In Psalm 36 the psalmist says, "Now I can enjoy the abundance of Your house, Your temple, and I can drink in Your temple the river of Your pleasures" (v. 8). The psalmist here does not talk about the law. He has come up from the first floor to the thirty-sixth floor. When we compare Psalm 1 with Psalm 36, we can see the difference.

2. The New Testament Having Both the Concept of Plants Absorbing Water and the Concept of Drinking the Living Water of the Divine River to Flow Rivers of Living Water

The New Testament has both the concept of plants absorbing water and the concept of drinking the living water of the divine river to flow rivers of living water (1 Cor. 3:6; John 4:10, 14; Rev. 21:6; 22:1, 17b; John 7:38-39). In 1 Corinthians 3:6 Paul said that he planted and Apollos watered. There we can see the concept of plants absorbing water. In John and Revelation, we see that when we drink the river of living water, we flow rivers from within us.

Do we want to absorb a little bit of water from a nearby stream, or will we be "crazy" to drink of the living water and flow rivers out from within us? Are we satisfied to stay in

Psalm 1? Where should we go? We should go to Revelation 22! Revelation 22 is the last "psalm." In Psalm 1 we absorb a little water bit by bit. Sometimes a river may be dry, with no water for the tree to absorb. But in the last "psalm," in the last chapter of Revelation, a river of water of life is flowing for us to drink. This is much higher than absorbing water as a tree.

3. The Concept of Likening the Saints to a Tree Not Being as High as the Concept of Unveiling the New Testament Believers as Branches of the True Vine—Christ—in John 15

Moreover, the concept of likening the saints to a tree is not as high as the concept of unveiling the New Testament believers as branches of the true vine—Christ—in John 15. Today are we merely trees or are we branches? If we are trees, we stand by ourselves. That is poor because Christ is separated from us, and, in a sense, we are competing with Him, since He is a tree and we also are a tree. But the New Testament revelation eventually shows us that we are not actually God's plants by ourselves. We are God's plants by being grafted into Christ to be made branches of Christ as the great true vine. It is higher to be the branches of the true vine than it is to be an individual tree.

The local churches are not many trees. The churches are actually one tree with millions of branches. This one tree is Christ, the great vine tree, and we are the branches of this tree. We are the members of Christ (1 Cor. 6:15a; Rom. 12:5). All the churches are one Body, one tree. All the believers are members of this Body and the branches of this unique tree.

4. The Human Concept in Psalm 1 Being That the Man Who Delights in the Law of God Prospers in Everything, but the Experience of the Psalmist in Psalm 73 Being the Opposite

The human concept in Psalm 1 is that the man who delights in the law of God prospers in everything. But the experience of the psalmist in Psalm 73:1-7, 13-17, and 23-26 is the opposite. He was godly and, no doubt, he delighted in the law of God; yet he suffered a lot and the ungodly prospered. Eventually, he was instructed, in the sanctuary of God, to take only God Himself as his portion, not anything other than God.

The godly psalmist in Psalm 73 was bothered. He was delighting in the law, but he suffered greatly while the evil ones prospered. He was bothered until he entered into the sanctuary of God, that is, into God's house. Then he became clear. There under God's revelation, he was instructed just to have God Himself as his portion. Eventually he declared that he had no one in the heavens nor anyone on this earth except God, his eternal portion (vv. 25-26).

If the Lord wills, we will study the minor prophets in this upcoming summer training of 1992. Then in the winter we hope to study Job. In the book of Job, there is a big controversy. Job suffered greatly. His family, his property, and his health were destroyed (Job 1:13—2:8). Then Job's three friends came to speak with him. What they spoke was nonsense. They told Job that he must have been wrong in something. Otherwise, God would not punish him in this way. Job contended with them by saying that he was wrong in nothing. These three friends spoke to Job one by one again and again throughout the book of Job. Job, however, would not be subdued by them. Eventually, God came in and stopped everyone's mouth. God's speaking to Job opened his eyes. Job said, "I have heard of thee by the hearing of the ear; but now mine eye seeth thee" (Job 42:5). Job heard about God, but he never saw God. After passing through his sufferings, he saw God. If someone who loves the Lord is suffering, his suffering is not basically a matter of his being right or wrong. What God is concerned with is our having more of God in our inward being.

About three or four years ago, I went to see my eye doctor for a check-up. He has been taking care of me since 1975, and he performed surgery on my eyes to remove cataracts. I told him that my eyes were bothering me, and I asked him why. He responded by saying, "These are Job's sufferings." By this he indicated to me that my suffering was without any reason and that he could not help me any more. Job's sufferings always come from God's assignment. Every parent expects to have good children, and they may wonder why their children are bad. A brother may wonder why his wife is not as nice as other wives, and a sister may wonder why her husband is so incapable. These are Job's sufferings. Today I am still experiencing Job's sufferings.

5. The Lord's Teaching in the New Testament Being "Blessed Are Those Who Are Persecuted [Not Prosperous] for the Sake of Righteousness"

The Lord's teaching in the New Testament says, "Blessed are those who are persecuted [not prosperous] for the sake of righteousness" (Matt. 5:10). A brother may be one who hungers and thirsts for righteousness (v. 6), yet he is persecuted. I would not say that this persecution is Job's sufferings, but I would say that it is according to God's economy.

J. People to Whom the Law Was Given Will Be Judged according to the Law

People to whom the law was given will be judged according to the law (Psa. 1:5-6; Rom. 2:12). Paul tells us in Romans 2:12 that all human beings will stand before God to be judged one day. But those who have received the law will be judged by God according to the law. Those who never received the law will be judged by God according to their conscience (vv. 15-16).

K. Ended by Christ

The law has been ended by Christ (Rom. 10:4a). Christ is the end of the law, the close of the law, the replacement of the law. Christ came to fulfill the law (Matt. 5:17) that He might terminate the law and replace it (Rom. 8:3-4). Thus, everyone who believes in Him receives God's righteousness, which is Christ Himself.

L. The New Testament Believers Not Being under the Law

The New Testament believers are not under the law (Rom. 6:14b). Hallelujah! We are no longer under the law, but we are now under grace.

LIFE-STUDY OF THE PSALMS

MESSAGE THREE

CHRIST IN GOD'S ECONOMY
VERSUS THE LAW IN MAN'S APPRECIATION

(2)

Scripture Reading: Psa. 2:1-12; John 1:41; Matt. 3:16-17; Luke 4:18-19; Heb. 1:9; Acts 10:38; Dan. 9:26a; Acts 13:33; Heb. 1:5-6; Acts 2:36; 5:31; Rev. 1:5a; 2:26-27; Acts 4:25-29a; Rev. 6:15-17; Acts 17:30; John 3:16; 21:15a

In the previous message, we saw the truth concerning the law in its position, its nature, its content, its function, and its weakness. Psalm 1 is according to the human concept of uplifting and treasuring the law, whereas Psalm 2 is according to the divine concept of exalting Christ as God's central stress.

Perhaps we can receive further help by considering stanza 3 of *Hymns*, #541:

> Not philosophy nor
>   Any element
> Can to Christ conform us
>   As His complement;
> But 'tis Christ Himself who
>   All our nature takes
> And in resurrection
>   Us His members makes.

No philosophy, element, or religion can conform us to Christ. The law of Moses cannot conform us to Christ. Only Christ can conform us to Himself, and nothing else. Some may be bothered that we are belittling religion. They may say, "We are Christians; shouldn't we love Christianity?" But we need to be those who love Christ, not any "anity." Nothing can or should replace Christ.

Christ conforms us to Himself so that we can be His complement. To be Christ's complement means that we are a part of Him. This is like Eve being a complement to Adam. Only Christ can make us a part of Him as His complement. The law cannot make us members of Christ. Only Christ can make us His members in resurrection.

We need to see Psalm 1 in the light of the economy of God. This psalm says that those who meditate in the law will be like a tree absorbing the water from the streams, but according to the New Testament revelation this is not very high. Eventually, the New Testament tells us that the river of living water gets into us (John 7:38; 4:14). Do we want to be a tree by the side of a river or do we want to have the river flowing within us? Which is better and which is higher? The thought of a river flowing within us is the ultimate concept of the Bible (Rev. 22:1). To be a tree planted by the river to absorb its supply of water is good, but it is not the best. Paul said that he planted and Apollos watered (1 Cor. 3:6). The thought here is the same as that of a tree absorbing water, but this is not as high as the thought of the river of water of life flowing within us. This is God's ultimate thought.

In my youth I was taught that when we study the Bible, we have to get the secret of the Bible. Later, Brother Nee told us that we have to know the spirit of the Bible. The Bible, the written Word, has a spirit. The Lord Jesus said, "The words which I have spoken to you are spirit and are life" (John 6:63). This shows us that the Word is the Spirit (Eph. 6:17). Not only is the Spirit in the Word, but also the Word itself is the Spirit. Furthermore, John 1:1 says, "In the beginning was the Word...and the Word was God." The Word is God, and the Word is the Spirit. Thus, God, the Word, and the Spirit are one.

When we come to the Bible, we should not think that we are coming to an ordinary book. We should not read it as we would a magazine or a newspaper. We have to realize that the Bible is God's Word, and the Word is God's embodiment, Christ. Christ is the Word of God. Also, whatever He as the Word of God utters, whatever is spoken out of His mouth, is the Spirit. Psalm 1 is the Word of God. Paul told us that all Scripture is God-breathed (2 Tim. 3:16a). If we take this

position when we read Psalm 1, we will receive the Spirit,
we will see the secret, and we will also see the spirit of the
Bible.

Does the spirit of the Bible reveal to us the law of Moses,
exalting the law given at Mount Sinai? On the mount of
transfiguration, Peter put Moses and Elijah on the same level
as Christ (Matt. 17:1-13). When Moses and Elijah appeared
with Christ, Peter became excited. He said, "Lord, it is good
for us to be here; if You are willing, I will make three tents
here, one for You and one for Moses and one for Elijah" (v. 4).
Then God said, "This is My Son, the Beloved, in whom I have
found My delight. Hear Him!" (v. 5). In God's New Testament
economy, we should no longer hear Moses (the law) or Elijah
(the prophets). The Bible does not exalt the law or the
prophets. The spirit of the Bible exalts only one person—
Christ.

We must understand why Psalms 1 and 2 were sovereignly
arranged in this way. Psalm 1 is concerning the keeping of the
law. Immediately after Psalm 1, Christ is in Psalm 2 as the
exalted One. The spirit of the Bible, from Genesis 1 through
Revelation 22, reveals only Christ as the prominent One, as
the first One, as God's centrality and universality. Eventually,
the Bible concludes with a new city. The new city, the New
Jerusalem, will be a complement of Christ and a complement
to Christ. The spirit of the Bible does not exalt anything or
anyone other than Christ.

Paul, in his fourteen Epistles, fought a battle to put down
everything other than Christ. In his Epistle to the Galatians,
Paul put down the law, circumcision, tradition, and religion.
To him all things other than Christ were refuse (Phil. 3:8).
He exalted only Christ.

In Paul's last visit to Jerusalem, he went to the elders,
and the leading elder at that time was James. James told
him, "You observe, brother, how many thousands there are
among the Jews who have believed; and all are zealous for the
law" (Acts 21:20). James exalted the law. I believe that he
exalted the law higher than David did in Psalm 1. James
declared that there were thousands of Jewish Christians who
were enthusiastic for the law. The Greek word for *thousands*

means myriads or tens of thousands. Tens of thousands of
Jewish brothers were all burning for the law. James was
concerned that these ones would dispute with Paul, since
they had heard that Paul put down the law. History tells us
that James was a man of prayer, a pious, godly, and devoted
man. In his Epistle he taught the practical virtues of
Christian perfection. But we need to see that James, the
elders in Jerusalem, and many thousands of Jewish believers
were still in a mixture of the Christian faith and the Mosaic
law.

In this message, I want us to check with ourselves. Is our
spirit for the law or for Christ? We may say that we are for
Christ, but we are also for the law. Our being for Christ is
mostly in theory, but our being for the law is very practical.
We act mostly according to the law, according to yes and no,
right and wrong, and not according to Christ. We even educate
and teach our children according to right and wrong. A parent
may say to his child, "That is not right; you shouldn't do it."
But have we ever said, "That is not Christ; you shouldn't do
it"? Who ever tells someone not to do something because that
is not Christ? This should help us to realize that we are for
Christ in theory, but actually we practice the law. Do we
practice Christ or the law? To practice Christ is to get out of
the realm of yes and no, right and wrong, good and evil. This
means that we get out of the realm of the tree of the knowledge of good and evil. We may say that our spirit is for Christ,
but in practice we live according to the law, according to what
is right and wrong, good and evil.

The book of Psalms shows us the contrast between the
law and Christ. The first psalm is concerning keeping the law,
and the second psalm tells us to kiss Christ. Which is higher?
I am not asking which one is right or wrong, but which one
is higher. Surely, kissing the Son is higher than keeping the
law.

I think that David's devotion to the law in Psalm 1 was
higher than our devotion to Christ. This is because he said
that he meditated in the law day and night. Do we meditate
on Christ day and night? If we meditate on Christ for a short

time, we think this is wonderful, but David meditated in the law day and night.

I am sharing this to show us that we secretly, unconsciously, and subconsciously hold our natural concept in coming to the Bible. This is why we do not receive the revelation from the Bible into us. Instead, we insert our concept into the Bible. We should not exalt the keeping of the law, because the book of Psalms itself does not go along with this. If we are exalting the keeping of the law in Psalm 1, we are then confronted with Psalm 2. Psalm 2 is God's speaking, God's declaration, concerning Christ as the center of His economy. He declares, "I have installed My King / Upon Zion, My holy mountain" (v. 6). This is not ordinary speaking, but a declaration and a proclamation.

God proclaimed to all His people that He had installed His King upon Mount Zion, not Mount Sinai. These two mountains—Mount Zion and Mount Sinai—are very significant. Hebrews 12 says that we have not come to Mount Sinai but to Mount Zion (vv. 18-22). Mount Sinai was the place where the law was given, and Mount Zion is the place where Christ is today in the heavens in His ascension.

Paul speaks of these mountains in Galatians 4. Mount Sinai produces children of slavery, but our mother, the Jerusalem above, is in the heavens, at Mount Zion (vv. 25-26). Revelation 14:1 tells us that there are a hundred and forty-four thousand standing with the Lamb on Mount Zion. These hundred and forty-four thousand are not praising God for the law given at Mount Sinai. Mount Zion is not a place to show us the law, the commandments. It is a place to show us Christ — only Christ. Mount Sinai is in the Bible, but the spirit of the Bible does not exalt it. Instead, the Bible puts Mount Sinai down to a lower place. The spirit of the Bible exalts only Christ.

The sad thing is that many of God's chosen people forget about Christ. They believe in Christ, but they do not know Christ or care for Christ. Instead, they care for the law. Paul said, "For to me, to live is Christ" (Phil. 1:21a). We might say, "For to me to live is yes and no, good and evil, right and wrong." What mountain are we on today? Nearly all of us are on Mount Sinai. We are not disciples of Moses but disciples of Christ. However, we are on the wrong mountain. Christ is on Mount Zion. He is not on Mount Sinai, but we still linger there. Many of us dare not say good-bye to the law. Instead, we want to stay with the law as a follower of David, meditating in the law day and night.

We need to see that the entire revelation of the Bible is progressive. The revelation in the holy Word proceeds higher and higher from Genesis to its peak in Revelation. Genesis 1 speaks of God's creation, but Revelation 22 speaks of the New Jerusalem. God's creation is somewhat easy to understand, but the sign of the New Jerusalem is a great mystery. The revelation of the New Jerusalem is high and profound to the uttermost.

The five books of the Psalms were arranged in the same progressive way as the entire Bible was arranged. From the first book of the Psalms to the fifth book, the revelation proceeds higher and higher. The fifth book is full of the psalmists' praising of God. God is embodied in Christ, Christ is in His Body, and His Body is God's house and God's city for God's kingdom. This is all for God's economy. The central thought of the book of Psalms is Christ and the church as the house of God and the city of God for His kingdom.

II. CHRIST IN GOD'S ECONOMY

We need to see the revelation concerning Christ in God's economy versus the law in man's appreciation in the Psalms. In the previous message, we saw the truth concerning the law in man's appreciation. Now we need to see the divine revelation of Christ in God's economy in Psalm 2 (vv. 2, 6-9, 12).

A. A Declaration of God according to His Divine Concept

Psalm 2 is a declaration of God according to His divine concept. Psalm 1, however, is according to the natural, human concept. David thought that the one who meditated in the law day and night would prosper in everything. This is according to the human concept of doing something for one's

personal benefit and gain. There is no consideration in
Psalm 1 for God's economy.

B. Exalting Christ as the Center
of the Economy of God

Psalm 2 exalts Christ as the center of the economy of God.
Although the word *economy* is not in Psalm 2, the revelation
and reality of God's economy are there. In this psalm God
declared that He had installed His King (v. 6). For God to
have a King is for the fulfilling of His economy. Then God
said, "I will give the nations as Your inheritance / And the
limits of the earth as Your possession" (v. 8). This is for a kingdom. Of course, the King needs a kingdom, and this kingdom
is not small. It is a great kingdom of all the nations, covering
the limits of the entire earth. This will be the biggest kingdom in human history. Christ will possess all the continents.
His kingdom will be everywhere to include everyone. The
King and the kingdom in Psalm 2 show us the economy of
God.

1. Anointed in His Divinity in Eternity by God
to Be the Messiah—Christ—the Anointed One

Psalm 2 reveals Christ, the Anointed One (v. 2). Among
the Brethren, there was a debate concerning when Christ
was anointed. Daniel 9:26 says that Messiah would be cut
off, crucified. *Messiah* is a Hebrew word, and the Greek
equivalent is *Christ*. They both mean the Anointed One.
Daniel 9:26 shows that before Christ was incarnated and
crucified, He was already the Anointed One. Therefore,
Christ was anointed in His divinity in eternity by God to be
the Messiah—Christ—the Anointed One. This is also based
upon John 1:41, where the Lord's disciple Andrew told Simon,
his brother, that he had found the Messiah, the Anointed One.
This indicates that Christ was anointed in eternity in His
divinity before His incarnation.

2. Anointed in His Humanity in Time
at His Baptism

He came as the Anointed One to accomplish God's eternal

plan. He became a man and He was anointed again in His humanity in time at the time of His baptism (Matt. 3:16-17; Luke 4:18-19; Heb. 1:9; Acts 10:38).

3. Cut Off—Crucified

After passing through thirty-three and a half years of human living, Christ was cut off (Dan. 9:26). That means He was crucified.

4. Resurrected to Be Begotten as the Firstborn Son of God

After being cut off, crucified, Christ was resurrected to be begotten as the firstborn Son of God (Psa. 2:7; Acts 13:33; Heb. 1:5-6). Psalm 2 shows us Christ's resurrection. The word *resurrection* is not there, but the fact is there. Verse 7 says, "I will recount the decree of Jehovah; / He said to Me: You are My Son; / Today I have begotten You." "Today" is the day of Christ's resurrection. In Acts 13:33 Paul quoted Psalm 2:7, telling us that this refers to Christ's resurrection. In His resurrection, Christ was begotten. Since He was already the Son of God, why did He need to be begotten as the Son of God in resurrection? Christ was the only begotten Son of God in His divinity (John 3:16), but when He became incarnated, He put humanity upon Him. This humanity had nothing to do with the sonship of God, but through His death and resurrection, His humanity was "sonized" to also be the Son of God. By resurrection Christ brought His humanity into the divine sonship and was designated the Son of God with His humanity (Rom. 1:4). Now the Son of God has the divine nature with the human nature. When Christ was merely the only begotten Son of God, He was God's Son only in the divine nature. Now as the firstborn Son of God, He possesses both the divine nature and the human nature.

Christ is the firstborn Son of God, and we are the many sons of God. We believers in Christ are regenerated sons of God, having God's life and God's nature, but we also have our human nature. Our human nature is still in the process of being begotten. We have been regenerated in our spirit, but we still have not been transfigured in our body. When our body is transfigured, redeemed, glorified, our body will also be "sonized." Our sonship will be completed by that time (Rom. 8:23). The sonship began with the regeneration of our spirit, is continuing with the transformation of our soul, and will be consummated with the redemption of our body. The process of our sonship passes through our regeneration and transformation to our glorification.

In Psalm 2 we can see God's economy with God's kingdom and the resurrection of Christ, in which He was begotten to be God's firstborn Son. The day of resurrection was a great day. Not only was Christ born on that day, but we also were born on that day. First Peter 1:3 says that through Christ's resurrection, God regenerated us. When Christ was born as the firstborn Son of God, we were all born with Him to be His many brothers, the many sons of God (Rom. 8:29). Christ's resurrection was a big delivery, a big birth, of Himself as the firstborn Son of God with His many brothers, the many sons of God.

5. Installed as God's King in the Heavens in His Ascension

Psalm 2 also reveals that Christ was installed as God's King in the heavens in His ascension (v. 6; Acts 2:36; 5:31; Rev. 1:5a). In verse 6, God declared, "I have installed My King / Upon Zion, My holy mountain." This was in Christ's ascension. In His ascension He was made the King in the heavens for God's kingdom.

6. Having Been Given the Nations as His Inheritance and the Limits of the Earth as His Possession for His Kingdom

According to Psalm 2:8, Christ has been given the nations as His inheritance and the limits of the earth as His possession for His kingdom. When the Lord came back to the disciples in His resurrection, He told them, "All authority has been given to Me in heaven and on earth" (Matt. 28:18). The Lord's word here covers what is mentioned in Psalm 2:8. God has given all the nations on this earth to Christ as His inheritance. Furthermore, God has given the limits of the earth to Christ as His possession. Today if you own even a small portion of land in Taiwan, you are a rich man. But the entire earth will be possessed by Christ. This is His land. How rich He is! We cannot see such wonderful things about Christ in Psalm 1. Psalm 1 says, according to the human concept, that the man who meditates in the law will prosper in everything, but Psalm 2 reveals, according to the divine concept, that God has given the limits of the earth to Christ.

7. To Rule the Nations in His Kingdom with an Iron Rod

Eventually, Christ will rule the nations in His kingdom with an iron rod (Psa. 2:9; Rev. 2:26-27). There is a marvelous sequence in Psalm 2 revealing the steps of Christ in God's economy beginning from His being anointed in eternity in His divinity. We may wonder where Christ's death is spoken of in Psalm 2, but we need to realize that Christ's resurrection implies His death. Without death, how could there be resurrection? Thus, in Psalm 2 we see His being anointed in His divinity and humanity, His death, His resurrection, and His ascension with His enthronement. God installed Him as King, enthroning Him to give Him all the nations with the limits of the earth. This is to set up a universal kingdom for Christ. Then Christ will rule the nations with an iron rod.

8. Opposed by the Rulers of the World

Psalm 2 says that Christ is opposed by the rulers of the world. Verses 1-3 say, "Why are the nations in an uproar, / And why do the peoples contemplate a vain thing? / The kings of the earth take their stand, / And the rulers take counsel together, / Against Jehovah and against His Anointed: / Let us break apart their bonds / And cast their ropes away from us." Soon after Christ's ascension, on the earth at Peter's time, Herod and Pilate took their stand against Christ. Acts 4:25-29a records the prayer of the early church, in which they quote from Psalm 2. Acts 4:27 says, "For truly in this city there were gathered together against Your holy Servant Jesus, whom You anointed, both Herod and Pontius Pilate, with the

Gentiles and the peoples of Israel." They all were opposing Christ.

C. A Warning to the World

Psalm 2 also gives a warning to the world (vv. 10-12).

1. God and His Christ Being in Wrath to the World

First, God and His Christ will be in wrath to the world (v. 12b; Rev. 6:15-17). Men should not think that there is no God in this universe or that Christ is just a name in religion. The Bible tells us clearly that Christ is waiting for the opportunity to come to execute His judgment in His anger, in His wrath.

The book of Joel speaks of this judgment. The subject of Joel is the day of the Lord (1:15; 2:11, 31; 3:14), but few Christians understand what the day of the Lord is. Paul gave us the definition in 1 Corinthians 4:3-5. In verse 3 he said, "It is a very small thing that I should be examined by you or by man's day." Before the Lord comes, it is man's day, in which man judges. Today is man's day. In man's day, everything is judged by man. But after man's day, there will be a day which will be called the day of the Lord. This day will last about one thousand three and a half years. The day on which the great tribulation begins will be the beginning of the day of the Lord. From that day, the Lord's wrath will be expressed. The day of the Lord is the day of His judgment.

It may seem today that the Lord does not care for the world situation. If people want to settle their problems, they have to go to the police station. Then the police station will transfer them to the law court, where they will be judged and ruled according to the law of man. When people have disputes and grievances today, they do not go to Christ. But when the great tribulation begins, that will be the beginning of the day of the Lord. Christ will come to interfere with the world situation.

Joel reveals that after the three and a half years of the great tribulation, the Lord will judge the living Gentiles (3:12). Matthew 25 tells us that He will separate them, the sheep from the goats, in His judgment (vv. 32-46). Afterward, He will set up the thousand-year kingdom. In the thousand-year kingdom, He will judge, rule, and control the entire earth. At the end of that thousand years, there will be a rebellion, which He will also judge (Rev. 20:8-9). Then He will have the final judgment on the great white throne to judge the dead unbelievers (vv. 11-15). That will be the end of the day of the Lord. Thus, the day of the Lord will last one thousand three and a half years. After this day, the heavens and the earth will be burned to become the new heavens and new earth. Then the New Jerusalem will come in, and righteousness will fill the new heavens and new earth (2 Pet. 3:13). Everything will be right. There will be no more need for any kind of judgment.

2. Repent

Since God and His Christ will be in wrath to the world, man must repent (Psa. 2:11; Acts 17:30). This is the New Testament gospel.

3. Take Refuge in the Son—
Believe into the Son, Christ

Psalm 2:12b says, "Blessed are all those who take refuge in Him." To take refuge in the Son equals to believe into the Son, Christ (John 3:16). Many of us probably have never considered that to believe into Christ is to take refuge in Him. We can see this with the type of Noah's ark. When all the people trusted, or believed in, that ark, they all entered into that ark, to take the ark as their refuge, protection, and hiding place. Today our Christ is our refuge, our protection. We are hiding ourselves in Him.

After getting into bed, I usually pray, "Lord, cover us, our building, and our yard with Your prevailing blood against all the enemy's attack." The next morning I thank the Lord for being our security. Every time I take a trip, I ask the Lord to be my protection. I ask the Lord to cover the car which I will take to the airport and to cover the plane in which I will fly. Even, of course, I take the Lord as my refuge under God's eternal judgment. These are experiences of taking refuge in Christ.

4. Kiss the Son—Love Christ, the Son of God

Psalm 2:12a says that we need to kiss the Son. The New Testament tells us that we need faith and love. Paul said in 1 Timothy 1:14, "And the grace of our Lord superabounded with faith and love in Christ Jesus." The Lord's grace visited Paul and superabounded in him with faith and love in Christ. One day he received mercy and grace from the Lord, not only to believe in Him but also to love Him. We have been given faith to believe into Christ, taking Him as our refuge. Also, we have been given God's love to love the Lord Jesus.

In the Gospel of John, we are taught that we need to believe into Christ, the Son (1:12), and to love Him (14:23). In the last chapter of John, chapter twenty-one, the very Christ who is our refuge came back to Peter to restore Peter's love toward Him. The Lord asked Peter three times, "Do you love Me?" (vv. 15-17).

Peter failed utterly in denying the Lord three times (18:17, 25, 27), so the Lord came back to ask him three times—"Do you love Me?" I think that this threefold asking reminded Peter of his being defeated three times. This is why Peter responded by saying, "Lord, You know." Peter said, "Lord, You know that I love You" (21:15b, 16b). A young believer may be strong to boldly tell the Lord that he loves Him and will never deny Him. But when he is defeated, his natural confidence in his love toward the Lord will be dealt with. Then he will learn to follow the Lord and to love the Lord without any confidence in his natural strength.

To believe in the Lord is to receive Him; to love the Lord is to enjoy Him. The Gospel of John presents these as the two requirements for us to participate in the Lord. The Lord is within us to be our faith and to be our love. To love Him, according to Psalm 2:12a, is to kiss Him. We should not uplift and treasure the law. Instead, we should kiss Christ, love Christ, day by day.

I read a portion of John Nelson Darby's writings which inspired me to love the Lord. One day when he was over eighty years old, he was traveling and he stayed overnight in a hotel. Before going to sleep, he said to the Lord, "Lord Jesus, I still love You." That inspired me to the uttermost. After many years, he could still speak such a word to the Lord. We need to ask the Lord to keep us loving Him all the time.

D. Concerning the Accomplishment of the Economy of God

Psalm 2 is concerning the accomplishment of the economy of God, whereas Psalm 1 is concerning the personal benefit of the saints (vv. 1-3). The human concept of Psalm 1 is that the man who delights in the law of God prospers in everything. But according to the New Testament revelation, the law is over and Christ is here (Rom. 10:4a). Christ is the centrality and universality of God's economy. The entire book of Psalms takes these two lines: the law and Christ. Eventually, by the end of the Psalms, the law is over, and we see Christ with His complement, which is His Body, His church, the house and the kingdom of God in God's economy to fulfill God's eternal purpose.

Thus, we have to see that Psalms 1 and 2 show us a comparison of the human concept in exalting the law with its keeper as the one blessed by God in man's interest and the divine revelation in proclaiming Christ as the One anointed of God in God's economy.

LIFE-STUDY OF THE PSALMS

MESSAGE FOUR

DAVID'S CONCEPTS CONCERNING A GODLY LIFE
IN COMPARISON WITH
HIS INSPIRED PRAISE OF THE EXCELLENCY OF CHRIST

(1)

Scripture Reading: Psa. 3—7

Thus far, we have covered Psalm 1 concerning the law in man's appreciation and Psalm 2 concerning Christ in God's economy. We have seen that it was altogether by the Holy Spirit for the Psalms to be arranged this way. Suppose that we were the arrangers of the one hundred fifty psalms. Which psalm would we place as the first one? The Lord's way is the best way. He put Psalm 1 first, where we see the law in man's appreciation. Then we see Christ in God's economy in Psalm 2. What would be next in Psalms 3—7? It is interesting to see that right after Psalms 1 and 2, there are five psalms which show us David's concepts concerning a godly life.

The title of Psalm 3 says, "A Psalm of David, when he fled from Absalom his son." Absalom was a rebellious son. The Psalms were arranged in this way to show us that David needed to be corrected and disciplined. David appreciated the law so highly in Psalm 1, but did he keep the law? Did he as a tree stand by the streams steadfastly? He was not planted by the streams in Psalm 3. Instead, he was fleeing from his rebellious son.

From my youth I have loved Psalm 51. This is a psalm of David's repentance after his great sin recorded in 2 Samuel 11. David committed intentional murder, using his power and authority as a king to carry out his conspiracy to kill Uriah, one of his fighters. After that murder, he robbed Uriah of his wife. The last five commandments of the law prohibit killing, fornication, stealing, lying, and coveting. David broke the last five commandments. He killed Uriah, committed fornication, stole Uriah's wife, lied to Uriah, and coveted Uriah's wife. That offended God to the uttermost (1 Kings 15:5). Right away God sent the prophet Nathan to reprove David, as recorded in 2 Samuel 12. David became subdued, and he repented. Then he wrote Psalm 51. That is a wonderful psalm. The standard in this psalm is high; it is full of life and full of spirit. It even takes care of God's economy. The end of that psalm shows that after his confession of his own sin, he still remembered Zion and Jerusalem. In verse 18 David said, "Do good in Your good pleasure unto Zion: / Build the walls of Jerusalem."

That psalm is very good and very high. But it is difficult to believe that about three years later, he wrote Psalms 3—7, which are full of the human concept. After David committed murder and fornication, God disciplined him by allowing there to be trouble among his children (2 Sam. 12:11). One of David's sons committed fornication with one of his daughters. Then the fornicator was killed by another son of David, Absalom (2 Sam. 13:1-36). After the killing of his brother, Absalom fled to Geshur and stayed there for three years (vv. 37-39). Then after three years, he came back to David, and a little later he rebelled. Then David fled. In his flight from his rebellious son, he wrote Psalms 3—7. We have to know the history of these psalms in order to see them in the light of God's New Testament economy.

Some Chinese Christians have said that if you want to learn how to pray, you should study the Psalms, but I would say that we should not do this. Psalms 3—7 are all psalms of prayer, but they are the wrong example of how to pray because they are according to David's human concept for his personal interest. The Chinese Christians also say that if you want to learn how to preach, you should study Proverbs. But I would say that if you want to be a good preacher, you should study Paul's fourteen Epistles. Furthermore, if you want to learn to pray, you should go to Paul. Paul gave us two model prayers in one book, the book of Ephesians. In Ephesians 1 he said that he would ask the Father, the God of our

Lord Jesus Christ, to give us a spirit of wisdom and revelation that we may know what is the hope of His calling, what are the riches of the glory of His inheritance in the saints, and what is the surpassing greatness of His power toward us (vv. 17-19). Then in Ephesians 3, Paul said, "I bow my knees unto the Father...that He would grant you...to be strengthened with power through His Spirit into the inner man, that Christ may make His home in your hearts...that you may be filled unto all the fullness of God" (vv. 14-19). If we compare these two prayers of the apostle Paul with the prayers in Psalms 3—7, we will realize that the prayers in these psalms should not be the examples of how we should pray.

In this message I would like to paraphrase the main points in these five psalms. We need to evaluate these psalms point by point in the light of God's New Testament economy. The prayers in Psalms 3—7 are all involved in sufferings, in good and evil, and are even involved in avenging, self-righteousness, and accusing of others. There is no point in these psalms indicating life, repentance, self-condemnation, or self-denial. Furthermore, there is no point indicating much fellowship with God, touching God or being touched by God, and being humble and contrite in spirit. As we consider these psalms, we need to see these points.

I. DAVID'S CONCEPTS CONCERNING A GODLY LIFE
IN PSALMS 3—7

As we have pointed out, Psalms 3—7 show us David's concepts concerning a godly life. I use the word *godly* because it is my quotation from Psalm 4:3. David's concepts of such a godly life in Psalms 3—7 are in comparison with His inspired praise of the excellency of Christ in Psalm 8.

A. These Five Psalms
Being Written by David in His Flight
from His Son Absalom's Rebellion

These five psalms were written by David in his flight from his son Absalom's rebellion, which was the outcome of David's sins of murder and robbing another of his wife (Psa. 3 title).

B. David, Who Appreciated
the Law with Its Keeper in Psalm 1,
Murdering Uriah and Robbing Him of His Wife

David, who appreciated the law with its keeper in Psalm 1, murdered Uriah and robbed him of his wife (2 Sam. 11:14-27). In Psalm 1 he highly uplifted and exalted the law with its keeper. In his great sin, however, he broke all the last five commandments, which require men to have virtues expressing God's divine attributes. Did David, the one who wrote Psalm 1, keep the law? I do not believe that many readers of the Psalms ever thought about this. They agreed with David's exaltation of the law in Psalm 1. They never thought that Psalm 1 was wrong in treasuring and uplifting the law.

The greatest teacher in the New Testament, Paul, told us that no flesh can be justified by keeping the law (Gal. 2:16; 3:11). It is impossible for fallen man to keep the law. Asking man to keep the law is like asking a crippled bird to fly from Los Angeles to New York. Romans 8:3 says that the law cannot do what God requires because it is weak through the flesh. The law is good in its nature (Rom. 7:12), but the law cannot give us life (Gal. 3:21); it cannot impart the very dynamic power, life power, organic power, into us.

David appreciated the law in Psalm 1, but he committed murder, fornication, stealing, lying, and coveting against the law. Eventually, he was fleeing from his rebellious son. Because David committed murder and fornication, God chastised him through his son's rebellion. His children became a mess. Among them, there were also murder and fornication. If we see this picture, we will be convinced not to treasure and uplift the law. We should not appreciate the law. The more we appreciate the law, the more we will commit something against the law.

C. David Repenting and Being Forgiven by God

After Jehovah reproved him through the prophet Nathan (2 Sam. 12:1-12), David repented and was forgiven by God (2 Sam. 12:13; Psa. 51:1-17).

D. The Five Psalms Being Composed
according to David's Concepts of a Godly Life

1. Asking God to Deal with His Adversaries
and Be a Shield around Him, His Glory
and the One Who Lifted Up His Head

Psalms 3—7 were composed according to David's concepts
of a godly life. In these psalms David asked God to deal with
his adversaries and be a shield around him, his glory and the
One who lifted up his head (Psa. 3:1-3, 6-8). Does asking God
to deal with his adversaries correspond with the New Testament teaching? Surely, it is against the New Testament
teaching. The New Testament teaches us to love our enemies
and pray for those who persecute us (Matt. 5:44; Luke
6:27, 35; Rom. 12:20).

I have been in the Lord's recovery for sixty years. In these
sixty years, I have encountered opposition and even rebellion.
How do we react to such opposition? As descendants of Adam,
we would ask the Lord to deal with all these opposers for us.
But if we are in the reality of the New Testament, we dare not
pray this way. We cannot pray this way to the Lord because
He told us to love our enemies.

David also asked the Lord to be a shield of protection
around him. Is this good or bad? What is wrong with asking
God to protect us? I would say that this is neither bad nor
good. At that juncture when he was fleeing from his son,
David prayed such a prayer. Why did he not pray, "Lord, You
know I committed that sin which caused my son to be rebellious. Lord, don't condemn him. Lord, condemn me. I repent. I
would like to have a time to say to my son, 'Son, forgive me.
The cause of today's trouble is not you, but me.' Lord, deal
with my heart." This is a spiritual prayer. Instead, David was
asking the Lord to be a shield around him. As a murderer and
a fornicator, was David worthy to be protected? He also asked
God to be his glory and the One who lifted up his head.
Should David not have felt ashamed to ask this of God when
he was fleeing from his son, being chastised by God because
of his murder and fornication?

2. Calling Out to Jehovah
and Believing That He Would Answer Him
from His Holy Mountain

David also called out to Jehovah and believed that He would answer him from His holy mountain (Psa. 3:4).

3. Praying in the Night for Jehovah's Sustaining

David was also praying in the night for Jehovah's sustaining (Psa. 3:5). Nearly all the Bible students and teachers call Psalm 3 a psalm of night prayer. Is praying nightly good or bad? It all depends upon how we pray. If David were really in the spirit, he would have considered the situation he was in at that time. He was fleeing from his rebellious son. He should have considered what caused his son to rebel. Then he would pray at night, "God, forgive me. It was I who caused my son to rebel. It was I who murdered Uriah, using my power and position as king to carry out conspiracy and murder. What a shame that even I robbed Uriah of his wife." As he was fleeing from his son, David should have felt shameful and repentant before God.

4. Asking God to Vindicate His Righteousness

David asked God to vindicate his righteousness based upon the past experience of his prayer. He convinced others that he was a godly man whom God set apart for Himself and who called out to Jehovah and whom Jehovah heard when he called out to him. He also admonished others not to sin in anger but to consider in their heart upon their bed and be silent (Psa. 4:1-4). When he was fleeing from his son, he still asked God to vindicate him of his righteousness, but where was his righteousness? David should not have prayed this way. Instead, he should have asked God to enlighten him so that he could see how evil and sinful he was. As a king, he killed one of his fighters by his conspiracy. Then after killing him, he robbed him of his wife. Where was his righteousness?

He also was convincing others that he was a godly man whom God set apart for Himself. He was fleeing, yet he considered that he was set apart by God. This shows that he was in darkness. In considering Psalm 4, we need to remember that this was a psalm written by David at the time when he was fleeing. At that time, he indicated that he was a godly man whom God had set apart for Himself. Was that the time for him to pray in this way?

This shows that we human beings always are not easily convinced of or subdued in our sinfulness. Even if we murdered someone and committed fornication by robbing, we would not be convinced. We still would think we are good. We might vindicate ourselves by saying, "Yes, maybe I was wrong in certain matters, but I am a godly person whom God has set apart for Himself." I have been touching people for sixty years in the Lord's recovery, but I have nearly never had a time with one who was thoroughly convinced by God of his failures. In the law court, neither the plaintiff nor the defendant think that they are wrong. They cannot be convinced that they are wrong. We all need God's mercy to see our failures, our sinfulness, and our filthiness, to even roll on the floor in confession of our sins. This means that we have received mercy and found grace in the presence of God. As long as we would not be convinced of our sinfulness, we are wrong and in darkness.

In Psalm 4 David even admonished others not to sin in anger but to consider in their heart upon their bed and be silent. This is a good teaching, but why did David not teach himself? Was he the right person to pray this way? If you know his background, you can see that he was not the right person.

5. Advising Others to Offer Sacrifices of Righteousness and Trust in Jehovah

David also advised others to offer sacrifices of righteousness and trust in Jehovah (Psa. 4:5). This word is very good, but for him to write such a thing at that time in his particular situation was not fitting.

6. Asking God to Lift Up upon Him the Light of His Countenance

David asked God to lift up upon him the light of His countenance, thanking God for putting joy in his heart more than others' rejoicing in the abounding of grain and new wine, and trusting in God to lie down and sleep in peace and dwell in safety (Psa. 4:6-8). By this we can see that David had no feeling concerning his situation and condition of a great failure. He had become numb. How could such a sinful person pray this way to God at the time when he was fleeing from a situation of rebellion caused by his sinfulness? At such a time, he said that he would lie down and sleep in peace and dwell in safety.

7. Praying in the Morning and Watching

David was one who was praying in the morning and watching (Psa. 5:1-3). Many teachers of the Bible call Psalm 5 a morning prayer. Psalm 3 is a night prayer, and Psalm 5 is a morning prayer.

8. Knowing That God Does Not Delight in Wickedness but Hates Iniquity

David knew that God does not delight in wickedness but hates iniquity (Psa. 5:4-6). If David knew this, why did he commit such a great sin? Merely knowing the law does not work out anything. The law and David's knowledge of it did not work for him.

9. Coming into God's House in the Abundance of His Lovingkindness

David said that he came into God's house in the abundance of His lovingkindness and worshipped toward God's holy temple in fear of Him. At that time, David was not worshipping in God's temple, but toward it (Psa. 5:7).

He asked God to lead him in His righteousness and make his ways straight on account of those who lay in wait for him (v. 8). He said that these ones had nothing right in their mouth, whose inward part was corruption and whose throat was an open grave, and who flattered with their tongue (v. 9). This clause was even quoted by Paul in his gospel preaching (Rom. 3:13).

David asked God to hold them guilty, letting them fall by their own counsels and thrusting them out because of their

multiplied transgressions and their rebellion against God
(v. 10). This prayer is full of condemnation of others, but
there is no condemnation of David himself. It seems that
everybody was wrong and sinful except him. We cannot find
any hint here that he confessed his sin before God.

10. Asking God to Let All Who Take Refuge in Him Rejoice and Shout for Joy Forever

David asked God to let all who take refuge in Him rejoice
and shout for joy forever that God might spread a cover, a
canopy, over them to cause those who love God's name to
exult in God. He also asked God to bless the righteous man,
surrounding him with favor as with a shield (Psa. 5:11-12). I
do not know why David prayed all these things here. Instead,
he should have prayed, "Lord, forgive me. My sinful conduct
caused my son to rebel. Lord, have mercy upon him. Move us
all to repent to You." There is no hint in these psalms of David
being convicted of his sinfulness.

11. In God's Chastisement Asking God to Be Gracious to Him

In God's chastisement, David asked God to be gracious to
him, to heal him, return to him, and save him for the sake of
His lovingkindness (Psa. 6:1-5). David realized that he was in
God's chastisement, but there was still not much confession
about his failure. He said that he was wearied with his groaning, causing his bed to swim all night long, dissolving his
couch with his tears. His eye had wasted because of grief and
had aged because of his enemies (vv. 6-7). I think that this is
David's exaggeration. Can anyone cause his bed to swim by
his tears? Do we agree with this kind of prayer? If a brother
prayed this way in a prayer meeting, we might admonish him
to stop this kind of prayer.

12. Believing That Jehovah Had Heard the Sound of His Weeping and That All His Enemies Would Be Ashamed and Greatly Dismayed

David believed that Jehovah had heard the sound of his

weeping and that all his enemies would be ashamed and greatly dismayed (Psa. 6:8-10). David could not forget his enemies. This is different from the Lord's teaching in the New Testament.

13. Taking Refuge in God and Asking God to Deliver Him from All Who Pursued Him, for He Had Done No Wrong

David took refuge in God and asked God to deliver him from all who pursued him. The enemies, including his son, were chasing after him. David felt that he had done no wrong (Psa. 7:1-5). How can anyone tell God that they have done no wrong?

14. Asking Jehovah to Arise in His Anger against the Overflowing Wrath of His Enemies

David asked Jehovah to arise in His anger against the overflowing wrath of his enemies, and asked Jehovah to judge him according to his righteousness and integrity (Psa. 7:6-8). It is hard to imagine that such a godly man as David would pray such a prayer. He asked God to judge him according to his righteousness and integrity. Where was his integrity? He had committed fornication and murder, issuing in the rebellion of his son. As we consider Psalms 3—7 in this light, we can see how blind we have been in our appreciation of the Psalms.

15. Asking God to Establish the Righteous Man

David asked God to establish the righteous man and believed that his shield was with God, who, as a righteous Judge, saves the upright in heart (Psa. 7:9-13).

16. Believing That the Evil Man Travails in Iniquity and Digs a Pit

David believed that the evil man travails in iniquity and digs a pit, hollowing it out and falling into the hole, his mischief returning upon his own head (Psa. 7:14-16). I say again, suppose that a brother prayed this way in a prayer meeting. The saints might ask him to stop.

17. *Giving Thanks to Jehovah according to His Righteousness and Singing Praise to the Name of Jehovah the Most High*

David gave thanks to Jehovah according to His righteousness and sang praise to the name of Jehovah the Most High (Psa. 7:17). This is one of the few good points in Psalms 3—7. Thank the Lord that these psalms have a good ending.

However, we can see that there is nothing in Psalms 3—7 concerning God's economy, God's kingdom, and God's interest. There is nothing concerning Christ. There is no real interceding spirit, that is, no intercession for others in the spirit. Also, there is very little life supply to the readers. Instead, these psalms encourage, strengthen, and confirm the readers in asking God to take care of them and their interest. Many readers of the Psalms, who read without the proper discernment of the human concept and the divine concept, have been encouraged to take care of their benefit and their interest.

After considering Psalms 3—7 in the light of God's New Testament economy, we can see that these psalms should not be taken as models for our prayer. In them we see David's sufferings, his desire to be avenged of his adversaries, and his self-righteousness. We do not see any repentance, confession of his fault, or self-condemnation. Psalm 8, however, reveals Christ's incarnation, His death and resurrection, His ascension, and His kingdom. Psalms 3—7 reveal David's concepts concerning a godly life, whereas Psalm 8 is his inspired praise of the excellency of Christ.

LIFE-STUDY OF THE PSALMS

MESSAGE FIVE

DAVID'S CONCEPTS CONCERNING A GODLY LIFE IN COMPARISON WITH HIS INSPIRED PRAISE OF THE EXCELLENCY OF CHRIST

(2)

Scripture Reading: Psa. 8

In this message we come to Psalm 8. The more we read this psalm, the more we have to admit that it is altogether heavenly language. No mere human word could express the divine concept in this psalm. The heavenly language in it must come from the divine revelation.

In the previous message, we saw David's concepts concerning a godly life in Psalms 3—7. In this message we want to see his inspired praise of the excellency of Christ in Psalm 8. If we read Psalms 3—7 with much prayer, we can realize that they all are on the same level and in the same category. They describe many bad things, showing that the earth is a messy earth. But when we read Psalm 8, we feel that we are not on this messy earth. When we come to Psalm 8, the tone changes.

I would like to read this psalm so that we can consider it verse by verse. In verse 1 David said, "O Jehovah our Lord, / How excellent is Your name / In all the earth, / You who have set Your splendor above the heavens!" This one verse covers both the earth and the heavens. In Psalms 3—7 the earth is a mess, but in Psalm 8 there is something excellent on the earth. This excellent item is the excellent name of the Lord Jesus. He is not here today physically, but His name is here. This earth today is nothing but a mess. But, thank the Lord, at least on this earth there is something excellent—the name of Jesus! His name is the exalted name, the glorified name.

Verse 1 mentions both the earth and the heavens. We need to realize that this psalm tries the best to link the earth to the heavens and to bring down the heavens to the earth. In verse 1 we can see this linking. Jehovah's name is excellent in all the earth, and He has set His splendor above the heavens. Actually, the heavens are the source of the excellency. The excellency does not initiate from the earth, but from the heavens.

Verse 2 says, "Out of the mouths of babes and sucklings / You have established strength / Because of Your adversaries, / To stop the enemy and the avenger." This verse shows us three negative categories of persons: the adversaries, the enemy, and the avenger. Above the heavens is God's splendor, and on the earth Jesus' name is excellent. But in this universe, there are still many adversaries, enemies, and avengers. Adversaries are those who are within, enemies are those who are without, and the avengers are those who run back and forth (cf. Job 1:7). Satan can be signified by these three categories. First, Satan was within God's kingdom. Then Satan became an enemy without, outside the kingdom of God. He is also the avenger, running back and forth. Above the heavens there is splendor, and on the earth there is the excellent name. But in between the heavens and the earth, there are the adversaries within, the enemy without, and the avenger running back and forth.

What would God do about this? God does something in a consummate way. He establishes His praises out of the mouths of babes and sucklings, the youngest, smallest, and weakest ones. Babes are a little stronger than sucklings, and sucklings are somewhat smaller than the babes, but both of them are in the category of the smallest and weakest.

In this message I would like to ask if we consider ourselves as babes and sucklings? Perhaps some of us have a doctor's degree, or others are high school seniors. Are we seniors, or are we sucklings? If you would ask me, I would say that I am the smallest suckling. In the kingdom of God, there is no old person. The Lord Jesus told people, "Truly I say to you, Unless you turn and become like little children, you shall by no means enter into the kingdom of the heavens" (Matt.

18:3). He also said, "Allow the little children and do not prevent them from coming to Me, for of such is the kingdom of the heavens" (19:14). The Lord stressed that to participate in the kingdom of the heavens, we must be like little children. All the people who are in the kingdom of the heavens are as babes. A brother may be over sixty years old, but in God's kingdom, he is a suckling.

Psalm 8 is poetry. Poetic writing should not be understood in a mere physical and literal way. We have to understand the terms according to a poetic way. Babes are not the real babes, and sucklings are not the real sucklings. These are the children of the kingdom of the heavens. All the people who are in the kingdom of the heavens are either babes or sucklings. If we consider that we are people with a high degree or status, that we have a doctor's degree, that we are seniors, we are not in the kingdom. The brothers and sisters who are seniors in high school should not take this standing in the church life. We should not be seniors, but sucklings. The psalmist means that we, the children of God, all are babes and sucklings, yet God could cause us to praise Him.

Psalm 8:2 says that the Lord has established strength out of the mouths of babes and sucklings. Seemingly, strength does not refer to something that comes out of the mouth. When the Lord quoted this verse in Matthew 21:16, He used the word *praise* instead of *strength*. Weaker ones in themselves cannot praise. To cry or weep does not require strength, but to praise requires strength. When we gossip, argue, or reason with people, that does not require strength. But without strength, we cannot praise the Lord. Some praises may come out of our mouth, but they cannot be considered as perfected praises, because they are not so full of strength. Praises should be full of strength. Many times when the saints are praising the Lord, we can see the strength.

The Septuagint version of the Psalms translated the Hebrew word for *strength* into *praise* in Psalm 8:2. This translation was quoted by the Lord in Matthew 21:16. This means that the Lord admitted that this translation was right. The scholars who translated the Old Testament into Greek for the Septuagint did have some kind of spiritual knowledge.

To praise is to have the strength in our mouth. God can work in His redemption to such an extent that the weakest ones and the smallest ones can have the strength to praise Him. God has established this.

The Hebrew word for *established* is a hard word to translate. In the Lord's quotation in Matthew 21:16, it says that He has "perfected" praise out of the mouths of the babes and sucklings. Psalm 8 says that He established strength out of the mouths of babes and sucklings, but the Lord Jesus quoted it by saying that He perfected praise. Is our praise perfect? We have to admit that our praise is altogether imperfect. Psalm 8 is not a long psalm, but it is a completed, perfected, and perfect psalm. If we are short of strength, we cannot praise. If we do not have the extra strength, we cannot have a completed, perfected, and perfect praise.

On earth the Lord's name is excellent; above the heavens is the Lord's splendor, His glory. In between there are the adversaries, the enemy, and the avenger, who are stopped by the praise of strength that comes out of the mouths of the smallest ones and the weakest ones. This is God's marvelous consummation. The highest consummation of the Lord's work in His redemption is to perfect the praise to Him out of the mouths of the smallest and the weakest.

The Lord does this because of His adversaries, with the purpose of stopping the enemy and the avenger. The Chinese translation shows that to stop the enemy and the avenger means to shut up their mouths. Today before the Lord and God, Satan's mouth has been shut up. In the whole universe, there are many voices. The adversaries have their voices, the enemy has his voice, and the avenger has his voice. But all these voices have been stopped by the overcoming Christ. He has overcome all of God's enemies in the entire universe, so He can perfect the praise to Him out of the mouths of the smallest and weakest persons, in order to stop the voices of His enemy and His avenger.

Verse 3 says, "When I see Your heavens, the works of Your fingers, / The moon and the stars, which You have ordained." David did not say that he saw *the* heavens, but he saw *"Your* heavens." We have a hymn on this psalm in our hymnal (*Hymns*, #1097). In the second stanza of that hymn, the writer referred to the sun, the moon, and the stars. The writer added the word *sun*, but this is wrong. In Psalm 8 David saw only the moon and the stars, not the sun. We cannot see the sun, the moon, and the stars at the same time. When we see the moon and the stars, we cannot see the sun. The moon and the stars in Psalm 8 indicate that it was in the night. In the nighttime, everything is dark. But the psalmist lifted up his eyes to look at our Father's heavens. In the night he saw the moon and the stars which God had ordained. The scientific experts can bear witness to this ordination. The divine ordination of the moon and the stars is truly a wonder.

After the psalmist turned his view from the messy earth to the bright heavens, he said, "What is man, that You remember him, / And the son of man, that You visit him?" (v. 4). He turned his view from the moon and the stars in the heavens back to man on this earth. First, God remembers man. Second, He visits man. We have to understand this in a poetic way. God in the heavens remembered man before He became incarnated. Then He came to visit man by becoming a man through His incarnation. The Triune God came to visit us. Before coming to us, He remembered us. The Triune God was very busy, yet He remembered us. Then according to His remembrance of us, He became incarnated to visit us.

As believers of Jesus, we surely have been visited by Him. Each day when I pray, I experience the Lord's visitation. He comes to me in the way of incarnation; in the way of His human living; in the way of His crucifixion; in the way of His resurrection; in the way of His ascension; and in the way of His descension. The Lord is there in my study room as I spend time with Him in prayer. We all need to enjoy the Lord's visitation day by day. If the Lord Jesus had never gone through all the above processes, how could He be with us today? He is now with us. In order to visit us, the Lord did not simply drop down from the heavens. He took a long journey. The Lord has remembered us and also visited us.

Heis with us all the time. If we did not have the visitation of the Lord, we would be pitiful.

Psalm 8:5 says, "You have made him somewhat lower than angels / And have crowned him with glory and honor." The word *angels* in Hebrew is *Elohim,* which is normally translated *God* (Gen. 1:1). The Septuagint translated *Elohim* here into *angels.* In Hebrews 2:7 Paul quoted this verse, not according to the Hebrew version but according to the Septuagint version. God made him somewhat lower than the angels. Who is "him" in this verse? "Him" actually refers to the man Jesus. God has made the man Jesus somewhat lower than the angels. To make Jesus lower than the angels refers to His incarnation with His human living. In the sense of being in the flesh, He was somewhat lower than the angels.

After His human living, He was resurrected, and in His resurrection, He was glorified. Then He ascended to the heavens, and in His ascension, He was honored. "Crowned...with glory and honor" indicates or implies two steps: Christ's resurrection and His ascension. Before His resurrection and ascension, there was the death of Christ. If there is no death, there is no resurrection, and if there is no resurrection, there is no ascension. Furthermore, without His incarnation and human living, He was not qualified to die. He had to become a man and live for thirty-three and a half years. Thus, in Psalm 8:5 we can see all the steps of the Triune God's process: incarnation, human living for thirty-three and a half years, death, resurrection, and ascension.

Verses 6-8 say, "For You have caused him to rule over the works of Your hands; / You have put all things under his feet: / All sheep and oxen, / As well as the beasts of the field, / The birds of heaven and the fish of the sea, / Whatever passes through the paths of the seas." Whatever passes through the paths of the seas are the sea animals other than the fish. These verses refer to the kingdom in which Christ will rule over all the created things and to the restoration in this one-thousand-year kingdom, the millennium.

Psalm 8 is a short psalm, but it comprises and implies Christ's incarnation, human living, death, resurrection, ascension, and His being crowned to be the Lord and Christ and the King of kings, the unique Ruler of the entire universe. The day will come when He will be in the kingdom for a thousand years to rule over all the creatures. This is the revelation in Psalm 8.

The last verse of this psalm repeats the first part of the first verse by saying, "O Jehovah our Lord, / How excellent is Your name / In all the earth!" At the end of the psalm, David does not say anything further about the heavens, because eventually the earth will be as excellent as the heavens.

Now that we have read through Psalm 8 in an interpretive way, let us consider in more detail the major points in this psalm.

II. DAVID'S INSPIRED PRAISE
OF THE EXCELLENCY OF CHRIST

Psalm 8 is David's inspiration, his inspired praise of the excellency of Christ.

A. The Lord's Name Being Excellent (Majestic) in All the Earth, and His Splendor (Glory) Having Been Set above the Heavens

The Lord's name is excellent in all the earth, and His splendor has been set above the heavens. I want to say again that this psalm tries the best to join the earth to the heavens and to bring the heavens down to the earth, making the earth and the heavens one.

In Psalms 3—7 it was a mess on the earth according to David's human concept. Here in Psalm 8, something, that is, the Lord's name, is excellent (majestic) in the earth according to the divine revelation, and the Lord's splendor (glory) is above the heavens in the sight of David. Today the earthly people do not see this revelation. They do not have such a view, but we have such a heavenly view about Jesus. Above David in the heavens was the glory, and with David on this earth was an excellent name. Thus, his view, his vision, brought him away from the view of the messy earth. The news media reports all the bad things that happen on this earth every day. To live anywhere on earth without the church life would be terrible.

B. Out of the Mouths of Babes and Sucklings the Lord Having Established Strength (Praise) Because of His Adversaries, to Stop the Enemy and the Avenger

Out of the mouths of babes and sucklings the Lord has established strength (praise—Matt. 21:16) because of His adversaries, to stop the enemy and the avenger (Psa. 8:2). We have seen that babes and sucklings are the youngest, smallest, and weakest among men, indicating the highest consummation of the Lord's work in His redemption. In God's salvation, the top consummation is to perfect the smallest and the weakest to praise God.

When we enjoy Christ's redemption to the uttermost, we will be bold to praise the Lord. When we are discouraged and disappointed, we may sigh and groan. But when we praise the Lord, this is the highest experience of our enjoyment of Christ. The enjoyment of Christ will make us so strong to utter a complete and a perfected praise to the Lord. We all have to learn how to praise. This is the highest consummation that God has completed in His redemption through Christ.

We all need to be the babes and sucklings in the church life. We may not be old in our physical age, but in our Christian experience we may be like tired and fatigued old folks. If we are still young in the Lord, we will praise the Lord on the way to the meetings. When we were in Elden Hall in Los Angeles, a certain brother was shouting praises to the Lord while he was driving to a meeting. A policeman saw him, followed him, and told him to pull over. The policeman asked the brother what happened to him. Then the brother said, "I was praising Jesus!" Then the policeman let him go. This is the right way to come to the meeting. When we drive to the meeting, we should sing, praise, and shout, "Amen! Hallelujah! Amen! Lord Jesus! Amen!" Many of us will not do this because we have become too old. To be old means to be weak. We need to shout more, say "Hallelujah" more, say "Amen" more, praise more. Our meetings should be full of joyful noise.

A number of the sisters among us are still in their early twenties, but their fatigued attitude makes them seem like they are over one hundred years old. With them there is no freshness and no strength. With them nothing is in the morning; instead, everything is in the sunset. They need to learn to praise the Lord. The weakest among men being perfected to praise the Lord indicates the highest consummation of the Lord's work in His redemption.

The Lord does such a consummate work because of His adversaries. He does this to insult Satan. It is as if God says, "Satan, you have done that much. Let me show you how much I can do. I can do much, much more than what you can do. Look at all My children now. They are all babes and sucklings praising Me." This praising shuts Satan's mouth. The enemy's speaking is stopped by our praising. The Lord establishes strength, perfects praise, out of our mouths because of His adversaries (within), for the stopping of the enemy and the avenger (without).

C. David Seeing the Heavens, the Works of the Lord's Fingers, the Moon and the Stars, Which the Lord Has Ordained

David saw the heavens, the works of the Lord's fingers, the moon and the stars, which the Lord has ordained (Psa. 8:3). This indicates that David had a view turned from looking at the earth to contemplating the heavens, in the night. In the night, if you look at the earth, you will see nothing because of the darkness. But if you look up to contemplate the heavens, you will see the moon and the stars. In this view David had a pure vision to see the pure work in God's creation and ordination. In the universe there is not only God's creation but also God's ordination. David saw the divine order in the universe.

This is the aim in the Lord's redemption—to turn us from the messy earth to the bright heaven. Before we were saved, we were in a messy situation. But after we were saved, our messy earth became a bright heaven. Our view was turned from looking at this messy earth to looking at the bright heaven. When bad news comes to me, I have to exercise to turn my view to look at the bright heaven. When I turn my view from the bad news and look up to the heavens, I can praise. We must learn to turn our view. The aim in the Lord's redemption is to turn our view from the earth to the heavens. The earth is messy, but the heavens are bright.

D. What is Man, That the Lord Remembers Him, and the Son of Man, That He Visits Him?

In Psalm 8:4 David asked, "What is man, that You remember him, / And the son of man, that You visit him?" In his view in the heavens, David turned his consideration to man on the earth. The ordination of the moon and the stars is marvelous. Then how about man on this earth? We should not forget that the psalmist in this psalm is trying the best to bring the heavens down and to bring the earth up to join with the heavens. He looked at the heavens with the moon and the stars. That is wonderful, but what about man? We may think that man is pitiful, but according to the divine view in this psalm, we are wrong. Man was pitiful in Adam and in the fallen situation, but today man in Christ is not pitiful. The man in Christ is wonderful.

Three portions of the Word speak of the same thing concerning man—Genesis 1, Psalm 8, and Hebrews 2. What is revealed in Psalm 8 was first spoken of in Genesis 1. Genesis 1 says that man was commissioned with the authority to rule over all the created things (vv. 26, 28). Psalm 8 repeats this. Then in Hebrews 2:6-8 Paul quotes Psalm 8. These three portions of the Word show us that man has been in three stages: created in Genesis 1, fallen in Psalm 8, and redeemed in Hebrews 2.

This redeemed man is no longer in a pitiful situation. He is joined to Jesus. Actually, Jesus, the incarnated God, first joined Himself with us. Now in His redemption we are joined to Him. There is an organic union between Him and us. Christ has passed through human living, and He died to solve our problems. Then He resurrected and ascended to be crowned and enthroned with glory and honor. He was breathed into us and poured out upon us. Today He is both in the heavens and also within us and outside of us. What kind of men are we? We are men who have been mingled with Christ.

Man is the central object of God in His creation for the accomplishment of His economy to fulfill His heart's desire. The first "man" in Psalm 8:4 is *enosh* in Hebrew. *Enosh* means a fragile, weak man. The second "man" in 8:4 is *adam* in Hebrew. Both *enosh* and *adam* in this verse refer to the God-created man in God's creation in Genesis 1:26; the Satan-captured man in man's fall in Psalm 8:4; and Christ as a man in His incarnation for the accomplishment of God's redemption in Hebrews 2:6. We should not forget Genesis 1, Psalm 8, and Hebrews 2. These three portions cover the three stages of man.

Such a man God remembers in His economy and visits in His incarnation (John 1:14; Phil. 2:7). Thank God for His remembrance, and thank God for His incarnation. He remembered us in His economy, and He visited us in His incarnation.

E. The Lord Having Made Man Somewhat Lower Than the Angels

The Lord has made man somewhat lower than the angels (Psa. 8:5a; Heb. 2:7a). This refers to Christ's incarnation (John 1:14). In His incarnation Christ was made somewhat lower than angels in the sense of being in the flesh. In the flesh Christ was lower than the angels.

F. God Having Crowned Man (Christ) with Glory and Honor

God has crowned man (Christ) with glory and honor (Psa. 8:5b; Heb. 2:7b). This refers to Christ's resurrection in His glory. Through resurrection He entered into glory; He was glorified in His resurrection (John 7:39b; Luke 24:26). This also refers to Christ's ascension in His honor (Acts 2:33-36; 5:31a). Christ's resurrection is mainly in His glory, and His ascension is mainly in His honor. Glory refers to the condition. Honor refers to the position. Condition-wise, Christ is in glory. Position-wise, Christ is in honor. He has both glory in condition and honor in position.

This was through His all-inclusive death (Heb. 2:9). Without death He could have never entered into resurrection, and He could have never reached His ascension.

G. God Having Caused Man (Christ)
to Rule over the Works of God's Hands and
Having Put All Things under His Feet

God has caused man (Christ) to rule over the works of God's hands and has put all things under His feet: all sheep and oxen, the beasts of the field, the birds of heaven, the fish of the sea, and whatever passes through the paths of the seas (Psa. 8:6-8; Heb. 2:7b-8a). This word was fulfilled first in Adam (Gen. 1:26-28). But this word was broken by man's fall. Today nothing is subject to us. Even the mosquitoes still come to defeat us. Nothing today is under us because the order has been fully destroyed by man's fall. But there will be a time, the time of restoration, when everything will be in a good order. This word will be fulfilled in full in Christ in the millennium, the age of restoration (Rev. 20:4-6; Matt. 19:28). Isaiah 11:6-9 and 65:25 speak of the wonderful divine order in the time of restoration. This is because of Christ's redemption.

H. O Jehovah Our Lord, How Excellent (Majestic)
Is Your Name in All the Earth

Psalm 8:9 repeats the first part of verse 1 by saying, "O Jehovah our Lord, / How excellent is Your name / In all the earth." This strengthens the thought concerning the excellency of the Lord's name in all the earth. The earth now is full of the excellency of Christ. Now the earth is not a messy earth but an excellent earth because the excellency of the name of Christ fills all the earth. In this verse the psalmist considers that the earth is as excellent as the heavens, as indicated in the first part of the Lord's prayer: "Our Father who is in the heavens, Your name be sanctified; Your kingdom come; Your will be done, as in heaven, so also on earth" (Matt. 6:9-10).

I would like to repeat the goal of this psalm once more. The goal is to join the earth to the heavens and to bring down the heavens to the earth, making these two one. If we are victorious and overcoming every day, this is our reality. Today with us, the earth is joined to the heavens, the heavens are brought down to the earth, and the two are one. But with the unbelieving ones and with the defeated Christians, the heavens are far away and the earth is dark and messy. This is why the unbelievers need all kinds of worldly amusements and sinful pleasures. But we do not need them. We need only Christ and the church life.

When we live Christ and live in the church life, the heavens and the earth are one. With us, our earth is really joined to the heavens. With us, the heavens are always here. Here on earth we have the excellent name of Jesus. On this earth today the only excellency is with the name of Christ. Hallelujah! There is such a name! We have this precious name on earth, and we also have our splendor, our glory, above the heavens.

Eventually, with us, the earth and the heavens will be one in a complete way. In the coming age, in the millennium, in the age of restoration, the heaven is down and the earth is up. There we will enjoy God's salvation to the uttermost. In the millennium all of us will be babes and sucklings. There will be no older ones, no fatigued ones. Everyone will be fresh, young, living, and full of strength.

Today many Christians like power, but the Bible in Psalm 8 speaks of strength. We need to be full of strength to praise the Lord, to express God's consummated work in His redemption.

I. An Additional Word on Psalm 8:2-5

Psalm 8 has nine verses. Verse 1 and verses 6-9 are somewhat easy to understand. Verses 2-5, however, are very puzzling and not easy to understand. Why did the psalmist, after talking about the earth with the excellency of Jehovah's name and the heavens with the glory, turn to the babes and sucklings? We need to see that verses 2-5 show us how the babes and sucklings are produced.

In Psalms 3—7 David thought the earth was messy and full of problems, but in the Lord's view, His name is excellent on this earth. Furthermore, the Lord has set His splendor, His glory, above the heavens. The earth is excellent, and the heavens are glorious, but the Lord has three categories of opposers. The first is the adversaries, the second is the enemy, and the third is the avenger. On the earth, there is no problem; in the heavens, there is no problem; but what about in the air? In the air there are the adversaries, the enemy, and the avenger. How does God deal with them?

Psalm 8 is all-inclusive. It talks about the earth, the heavens, man, and the coming kingdom. But in addition to the earth, the heavens, man, and the coming kingdom, there are the adversaries, the enemy, and the avenger. Verse 2 says that because of the Lord's adversaries, He has established strength, or perfected praise. The Lord has established strength or perfected praise out of the mouths of babes and sucklings for the purpose of stopping His adversaries, the enemy, and the avenger. In this way God kills "three birds with one stone." Because of the adversaries, the enemy, and the avenger, God makes the babes and sucklings to praise Him in a complete way.

Now we need to consider who the babes and sucklings are. The sucklings are even younger than the babes, the infants, because they are still feeding on their mother's milk. They are the youngest. The little babes and sucklings do not do anything. But after growing up, they do many things. To stop a person from doing things is nearly impossible, because all human beings are doers. The whole earth is filled with man's doings. Who can stop this? Only the Lord can. No unregenerated man is a babe or a suckling. We become babes and sucklings by regeneration.

Before I was regenerated, I was very active. One day when I was nineteen years old, I was saved. That made me a quiet person. Regeneration reduced my natural activity. I began to hate my doings, my speaking, and my thinking. I was remade, re-created, by the Lord's regeneration. Every believer who has been genuinely regenerated has experienced the same thing. When a person becomes regenerated, he becomes quiet, not wanting to act or speak in himself. When I was regenerated, I just wanted to read the Bible, to kneel down to pray, to muse on God, and to consider the things of the Lord. I became a real babe and a real suckling. The Lord made me such through regeneration. We natural beings are always busy, doing a lot of work. The proper, genuine salvation stops our human doing and makes us the babes and sucklings to praise the Lord.

We also have to realize that for the Lord to regenerate us, He had to undergo a number of procedures, or processes. He had to become a man, to live on this earth, to die, to enter into Hades for three days and three nights, and He had to rise up to become the life-giving Spirit. As the Spirit, He comes into us to regenerate us. Thus, regeneration comes out of all the procedures of the Lord.

This is why right after speaking about the babes and sucklings, the psalmist continues by saying, "When I see Your heavens, the works of Your fingers, / The moon and the stars, which You have ordained, / What is man...?" (vv. 3-4a). In this verse *Your heavens, the works,* and *the moon and the stars* are all in apposition. Strictly speaking, the writing here in verses 3-4a is not grammatically complete. From the word *When* to the word *ordained* is a long subordinate clause, but where is the main clause? In this sentence, there is no main clause. There should be a main clause following the subordinate clause. Instead, after the subordinate clause, David asks, "What is man?" This writing is incomplete. David said in a poetic way, "When I see Your heavens, the works of Your fingers, / The moon and the stars, which You have ordained, / What is man?" This is not a complete sentence.

The psalmist may have been wrong grammatically, but the Spirit could never be wrong. The Spirit inspired David to compose it this way, leaving an opening for us to fill in the main clause. After he says, "When I see Your heavens, the works of Your fingers, / The moon and the stars, which You have ordained," what should be said? The main clause can be filled in. I would propose four ways. It could read, "When I see Your heavens, the works of Your fingers, / The moon and the stars, which You have ordained, *I say,* What is man...?" *I say* is the main clause. Or it can read, "When I see Your heavens...*I wonder,"* or *"I consider."* It could also read, "When I see Your heavens...*I shout."* The psalmist also could have said, "When I see Your heavens...I weep." This is very meaningful.

After David said, "When I see Your heavens, the works of
Your fingers, / The moon and the stars, which You have
ordained," there is the need of a "selah," a pause. We have to
stop here for a rest to consider what to say. When I see the
heavens, the works of God's fingers, the moon and the stars, I
have to say and I have to ask and I have to find out—"what is
man?" I have to say this; I have to ask this. I have to find out
what man is that God remembers him and visits him.

By what way did God visit man? The answer follows in
verse 5a—"You have made him somewhat lower than angels."
Today we understand that this is incarnation. How did God
visit us? He visited us by becoming incarnated. He put on
humanity and became a man to be a little lower than the
angels. This is the way God visited us.

He was also crowned with glory and honor (v. 5b). Glory
refers to His resurrection, implying His death. Without death
He could not have entered into resurrection. To be crowned
with glory is to be glorified. To be crowned with honor
implies the ascension. Therefore in one verse, verse 5, we see
Christ's incarnation, His all-inclusive death implied, His
resurrection for His glorification, and His ascension for Him
to be honored.

God visited man by being incarnated, living on this earth,
dying, rising up from the dead, and ascending to the heavens
to be crowned with glory and honor. Thus, God visited man
through the long journey of His process to become the
life-giving Spirit to reach us and to enter into us. Ultimately,
He was consummated as the life-giving Spirit. The incarnated One is now the life-giving Spirit. It is this One that can
produce the babes and the sucklings.

The babes and sucklings are produced through regeneration in the initial stage. Then they continue to be produced in
full through their sanctification, renewing, and transformation. Through transformation they are perfected in praising
the Lord. This is the Lord's recovery and the Lord's victory.
God overcomes His enemy through these babes and sucklings.
The work of Christianity is to produce active ones; they
endeavor to produce "giants." Our work is to produce babes
and sucklings.

Verses 6-8 say, "You have caused him to rule over the works of Your hands; / You have put all things under his feet: All sheep and oxen, / As well as the beasts of the field, / The birds of heaven and the fish of the sea, / Whatever passes through the paths of the seas." These verses refer to the kingdom. All things will be ruled over by Christ with His Body, and all things will be subjected under His feet. This really perfects the praise, completes the praise, in this psalm. This short psalm reveals so much. It speaks of the heavens, the earth, babes and sucklings, man, three categories of enemies, and the Lord's incarnation, human living, death, resurrection, ascension, coming back, and kingdom.

We Christians may praise the Lord, but our praise needs to be perfected. We need to praise Him for His splendor above the heavens and His excellency on earth. Then we can praise Him for His incarnation for Him to come to visit us. Then we should go on to praise Him for His human living, for His death, for His resurrection, for His ascension, and for His kingdom. We have to praise Him with all these matters. Then our praises will be perfected, completed. This praise is the strength out of the mouths of babes and sucklings. Such perfected praise is the ultimate consummation of the Lord's work of incarnation, human living, death, resurrection, ascension, and coming back to rule on this earth.

When we come to the Lord's table, we stop every kind of human speaking and human doing. We stop our work. We are here at the table to do only one thing—to praise Him. In order to praise, we must stop our work. Thus, at the Lord's table, we all are the real babes and sucklings. While we are here being stopped from all of our doings to praise the Lord, the adversaries, the enemy, and the avenger are all defeated. This is a shame to God's enemy.

We need to remain in the condition and spirit of the Lord's table. Our Christian life should be like the Lord's table. When we go home after the Lord's table, we should continue to praise the Lord. We have to learn not to do too much. On the other hand, we should not be lazy. The point is that we should stop our human doings and be those who simply praise the Lord.

LIFE-STUDY OF THE PSALMS

MESSAGE SIX

DAVID'S CONCEPT
CONCERNING GOD'S JUDGMENT
ON DAVID'S ENEMIES AMONG THE NATIONS
AND
CONCERNING MAN'S CONDITION BEFORE GOD

Scripture Reading: Psa. 9—14

We have seen that the arrangement of the Psalms was under God's sovereignty. Psalm 1 is apparently an excellent initiation, but actually it is a very negative initiation. Then Psalm 2 comes in to annul what was exalted in Psalm 1. In Psalms 3 through 7, we again see David's human concept. Then Psalm 8 declares, "O Jehovah our Lord, / How excellent is Your name / In all the earth!" This psalm is David's inspired praise of the excellency of Christ. After Psalm 8, Psalms 9—15 go down again to the human concept. Then the revelation goes up to Psalm 16, where we see Christ as the God-man in His human living, crucifixion, resurrection, and ascension. Psalms 17—21 are down from the level of Psalm 16, but they are not as far down as Psalms 3—7 and 9—15.

Psalms 22—24 rise up to show us Christ once again. Psalm 22:1 says, "My God, my God, why have You forsaken me?" This was what Christ cried out on the cross (Matt. 27:46). Then in Psalm 23 the resurrected Christ becomes our Shepherd (v. 1), and this shepherding One in Psalm 24 becomes our King (vv. 8-10). In 1969 we had a conference on the Psalms, and these messages are in the book entitled *Christ and the Church Revealed and Typified in the Psalms.* In this book there is a diagram of the spiritual level of Psalms 1—21 (p. 40). This diagram, reprinted on the following page, gives us a view of the way the Psalms were written.

In the following message, we will cover Psalms 15 and 16.

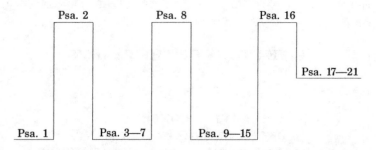

Psalm 15:1 asks us, "O Jehovah, who may sojourn in Your tent? / Who may dwell on Your holy mountain?" David's answer is—the one who is perfect according to the law (vv. 2-5). But in the whole universe there is only one person who is perfect according to the law— Jesus Christ. There is no one else. Everyone else has broken the law. We have seen that David exalted the law so highly, but by his failure regarding Uriah, he broke the last five commandments (Exo. 20:13-17). He murdered, he committed adultery, he stole by robbing another of his wife, he lied to Uriah, and he coveted Uriah's wife (2 Sam. 11).

The last five commandments prohibiting killing, fornication, stealing, lying, and coveting were given by God with the requirement that man would have the human virtues to express the divine attributes. If there were no killing, fornication, stealing, lying, or coveting in the human race, the kingdom of the heavens would really be on this earth. Today the newspapers, however, report all the evil things that take place on earth day by day. The earth is filled with murder, fornication, stealing, lying, and coveting.

No one is perfect according to the law. Paul said in the New Testament that no flesh can be justified by God based upon man's keeping of the law (Rom. 3:20; Gal. 2:16). The only One who can and did keep the law is the One unveiled in Psalm 16. This One is the very God who became a man and lived a human life (vv. 1-8). In His human life, He kept the law perfectly. He lived a life full of human virtues expressing the divine attributes. Then He died (vv. 9-10) and was resurrected (vv. 10-11a). Now He is in ascension at the right hand of God (v. 11b & c). This is the One who can sojourn in God's tabernacle and dwell with God on His holy mountain. We will see more concerning Psalms 15 and 16 in the following message.

In this message we want to cover Psalms 9 —14. In Psalm 9 we see David's concept concerning God's judgment on David's enemies among the nations. David mentioned clearly that he had many enemies among the nations. Today all of the Arab countries are enemies of Israel. It is regrettable that Israel has not yet turned to God, but the Bible tells us that although Israel has been re-formed as a nation, they will not turn to God until Christ returns (Zech. 12:10). Today Israel, just like David, is surrounded by enemies. In addition to the enemies surrounding David, he had the adversaries from within, even from his house, from his family. His son Absalom became the leading adversary.

In Psalms 10 —14 David speaks of man's condition before God. It is hard to find another portion in the Bible which presents us a complete picture of man's condition as in these psalms. When Paul preached the gospel in Romans, he quoted from this portion of the Word (Rom. 3:10-12, 14).

I. ACCORDING TO THE LAW GIVEN BY GOD ALONGSIDE THE CENTRAL LINE OF HIS ECONOMY

David's concept in these psalms is according to the law given by God alongside the central line of His economy. God has an economy, and in God's economy there is a central line. This central line is Christ to be enlarged to have a counterpart, that is, His church. Thus, Christ and the church are the central line of God's economy. But David's concept in Psalms 9—14 was not along this line. David's concept was according to the law, a subsidiary line that goes along with the central line. The law is not the central line. The law is a side line going along with the central line.

II. BASED ON THE PRINCIPLE OF GOOD AND EVIL— THE PRINCIPLE OF THE TREE OF THE KNOWLEDGE OF GOOD AND EVIL

David's concept in these psalms is also based upon the

principle of good and evil—the principle of the tree of the knowledge of good and evil (Gen. 2:9). These psalms show that David was full of the knowledge of good and evil. I would even say that in these psalms David himself was the tree of the knowledge of good and evil. Now I would like us to consider what kind of "tree" we are. We all should be able to declare that we are the tree of life. We should not be those who minister good and evil to others. Instead we should always minister Christ as life. Since I began to minister in the United States in 1962, all of my messages have been in the principle of the tree of life.

III. CONCERNING GOD'S JUDGMENT ON DAVID'S ENEMIES AMONG THE NATIONS

Psalm 9 reveals David's concept concerning God's judgment on David's enemies among all the nations.

A. God Sitting upon the Throne as the King to Judge the World in Righteousness and with Equity

David said that God sits upon the throne as the King to judge the world in righteousness and with equity (Psa. 9:4, 7-8). We may feel that this word is good, but we need to consider it in the light of the New Testament. In the New Testament, we are told that Christ is the King, even the Ruler of all the kings (Rev. 1:5; 19:16), sitting on the throne not to judge but to save. Today we have a saving King. Acts 5:31 says that God uplifted Christ to His right hand that He may be the Leader and the Savior. David's thought is that his God is the King on the throne to judge—not to save the world in mercy and grace but to judge the world in righteousness and with equity. *With equity* simply means with justice. The whole world is neither righteous nor just, so David had a good concept that the One who is sitting on the throne judges in righteousness and with justice. But this concept is according to the law and according to the tree of the knowledge of good and evil.

B. God Having Rebuked the Nations,
Destroyed the Wicked,
and Uprooted Their Cities

David said that God has rebuked the nations, destroyed the wicked, and uprooted their cities (Psa. 9:5-6).

C. God Having Upheld
David's Right and His Cause

David also said that God upheld his right and his cause and destroyed his enemies (Psa. 9:3-4a). This means that God was not good to the world, but God was very good to David. David's thought was that his Judge in the heavens upheld his cause and destroyed his enemies. This is not according to the divine concept of the New Testament.

D. For This, David Giving Thanks to God
and Telling Out All God's Wonders and Praises

For this, David gave thanks to God and told out all God's wonders and praises (Psa. 9:1, 14a). Wonders are wonderful doings, and praises here mean virtues. Because David thought that God upheld his right and his cause, destroying all his enemies, he had to thank God and tell out all of His wonderful doings and virtues.

E. God Being a High Refuge for the Oppressed

David said that God is a high refuge for the oppressed, not forsaking His seekers, remembering the slain, and not forgetting the cry of the afflicted (Psa. 9:9, 10b, 12). If God remembers the slain, David should not have forgotten Uriah, the one slain by him according to his conspiracy.

F. David Advising Others to Put Their Trust in God

David advised others to put their trust in God, sing psalms to Him, declare His deeds among the peoples, and exult in God's salvation (Psa. 9:10-11, 14). In a sense, what David wrote in Psalms 9—14 is neither according to the Old or the New Testament. This is David's "testament."

G. The Nations Having Sunk
in the Pit That They Made

David said that the nations have sunk in the pit that they made; their own foot is caught in the net that they hid; the wicked have been snared in their own work; and all the nations who forget God will be turned back to Sheol (Psa. 9:15-17). It seems these ones were in Sheol, Hades, already. Now David prayed that God would send them back and not let them out of Sheol. What kind of prayer is this? Is this the New Testament? This is again David's "testament."

H. The Needy Not Always Being Forgotten

David also said that the needy will not always be forgotten by God, nor will the hope of the afflicted perish forever (Psa. 9:18).

I. David Asking God to Look on His Affliction
and Not Let Mortal Man Prevail

David asked God to look on his affliction and not let mortal man prevail, but let the nations know that they are mortal (Psa. 9:13a, 19, 20b). It was as if David said, "God, You have to tell the nations that they are mortal men. Since they are mortal, they cannot prevail against me because I am under Your care; so look on my affliction." But what about David's sins? His wife at that time was actually the wife of the one whom he murdered. One thousand years later, when Matthew wrote the genealogy of Christ, he said, "David begot Solomon of her who had been the wife of Uriah" (1:6). David, a man after the heart of God (1 Sam. 13:14; Acts 13:22), did right in the eyes of the Lord all the days of his life except for this one evil (1 Kings 15:5).

IV. CONCERNING MAN'S CONDITION BEFORE GOD

Psalms 10—14 show us David's concept concerning man's condition before God.

A. David Challenging God

David challenged God, saying, "Why, O Jehovah, do You

stand far off? / Why do You hide Yourself in times of distress?" (10:1). David prayed, but God did not answer absolutely according to what he prayed, so that bothered him. It was as if David asked God, "Why do You hide Yourself when I need You in times of distress? It seems that the more I cry out to You, the more You disappear."

B. The Wicked Man's Sin against People and Arrogance toward God

In Psalm 10:2-11 David describes the wicked man's sin against people and arrogance toward God. The wicked man thinks there is no God, so he can do whatever he likes (v. 4). Verses 2-11 describe the condition of man. Actually, David is accusing all of mankind in these verses.

C. David's Request of God

Psalm 10:12-15 is David's request of God. After he presented the condition of man, he asked God to come to judge the wicked.

D. David's Praise to God

Psalm 10:14b and 16-18 are David's praise to God. The contents of this praise, however, are altogether negative. He said, "Jehovah is King forever and ever; / The nations have perished from His land" (v. 16). He did not praise God for the nations being saved by God's grace, but for the nations perishing. According to the revelation of the New Testament, God is not like this.

E. God Being in His Holy Temple, His Throne Being in Heaven, and His Eyes Discerning the Righteous Man and the Wicked Man

In Psalm 11 David said that God is in His holy temple, His throne is in heaven, and His eyes discern the righteous man and the wicked man. Verse 6 says that Jehovah "will rain down snares upon the wicked; / Fire and brimstone and a scorching wind will be the portion of their cup." If this were the case, the earth would already have been destroyed.

There would be no possibility for billions of human beings to live on this earth. Verse 7 says, "For Jehovah is righteous; He loves righteous deeds. / The upright man will behold His face." David said this, but he himself was not righteous. Actually, he was in darkness without any sensation about himself. He was not qualified to say this because he murdered a man and robbed that man of his wife.

F. David's Request and Jehovah's Willingness to Deal with the Wicked in Their Tongue and Lips

In Psalm 12 we see David's request and Jehovah's willingness to deal with the wicked in their tongue and lips. In verse 2a David said, "Each man speaks falsehood with his neighbor." But David was no different; he also spoke falsehood. As a whole, his concept was altogether based upon and entangled with the law and with good and evil.

G. David Taking Counsel with God That He Might Overcome His Enemy

Psalm 13 shows that David took counsel with God that he might overcome his enemy. In today's New Testament age, could we go to God and ask Him to put down our enemies, the ones that hate us? We cannot do this because the New Testament tells us to love our enemies and pray for those who persecute us (Matt. 5:44; Rom. 12:14, 20). In Psalm 13:3, David said, "Consider and answer me, O Jehovah my God; / Brighten my eyes lest I sleep the sleep of death." David was afraid that he would die while he was sleeping. He was afraid of sleeping a sleep of death.

H. God's Dealing with the Corrupt Fool and His Salvation to His People

In Psalm 14 we see David's concept concerning God's dealing with the corrupt fool and His salvation to His people. Verse 3 says, "Everyone has turned aside; / They are together perverse. / There is none who does good; / There is not even one." This word is quoted by Paul in Romans 3:12. The last verse of Psalm 14 is a good prophecy concerning the return of Israel from captivity—"O that the salvation of Israel might come forth from Zion! / When Jehovah turns the captivity of His people, / Jacob will exult, Israel will rejoice."

Psalms 9—14 show us a man who was supposedly very godly, yet his thought, his concept, was altogether wrapped up with the law and with the tree of the knowledge of good and evil. These psalms are David's thought regarding his welfare. In principle, these six psalms are the same as Psalms 3—7. Nothing in them is related to God's economy, to God's interest, to God's kingdom, or to God's plan. But everything is concerning David's personal benefit, personal interest, personal safety, and personal peace. Do you think this should be a model to us? Surely it should not. We have to stay in the line of the tree of life, the line covered in Psalms 2 and 8.

I believe that such a study of the Word, according to the principles of the divine revelation, will help all of us to understand the Holy Bible. The Holy Bible is the writing of God. When we read it, we should not understand it according to our way or our concept. A person may be very scholarly and learned and yet receive nothing of the divine revelation from the Bible. This is because he understands the Bible, interprets it, appreciates it, and teaches it according to his natural understanding.

In the Lord's recovery among us in the past seventy years, since Brother Watchman Nee's time, the proper interpretation of the Bible has always been preserved in the principles of the Bible. People may criticize us, but no one can accuse us of saying anything against the principles of the Word. This is why I am happy to have this life-study to show us the difference between Psalm 1 and Psalm 2 and the difference between Psalms 3—7 and Psalm 8. Now we have considered Psalms 9—14. Based upon what we have seen according to the principles of the Bible, there is not any point in these six psalms that is up to the standard of the divine revelation.

Today in the New Testament principle, God does have a throne, and He is really sitting on the throne. But the throne today is called the throne of grace (Heb. 4:16). Furthermore, from eternity past to eternity future, God's intention is to love the world. John 3:16 says, "God so loved the world that He gave His only begotten Son, that every one who believes into Him would not perish, but would have eternal life." The world in John 3:16 denotes the fallen human race. God loved the fallen human race, so He gave His only begotten Son to come to die for us that we should not perish but have eternal life through our believing into Him. The basic principle of the New Testament is that God loves fallen mankind. If this were not so, none of us could have been saved. We all have been saved based upon the principle that God loves the human race. Even though we, the human race, are fallen and have become the world, God loves us.

Therefore, God's throne today is not a throne of the King of authority. His throne today is the throne of a loving Savior. This throne of authority has become today the throne of grace. Every day and even every moment, we can come to approach this throne of grace that we may receive mercy and find grace for timely help (Heb. 4:16). This is today's dispensation of grace established by God. The Old Testament is the dispensation of the law, but even the Old Testament speaks of God's mercy. In Hosea 6:6 God said, "For I desired mercy, and not sacrifice." The Lord Jesus quoted this word in Matthew 9:13. God loves mercy because He is a God of mercy, a God of compassions. God desires to see people favored with His mercy, not judged by His being righteous. This is a principle in the Bible. When we interpret or teach the Bible, we need to take care of the governing principles.

LIFE-STUDY OF THE PSALMS

MESSAGE SEVEN

WHAT KIND OF MAN MAY DWELL WITH GOD FOR HIS HEART'S DESIRE AND GOOD PLEASURE?

Scripture Reading: Psa. 15—16

In this message we come to another pair of psalms, Psalms 15 and 16. We have seen that Psalms 1 and 2 were sovereignly arranged as a pair. Psalm 1 says that the man whose delight is in the law of Jehovah is blessed (vv. 1-2). Psalm 2 says that the man who takes refuge in the Son is blessed (v. 12). Thus, we see the human concept of being blessed by the keeping of the law versus the divine concept of being blessed by taking refuge in the Son. The comparison in Psalms 1 and 2 is between the law and Christ.

Psalms 15 and 16 also present a comparison. The end of Psalm 15 says, "He who does these things will not be shaken forever." *These things* refer to the good things according to the law in the foregoing verses. On the other hand, Psalm 16:8b says, "Because He is at My right hand, I shall not be shaken." Psalm 15 says that if you do all the good things according to the law, you will never be shaken. Then Psalm 16 says concerning Christ that because God is at His right hand, He will not be shaken. No doubt, Psalms 15 and 16 were arranged together to show us a comparison between the keeping of the law and the participating in the Son. Do we keep the law or do we partake of Christ? Do we keep the law or do we enjoy Christ as our portion?

At this point I would like us to read Psalms 15 and 16 together so that we can see the different concepts in these psalms. Afterward, we will cover them in more detail.

At the beginning of Psalm 15, the psalmist asks, "O Jehovah, who may sojourn in Your tent? / Who may dwell on Your holy mountain?" The tent refers to God's house, the temple.

David says that this one is "He who walks in integrity / And does righteousness / And speaks truth from his heart. / He does not slander with his tongue; / He does not do evil to his friend, / Nor does he take up reproach upon his neighbor. / In his eyes a reprobate is despised, / But he honors those who fear Jehovah. / Should he swear to his harm, / He does not change. / He does not lend his money on interest, / Nor accept a bribe against the innocent. / He who does these things will not be shaken forever" (vv. 2-5). This may seem like an excellent psalm, but actually it is a psalm in the line of the tree of the knowledge of good and evil.

Psalm 16, on the other hand, is a psalm revealing the God-man, Christ. Psalm 16:1 does not say, "Preserve Me, O God, for I keep the law, and I meditate in the law day and night." This is absolutely wrong. Psalm 16:1 says, "Preserve Me, O God, for I take refuge in You." It was as if the psalmist said, "I don't care for the law; I care for You and I enjoy You." Then Psalm 16:2 continues, "O My soul, you say to Jehovah, You are My Lord; / No good have I beyond You." When the Lord Jesus was a man on this earth, He always held such an attitude of recognizing God the Father as His Lord. His attitude toward the Father could have been expressed by His saying, "I do not have anything beyond You which is good. I have no blessing, no pleasure, and no enjoyment other than You."

Verse 3 says, "To the saints who are on the earth and to the excellent, / All My delight is in them." The Lord Jesus loved God the Father. He also had His delight in the saints, in the believers, in the members of His Body. He did not delight in the commandments of the law, but in the members of His Body, the saints in God's kingdom.

Verse 4 says, "Sorrows will be multiplied to them who bartered for some other god; / Their drink offerings of blood I will not offer, / Nor will I take up their names upon My lips." *Their names* refers to the names of the idols, the names of the other gods.

Verse 5 says, "Jehovah is the portion of My inheritance and of My cup; / You maintain My lot." God is the portion of two things: of the inheritance and of the cup. The inheritance refers to the substance of the lot, and the cup refers to the enjoyment of God as our blessing. At the Lord's table, we drink the cup of blessing (1 Cor. 10:16a). Stanza 3 of *Hymns,* #223 points out that in this cup God is our portion. Thus, we have God as the portion for our inheritance and for our enjoyment. God the Father was the very portion of these two things to Christ as a man on this earth. Verse 5b says, "You maintain My lot." The lot is the portion of the inheritance.

Verse 6a says, "The measuring lines have fallen on pleasant places for Me." To understand this verse, we have to read Psalm 2:8, which says that God will give to Christ the nations as His inheritance and the limits of the earth as His possession. *The limits* are the measuring lines of God in His divine economy. God has measured the earth. Whatever God has measured will be Christ's possession. The measuring lines have fallen on pleasant places for Christ.

Today the whole earth is not a pleasant place, not a place of pleasure. Even though people are trying to have their amusements, that is not the real pleasure. The earth today is a messy earth, not a pleasant earth. In Genesis 2 the earth was a pleasant garden, but after the fall of man, this pleasant garden became a messy earth. But when the earth will be measured and given to Christ, it will become a pleasant earth. Verse 6b says, "Indeed the inheritance is beautiful to Me." All the nations with the earth will be not only pleasant but also beautiful to Christ as the man who inherited God's inheritance.

Verse 7a says, "I will bless Jehovah, who counsels Me." Do you like to have someone as your counselor? To take others' counsel implies humility. A person is humble who wants to receive counsel from others. The Lord Jesus blessed Jehovah, the One who counseled Him. Isaiah 50:4 tells us the attitude of Christ as the Servant of Jehovah: "The Lord Jehovah has given me / The tongue of the instructed, / That I should know how to sustain the weary with a word. / He awakens me morning by morning; / He awakens my ear / To hear as an instructed one." Christ, in His human living, had the tongue of an instructed One, and He heard as an instructed One. He took God the Father as His counselor.

Psalm 16:7b says, "Indeed in the nights My inward parts instruct Me." This shows us that when God counseled Christ as a man, Christ's inward parts instructed Him. The inward parts of Christ were one with God. God counsels, and the inward parts instruct. This is our proper experience today. On the one hand, it is God who counsels us. On the other hand, it is our inward parts which instruct us. Our inward parts instruct us mostly in the nights while we are quiet. In the night, from four to six in the morning, I receive many things and many instructions from the Lord. Most of the light I have written down in the outlines for these messages has come during these hours. This is an experience of our inward parts instructing us in the nights.

Verse 8a says, "I have set Jehovah before Me continually." According to David's natural concept, he might have said, "I have set the law before me continually." We may want to say, "I have set the Bible before me continually." But even this is not as good as saying, "I have set Jehovah, the person, before me continually."

Verse 8b says, "Because He is at My right hand, I shall not be shaken." Because the Father was at Christ's right hand, He would not be shaken. Our security is not to keep the law, but to have Jehovah, the person, at our right hand. We shall not be shaken because we have Him as our security.

Verse 9 says, "Therefore My heart rejoices and My glory exults; / Even My flesh dwells securely." *Glory* here refers to our spirit. This verse covers our soul, which is included in our heart; our spirit, which is the glory; and our body, which is the flesh. What is in this verse transpired in the death of Christ. When He was in Hades He said, "My heart rejoices, My spirit exults, and even My body dwells securely." His body dwelt in a secured tomb.

Verse 10 says, "For You will not abandon My soul to Sheol, / Nor let Your Holy One see the pit." Christ was not bothered to be in Hades, in Sheol. *Hades* is from the Greek, and *Sheol* is from the Hebrew. They both refer to the same thing. The Septuagint translates *pit* as *corruption*. This means that Christ's body would not see corruption. It would not be decayed. This is because within three days, His body was resurrected from the tomb, and His soul was raised up from Hades.

Verse 11 says, "You will make known to Me the path of life." The path of life is the way of resurrection. God the Father made known to Christ the way of resurrection. Verse 11 continues, "In Your presence is fullness of joy." This was in Christ's ascension. In God's presence in the heavens is fullness of joy. Finally, verse 11 says, "In Your right hand there are pleasures forever." In God's right hand in ascension, Christ is enjoying pleasures forever.

We need to notice that in this whole psalm, Psalm 16, nothing concerning good and evil is mentioned. The revelation in Psalm 16 is far beyond our natural understanding.

From the day we were born, we were always taught to take care of good and evil. We were taught that we need to do good and abandon evil. In every culture on all the continents, this same thing is taught. We may be people of different colors, but in our thought concerning good and evil, we are absolutely the same. We are "birds of the same feather" in our natural, human concept of good and evil. Psalm 15 is full of the concept of good and evil. In Psalm 16, however, there is no good and evil. Instead what replaces good and evil is the Lord Himself, the very person.

In the following message, I will fellowship concerning the lines, the principles, and the spirit of the Bible. For us to read and study the Bible properly, we have to know the two lines in the Bible, the principles in the Bible, and the spirit of the Bible.

In the Bible there are two lines. Right after God created man, God brought man into the garden and put him in front of two trees. These two trees were not a tree of good and a tree of evil. Good and evil are of one tree. We should not forget this. In the eyes of God, good is the same as evil. They are considered as one unit, as one tree. The other tree is the tree of life. Thus, there are the tree of the knowledge of good and evil and the tree of life (Gen. 2:8-9).

With the tree of the knowledge of good and evil, there are knowledge, good, evil, and death. Thus, knowledge, good, evil, and death are all one family. If you are in the family of good, you are in the family of evil. Where good is, evil is there; where good and evil are, knowledge is there; and where knowledge is, death is there. This family is very complicated and terrible. It includes the good teachings of Confucius and the evil deeds of bank robbers. What family is this? It is the family of good and evil. But in the family of the tree of life, there is only one thing: life, life, life, life! There is no good, but life; no evil, but life; no knowledge, but life; and no death, but life. This is the tree of life.

The tree of the knowledge of good and evil and the tree of life are two sources, which produce two lines. These two lines start from Genesis 2 and go through the entire Old and New Testaments to reach two ends. The one end for the tree of the knowledge of good and evil is the lake of fire, and the other end for the tree of life is the New Jerusalem. The lake is full of burning fire, but the holy city is full of water, flowing and quenching and watering and saturating. If you are of the source of good and evil and are always going along in the line of good and evil, you will arrive at the lake of fire. There are only two ends in the entire universe: the lake of fire and the city of water.

The divine revelation of the Bible shows us two starts, two sources, two lines, and two ends, two results. If we can see these two lines, they will become governing principles to us in our understanding of the Bible. We will be governed and kept from making any mistakes. Throughout the years, in all the messages we have given, we have been governed by these two principles as the two main lines in the holy Scriptures.

We need to consider the book of Psalms in the light of these two lines. If we are the appreciators of the law, as David was in Psalm 1, we are on the line of good and evil. People may wonder what is wrong with good and evil. But if we trace this line to the end of the Bible, we arrive at the lake of fire. When you "drive" to and arrive at the end of the divine revelation on this line, you know you are wrong. The line of good and evil leads to the lake of fire.

The person in Psalm 2 takes refuge in the Son and kisses

the Son, loves the Son (v. 12). This one surely is on the line of life leading to the New Jerusalem. We need to be those who are on the line of life. The person in Psalm 15 is on the line of good and evil. Psalm 16, however, reveals Christ as the God-man. He has been, still is, and always will be on the line of life. Those of us on the line of life will eventually be in the New Jerusalem, the city of living water.

After the fall of man, the Bible tells us that Adam had two sons. Actually, I believe Adam had more sons, but only two sons are recorded in the Bible because these two sons represent two lines. The first son was Cain, and the second son was Abel. Cain was a representative of good and evil. At first, he was good. He presented the offerings of the labor of his own hands to God. This was good according to Cain's way, but he was rejected. God rejects man's evil. God also rejects man's good as evil. Then when Cain was rejected by God, he immediately turned to kill his brother. This was evil (Gen. 4:1-8). On the one hand, he did something good. On the other hand, he did something evil. Both good and evil are in the same line. Cain was in the line of the tree of the knowledge of good and evil. Abel, however, was not in this line. He enjoyed Christ as his burnt offering to contact God and to take God as his portion. Abel was in the line of life.

The title of this message is a question. This is the question David asks in Psalm 15—"What kind of man may dwell with God for His heart's desire and good pleasure?" We may think that the man of good can dwell with God, but not the man of evil. Good and evil are our two lines. Teachers of philosophy and those of many religions would all say that if there is a God, only a good man, not an evil man, could dwell with Him. All of them would hold the same concept. But thank the Lord, in the Bible, which is His divine revelation, we have a pair of psalms, Psalms 15 and 16, to show us what kind of man God wants. God does not want an evil man or a good man. God rejects the good man as the evil man. They are of the same source, in the same nature, and in the same entity. They are in the same line and will arrive at the same end. Only a God-man can satisfy God's desire and fulfill His good pleasure.

I. DAVID'S CONCEPT—PSALM 15

A. According to the Law Given by God at Sinai alongside the Central Line of God's Economy

In Psalm 15, David's concept was according to the law given by God at Sinai alongside the central line of God's economy. His concept in this psalm was not at Zion in the central line of God's economy. It was at Sinai. Do you love the name Sinai? According to Galatians 4, Sinai symbolizes a source that produced slaves, who are rejected by the grace of God (vv. 24-31). The law given by God at Sinai goes alongside the central line of God's economy. This side line always goes in parallel with the central line.

Satan is always where God is. The book of Job shows that Satan even went to the sanctuary in the heavens where God was (1:6-7). Before we are going to have a meeting, I pray desperately, asking the Lord to chase away all the darkness, all the demons, and all the evil spirits. This is because where God is, Satan is. Where the central line goes, the side line will come along to bother and distract you.

B. The Perfect Man according to the Law

Psalm 15:2-5 shows that David's concept in this psalm was that the perfect man according to the law could dwell with God for His heart's desire and good pleasure. Thus, verse 5 says that he who does these good things will not be shaken forever.

II. THE DIVINE REVELATION—PSALM 16

Following Psalm 15, we see the divine revelation in Psalm 16.

A. According to the Economy of God

The divine revelation in Psalm 16 is according to the economy of God with Christ as its centrality and universality, ordained by God in eternity (Eph. 3:9, 11).

B. The God-man, Christ

Psalm 16 reveals the God-man, Christ, not the good man.

God does not desire a good man, but a God-man. He does not desire a man with two "o's" as in the word *good,* but a man with one "o" as in the word *God.* Psalm 16 shows us Christ in His four stages: the stages of human living, death, resurrection, and ascension. Only God with His Spirit could write such a psalm. The human mind could never compose such a writing.

1. In His Human Living

Psalm 16:1-8 reveals the God-man, Christ, in His human living. He is not merely a good man, but a God-man. God became a man and lived on this earth for thirty-three and a half years. He lived in Nazareth until the age of thirty. Then He ministered for three and a half years. He was the very God living a human life in a small geographical area. The land of Palestine in the time of Jesus was a very small and narrow strip of land. He grew up in the small village of Nazareth in the despised place of Galilee for thirty years. What patience He had! Then He came out to travel in His ministry. Of course, there was not the modern means of transportation which we enjoy today. Jesus had to travel mostly by foot within the land of Palestine.

The four Gospels show us the marvelous human living of this God-man. No biography can compare with Jesus' life. Millions of readers of these four Gospels have been inspired by the way in which Jesus Christ lived on earth. After His human living, He entered into death for three days and three nights. Then He came out of death and entered into resurrection. Finally, He ascended to the heavens where God the Father is. Today He is in ascension at the right hand of God the Father. Psalm 16 is a short psalm, but it covers such a wonderful Person in His four stages: His human living, His death, His resurrection, and His ascension.

a. Implying His Incarnation

His human living spontaneously implies His incarnation. If He had not been incarnated and did not have the human nature with a human body, He could not have lived on earth. Because He was altogether in humanity, He did not threaten anyone. Even the small children could come to Him (Luke 18:15-16). He was so wonderful—because He was God born to be a man. God, in this man, in this humanity, lived on earth.

His human living implies His incarnation in which He became a man and brought divinity into humanity (John 1:14a). Formerly, before the incarnation, divinity was separate from humanity. But when Jesus was born, divinity was brought into humanity, and divinity and humanity were mingled together to produce a God-man.

b. Taking Refuge in God and Trusting in God's Preservation

Christ took refuge in God and trusted in God's preservation (Psa. 16:1). We may pray, "Lord Jesus, protect us; preserve us." When Christ was a man on this earth, the very God in whom He trusted was also His preservation.

c. Taking God as His Lord and Having No Good beyond God

Christ took God as His Lord and had no good beyond God (Psa. 16:2). Today on earth everyone, even the most sinful person, is claiming his rights. But the Lord Jesus, while He was a man on this earth, did not claim any right for Himself. He took God as His Lord. Every man needs God as his Lord. Without the Lord, we do not know who our Possessor is. Our parents or our wives are not our possessors. Christ the Lord is the One who owns us. He is our Possessor. Christ in His human living had no good beyond God. His good was uniquely God Himself as His portion.

d. Having Delight in the Saints, the Excellent on the Earth

Christ has delight in the saints, the excellent people on the earth (Psa. 16:3). *The saints* implies the church, the Body of Christ. Why does Christ delight in the saints? It is because the saints are the members that constitute His Body, the church. While we are gathered together in the meetings, many other people are gathered together to engage in worldly entertainment and sinful pleasures. Who is the excellent group in God's eyes? By the Lord's mercy, we are the excellent group. In Christ's view, we are a particular and excellent people. Christ delights in God's people, and He has made us excellent.

e. Having Nothing to Do with Other Gods and Their Offerings, nor Taking Up Their Names upon His Lips

Christ in His human living had nothing to do with other gods and their offerings, nor did He take up their names upon His lips (Psa. 16:4). He would not mention the names of any idols. He even would not mention the names of the idol worshippers. That would contaminate His lips.

f. Taking God as the Portion of His Inheritance and of His Cup, and Trusting in God to Maintain His Lot

Christ took God as the portion of His inheritance and of His cup (Psa. 16:5). *Inheritance* refers to a possession, and *cup* refers to enjoyment. In Christ's human living, God became His possession and also His enjoyment. God was His inheritance and His cup. With the inheritance, there is a portion, and with the cup, there is also a portion. The portion of our inheritance and of our cup today is Christ. Furthermore, Christ trusted in God to maintain His lot (v. 5). Today the whole earth is a mess. Seemingly there is no hope for this earth. We may think the earth is hopeless, but God still maintains it for Christ. Eventually, Christ will inherit the earth as His possession.

g. Appreciating the Possession Given by God to Him under the Measuring Lines on Pleasant Places and the Beautiful Inheritance Given to Him by God

Christ appreciated the possession given by God to Him under the measuring lines on pleasant places and the beautiful inheritance given to Him by God (Psa. 16:6; 2:8; Rev. 11:15). This messy earth will become a pleasant globe to Christ when He comes back to inherit it.

h. Blessing God Who Counsels Him, and
Being Instructed by His Inward Parts in the Nights
(through His Contact with God)

Christ blessed God who counseled Him and was instructed by His inward parts in the nights through His contact with God (Psa. 16:7; Luke 6:12).

i. Setting God before Him Continually and
Not Being Shaken Because God Is at His Right Hand

Christ set God before Him continually and was not shaken (cf. Psa. 15:5b) because God was at His right hand (Psa. 16:8; Acts 2:25). In John 8:29 the Lord said that while He was on this earth, He was never alone, because God the Father was always with Him. In Jesus' human living, God the Father was with Him.

2. In His Death

In Psalm 16:9-10 we see the revelation of the God-man, Christ, in His death (Acts 2:26-27).

a. His Heart Rejoicing and
His Spirit with His Tongue Exulting

Psalm 16:9a says that Christ's heart was rejoicing and His glory was exulting. This means His heart was rejoicing in Hades. The Hebrew word for *glory* in verse 9 can be interpreted as *spirit* or *tongue*. The Hebrew word means glory, but the Greek Septuagint translated the Hebrew word for *glory* into *tongue*. When Peter quoted Psalm 16:9 from the Septuagint in Acts 2, he said, "My tongue exulted" (v. 26). Some other versions translate the Hebrew word for glory as *mouth*. Thus, three things are referred to by the word *glory*: our spirit, our tongue, and our mouth. In Christ's death His heart was rejoicing, and His spirit with His tongue was exulting.

We have to exercise our spirit, our mouth, and our tongue in the meetings. This is the way to prophesy. Many saints come to the meetings and sit quietly. They are like the "marble Mary" outside some Catholic cathedrals. I would like to ask them, "Where is your spirit? Where is your mouth?

Where is your tongue?" In the meetings their spirit is not exercised, their mouth is not exercised, and their tongue is not exercised. When we are in the meetings, we should exercise our spirit, our mouth, and our tongue to speak for the Lord. Then we will be glorious; we will be in glory. When we do not exercise in such a way, we are in a low condition. We need to exercise our spirit, our mouth, and our tongue to speak Christ to one another in the meetings. Then we are glorious because we are exercising the three parts of our glory: the spirit, the mouth, and the tongue.

Christ's heart rejoicing and His glory, His spirit with His tongue, exulting indicate that Christ was obedient to God even unto death, and that the death of a cross (Phil. 2:8). He was obedient unto death, not an ordinary death but a particular death, the death of the cross. This also indicates that Christ was willing and happy to die for the accomplishment of God's economy. He told us in John 10:17-18 that no one took His life away, but He laid it down. He also had the authority to take His life back. He died for the accomplishment of God's economy.

b. His Flesh (His Physical Body)
Dwelling Securely

In His death, Christ's flesh (His physical body) dwelt securely (Psa. 16:9b). This indicates that Christ's body was buried in a secured tomb (Matt. 27:59-60). This also indicates that Christ was resting physically in His burial waiting to be resurrected.

c. His Soul Having Gone to Sheol (Hades)
and Remaining There for Three Days

His soul went to Sheol (Hades) and remained there for three days (Psa. 16:10a; Eph. 4:9).

d. Not to See Corruption (Decay)
in His Physical Body

He did not see corruption (decay) in His physical body (Psa. 16:10b). This indicates His death and burial.

3. *In His Resurrection*

Now we come to the third stage of Christ in Psalm 16—His resurrection (Psa. 16:10-11a; Acts 2:27-28a).

a. *God Not to Abandon Christ's Soul to Sheol*

God would not abandon Christ's soul to Sheol, nor let Him as God's Holy One see corruption, decay (Psa. 16:10; Acts 2:31). This indicates that Christ's soul would be raised up from Hades and also that Christ's physical body would be resurrected from the tomb (Matt. 28:6; John 20:5-9).

b. *God to Make Known to Christ the Path of Life—Resurrection*

God would make known to Christ the path of life—resurrection (Psa. 16:11a; Matt. 28:6). In His incarnation Christ brought divinity into humanity; in His resurrection He brought humanity into divinity. In His incarnation Christ made something divine, human; in His resurrection He made something human, divine.

In resurrection Christ was also begotten of God to be the firstborn Son of God (Psa. 2:7; Acts 13:33; Rom. 8:29). Through His incarnation Christ put on humanity. In His resurrection He brought His human part into divinity to be begotten of God that He could be the firstborn Son of God. In eternity past and before His resurrection, He was the only begotten Son of God (John 3:16). But in resurrection the only begotten Son became the firstborn Son of God by having His humanity begotten of God.

In Christ's resurrection the believers were regenerated to be the many sons of God and the many brothers of Christ (1 Pet. 1:3; Heb. 2:10; Rom. 8:29). First Peter 1:3 says that through the resurrection of Christ, God regenerated us, all the believers. Actually, we were not regenerated at the time when we believed. That is merely according to our estimation. According to the divine fact, we all were regenerated together nearly two thousand years ago. When Christ in His humanity was begotten of God to be God's firstborn Son, all His believers were also begotten of God to be God's many sons. Thus, now through the resurrection of Christ, God has a group of sons, a corporate sonship. As sons of God, we need to realize that divinity was brought into our humanity and now our humanity is being brought into Christ's divinity. Christ was divinely human, and we are humanly divine. Thus, we are the same as He is in life and in nature, but not in the Godhead.

4. In His Ascension

Psalm 16 finally reveals the God-man, Christ, in His ascension (v. 11b & c; Acts 2:28b).

a. In God's Presence Participating in Fullness of Joy

Christ is in God's presence participating in fullness of joy, indicating that Christ has ascended to the heavens for His attainments and His obtainments (Psa. 16:11b; Acts 1:11; Phil. 2:9-11). In His ascension, among many other things, He attained to the kingship, to the lordship, and to the ruling leadership and the qualification of being a Savior to save others (Acts 5:31). He also obtained many things in His ascension.

b. In God's Right Hand Enjoying Pleasures Forever

In His ascension Christ is enjoying pleasures forever in God's right hand, indicating that Christ is also at the right hand of God in His ascension to surpass all for the accomplishment of God's eternal economy concerning the church, the Body of Christ (Psa. 16:11c; Eph. 1:20b-23). This is the wonderful God-man portrayed in Psalm 16.

We need to see the divine revelation of this wonderful person in the Psalms. We may be like the blind man who was healed by the Lord in Mark 8. After the Lord laid His hands on him, He asked this man if he saw anything. The blind man responded that he saw men as trees, walking. The Lord had to lay His hands upon this man again so that he could see clearly (vv. 22-25). We may be like this man because our eyes are not fully open yet. But as we get into the Psalms week by week, our eyes are becoming more open, and we are seeing more and more.

Our eyes need to be opened until we have a full vision, a full revelation, concerning this wonderful person. He is the Word of God, even God Himself. In eternity past, He was full of divinity without any humanity. But one day in time He came to be incarnated and put on humanity. He became a God-man with a human body and lived on this earth for thirty-three and a half years. Then He entered into death to accomplish God's redemption according to God's eternal plan, God's economy.

Christ came out of death and entered into resurrection. In this resurrection He brought His humanity into divinity to be begotten of God to become God's firstborn Son, and God regenerated all His believers to be God's many sons. Furthermore, in resurrection, He became a life-giving Spirit (1 Cor. 15:45b). As the life-giving Spirit, He is now within His believers as their life and their life supply.

He ascended to the heavens to attain many positions and to obtain many qualifications. In His ascension He became the Lord, the King, the Ruler, the Savior, and even the Christ for the accomplishment of God's economy that God could produce an organism, that is, the Body of Christ in resurrection as the church.

This is the Christ revealed in Psalm 16. This is the man that can sojourn in God's temple and dwell on God's holy mountain. Such a man is not a good man according to the law, but a God-man according to God Himself as the life and life supply.

III. THE HISTORY OF PSALMS 1—16

From Psalm 1 to Psalm 16, there is a history which we need to see. The history begins in Psalm 1 with a man appreciating the law, treasuring the keeping of the law, and highly appraising the keeper of the law. Then in Psalm 2, God came in to declare that Christ was His Anointed. God anointed Him and installed Him to be the King. God also begot Him in His humanity to be the firstborn Son of God. Thus, we all have to take refuge in Him, to believe into Him. We also have to kiss Him, to love Him. This is the second step of the history.

After Psalm 2 was written, David, the appreciator of the

law, committed the most "rough and tough" sin. He committed adultery with Uriah's wife and murdered Uriah (2 Sam. 11). We have seen previously that by that terrible sin, he broke the last five commandments (Exo. 20:13-17). He murdered Uriah, committed fornication, robbed Uriah of his wife, lied to Uriah, and coveted Uriah's wife.

The title of Psalm 3 says that this psalm was written when David was fleeing from his son Absalom. David fled from his son because his son rebelled against him. This rebellion was the issue of David's sin of fornication and murder. Because of this sin, God allowed fornication and murder to occur in David's family among his children. One of David's sons committed fornication with his daughter, and then Absalom killed the son who did this (2 Sam. 13). Eventually, Absalom rebelled against David (2 Sam. 15).

I would like to add something here for us to see. At the time that David committed his terrible sin, God took away His sustaining hand from David. If God had so desired, He could have arranged the situation so that David would have never seen Uriah's wife. There was a kind of circumstance that gave David the opportunity to sin. God allowed this to happen to David. We need to consider why God allowed this. David appreciated the law and even appraised himself so highly. Therefore, God took His sustaining hand away from David so that David could be fully exposed, not only to himself but also to all the Lord's children throughout the generations until today.

David was exposed to the uttermost. I do not believe that any of us have been fully exposed or convicted of our sinfulness. This is because God in His mercy has not exposed us to the extent that He exposed David. It is hard to believe that such a godly servant of God as David could commit such a terrible sin. He conspired to murder one of his soldiers, and then he robbed this one of his wife! Who could believe that such a godly king like David could do this? God allowed that to happen. God kept His preserving, protecting, and sustaining hand away from David for a time. David thought he kept the law, but God arranged an environment to show him that he could not keep the law. An environment was there that fit

David's sinful flesh, allowing his flesh to come out and fully expose him.

David committed this great sin about one thousand years before Christ. Many years later the New Testament still refers to this sin. Even in the genealogy of Christ, Matthew 1:6 says, "David begot Solomon of her who had been the wife of Uriah." What an ugly record! How could someone beget a son of another's wife? David is exposed even today.

He was exposed, and later he was on the test with Absalom's rebellion. When Absalom was pursuing him, David prayed the prayers recorded in Psalms 3—7. After considering Psalms 3—7 in the light of God's New Testament economy, we have seen that these psalms should not be taken as models for our prayer. In them we see David's sufferings, his desire to be avenged of his adversaries, and his self-righteousness. We do not see any repentance, confession of his fault, or self-condemnation. This is the history of the one who appreciated the law and who was exposed. There is no hint or indication that he was humbled, that he was full of self-denial, or that he was self-condemned. He was on the test during Absalom's rebellion, and the testing did not bring out anything positive in these psalms.

Then in Psalm 8, God came in to inspire David. This psalm is David's inspired praise of the excellency of Christ. After Psalm 8, the history goes on with Psalms 9—14, which show us David's human concept concerning God's judgment on his enemies and his concept concerning man's condition before God. Then Psalm 15 speaks of David's concept of a perfect man according to the law being able to dwell with God for God's heart's desire. But in Psalm 16, there is the divine revelation that the only one who can dwell with God for God's heart's desire is the God-man, Christ. The God-man Christ in His human living, His death, His resurrection, and His ascension is the centrality and universality of the economy of God, the man who may dwell with God for His heart's desire and good pleasure. I hope that we can keep in mind the history of these sixteen psalms. Then we can understand their real significance.

LIFE-STUDY OF THE PSALMS

MESSAGE EIGHT

THE LINES, THE PRINCIPLES, AND THE SPIRIT OF THE BIBLE CONCERNING CHRIST AND THE LAW

Scripture Reading: Col. 1:15-19; Rom. 5:20a; 10:4a; 6:14

In order to help us understand the book of Psalms and even the entire Bible, we need to see the lines, the principles, and the spirit of the Bible concerning Christ and the law. The spirit of the Bible does not refer to the Holy Spirit, the Spirit of God, directly. The Bible as an entity has its own spirit.

The book of Psalms, composed of one hundred fifty psalms, is the longest book among the sixty-six books of the Bible. Furthermore, each psalm is not just a story, a history, or a kind of teaching, exhortation, or instruction. Each psalm is man's speaking to God. In the Psalms we see prayers, thanksgivings, or praises to God. Thus, it is not an ordinary book. Many Bible readers spontaneously and naturally love this book, but they do not know why it is so lovable. The Psalms are very sweet to us because they are man's talk to God. The title of Psalm 18 says that it is a psalm which David "spoke to Jehovah." This psalm was not just David's prayer, thanksgiving, or praise, but his speaking to God. When we pray, that is the sweetest time because we are speaking to God.

Even in our sweet talk to God, however, we make mistakes. We may be mistaken, but our talk to God is still very sweet. A husband and a wife may speak to each other in a way that is full of mistakes, but their talk to each other can still be very sweet. In order for us to understand such a sweet book as the Psalms which is full of both the divine concept and the human concept with human mistakes, we need to see the way to understand the Bible. In order to understand the Bible, we need to see the lines, the principles, and the spirit of the Bible.

I. THE TWO LINES CONCERNING
GOD'S ETERNAL ECONOMY IN THE PSALMS
AS IN THE ENTIRE SCRIPTURES

A. The Line of Life versus
the Line of the Knowledge of Good and Evil

In order to see the two lines of the Bible, we need to go back to the very beginning of the divine revelation at the creation of man. The book of Genesis reveals that God created man in His image so that He could have a vessel to contain Him for His expression (1:26-28; 2:7-9). After God created man, He did not give man a long list of instructions. He did not say to man, "Man, you have to know that I am your God. You have to fear Me, love Me, and obey Me. Furthermore, I will make you a wife, and you have to love her. After you have a wife, you will produce children, and you have to listen to Me so that you can pick up the best way to raise them." God did not do this.

After God created man in His own image and after His own likeness, He did not tell man what to do and what not to do. Instead, God brought man into a garden, signifying that God's intention with man for the accomplishment of His economy needs a pleasant situation, a pleasant environment. Even to carry out the church life, we need a pleasant situation. If there is much complaining, arguing, debating, gossiping, and reasoning among us, the church life cannot be carried out. The garden on this earth today is the place where God's people are gathered into the Lord's name.

God brought Adam into a garden, into a pleasant environment, and put him in front of two trees—the tree of life and the tree of the knowledge of good and evil (Gen. 2:9). God told Adam that he could freely eat of every tree in the garden, including the tree of life, but He warned Adam not to eat of the tree of the knowledge of good and evil (vv. 16-17). In telling Adam that all the trees in the garden were good for food, God was very wise. His intention was to stress to Adam that the tree of life was good for food. Then God warned Adam not to eat of the tree of the knowledge of good and evil, telling Adam that if he ate of it, he would surely die.

We need to realize that the entire Bible was written according to these two trees. The entire divine revelation is the development of the notion of these two trees. Genesis shows us man in a pleasant garden with the tree of life before him. Then in Revelation at the end of the divine revelation, we see the tree of life again (22:2). The tree of life not only was in the garden but also will be in the eternal city, the New Jerusalem. The line of the tree of life runs through the entire Bible from Genesis to reach the last chapter of the book of Revelation.

Someone may ask, "What does the Bible teach?" This question can be answered in many ways. We can say that the Bible teaches God's economy or that it teaches Christ. In this message, I would say that the Bible teaches the tree of life. The Bible is a book which defines the tree of life. Along with the main line of the tree of life, there is another line, the line of the tree of the knowledge of good and evil.

When I was very young, I thought that God made a mistake in allowing Satan to exist. If He had not allowed Satan to exist, everything would be fine. Furthermore, after God created man, He did not put man in front of one tree. If there were only one tree, the tree of life, Adam would not have been able to fall even if he had wanted to fall. Why did God allow there to be two trees—the tree of life and the tree of the knowledge of good and evil? We might say that if we were God, we would have had only one tree in the garden. We probably think, "How good it would be if in this whole universe, there were only God, but not Satan." We might think this, but this is not according to God's thought. Without Satan, the excellency, the majesty, the wisdom, and the marvelous, wonderful points of God could never be exhibited. God and Satan are two sources in the universe.

The two trees set before man after man's creation signify God and God's enemy, His opposite. God is positive, and Satan is negative. From these two sources, there are two flows, and these two flows become two lines. A line is also a way. The tree of life is a way, and the tree of the knowledge of good and evil is also a way. The tree that you live by is the way that you live. To live by the tree of life is to live by the way of life. To live by the tree of the knowledge of good and evil is to live by the way of the knowledge of good and evil.

About six thousand years have passed since the time of Adam, and the entire world today is taking the way of the knowledge of good and evil. Families, societies, and nations of the world are formed not by the way of life but by the way of the knowledge of good and evil. But thank the Lord that we are a group of people who have been called out of the group of those who live by the way of the knowledge of good and evil, the way of complication.

Much of the time, however, instead of living by the way of life, we live by the way of the knowledge of good and evil. Day by day we parents raise our children to deal with three things—knowledge, good, and evil. The mothers teach their children with the knowledge of what is good and what is evil. The children are taught in their homes and schools to pick up the proper knowledge to do good and hate evil. The law courts and human governments are set up according to the concept of the knowledge of good and evil. Even Christianity and many other religions have fallen into the same "cage" of the way of the knowledge of good and evil. But we need to be those who are outside of this cage. We do not care for the knowledge of good and of evil. We care only for life.

Cain and Abel are representatives of these two lines, which are two ways. I believe that Adam brought forth many sons, but the Bible in Genesis 4:1-2 records only two sons of Adam—Cain and Abel. Both Cain and Abel came to worship God by offering something to God. Cain was a farmer. His labor produced a crop, so he offered the fruit of his crop to God. It seems that Cain worked for God and respected God by offering something to God. God, however, rejected Cain's offering. When I was young, I could not understand why God did this. Abel was a shepherd who offered the firstlings of his flock to God. God was pleased with Abel's offering.

These two brothers of the same parents represent the two lines of the Bible. The first one, Cain, chose the way of the knowledge of good and evil, and the second one, Abel, chose the way of life. Adam's race became two groups. One group was of Cain, and the other group was of Abel. In Abel's group there were Enosh, Enoch, Noah, Abraham, Isaac, and Jacob who eventually became Israel. This is the positive line in the Old Testament. In Cain's group there were all the evil ones. Eventually Nimrod was raised up in this evil group. He was a mighty man who built Babel (Gen. 10:8-10a). He also built Assyria with Nineveh as the capital (vv. 11-12; cf. Micah 5:6).

The history of mankind in the Old Testament is of two groups, two lines, which are out of two sources. To what group did David belong—the group of Cain or the group of Abel? According to the revelation we have seen thus far, David was in both groups. In Psalms 1, 3—7, and 9—15, he was in the group of Cain. In these psalms, he was praying to God, praising God, and thanking God in the group of Cain. He was fearing God, loving God, and worshipping God, but in the wrong way.

We have seen that in these psalms he justifies himself and mentions his righteousness frequently. He asks the Lord to hear him and remember him because of his righteousness. We need to ask whether David's righteousness as an offering to God is from the crop, as from Cain, or from the flock, as from Abel. David's prayer, thanksgiving, and praise in Psalms 1, 3—7, and 9—15 may be good, but they are of the knowledge of good and evil. There are two kinds of fruit of the same tree—good fruit and evil fruit. It is possible to pray to God, love God, praise God, and work for God according to the line of the knowledge of good and evil. Cain was a God-worshipper who offered something to God, but what he offered according to his way was not acceptable to God. David offered his righteousness to God, but we know that man's righteousness is as a soiled garment in the sight of God (Isa. 64:6).

In Psalms 2, 8, and 16, however, David was in the group of Abel in the line of life. We may say that at times David was a "Cain," a good Cain, a positive Cain, not an evil Cain. He was a Cain of good, not a Cain of evil. But sometimes, David was turned to another group, to the group of Abel. In this group he did not mention his righteousness or what he

could do. He spoke of taking refuge in the Son (Psa. 2:12) and
of God hiding him under the wings of God (Psa. 17:8). In
Psalm 27 David was on the line of life, saying that he desired
to dwell in the house of Jehovah to behold the loveliness of
Jehovah (v. 4). In Psalm 36 David said that in God's house,
there is the fatness, the river of God's pleasures, the fountain
of life, and light (vv. 8-9). This is God as our enjoyment.
Therefore, we can see that at times David was with the group
of Cain in the line of the knowledge of good and evil, but at
other times God turned him to be with the group of Abel in
the line of life.

Now we need to ask, "To what group do we belong?" Do
we belong to the group of Cain or the group of Abel? Are we
companions of Cain or companions of Abel? At times we may
be with Abel, and at other times we may leave Abel and
join Cain. When we endeavor to do things in ourselves, by
ourselves, with ourselves, and for ourselves, we are companions of Cain. We have to confess that today we are mostly
"Cains" in the line of the knowledge of good and evil. Very
rarely are we "Abels" in the line of life. We live mostly by the
tree of the knowledge of good and evil, not by the tree of life.

Now I would like us to consider whether Abraham was
with Cain or with Abel. Actually, Abraham was sometimes with
Cain and sometimes with Abel. God had promised Abraham a
son, but Abraham and his wife Sarah became very old, and
they had lost the human capacity to produce children. Sarah
then urged Abraham to take her handmaid, Hagar, so that
they could have a son (Gen. 16). Before taking Hagar to produce Ishmael, Abraham was with Abel. But when Abraham
took Hagar, he became a companion of Cain, and that
offended God. God did not appear to Abraham for thirteen
years after Ishmael was born (Gen. 16:16—17:1).

Abraham was walking with God in the line of the tree
of life, but he was under God's test. God promised him a
son, but by the time he was very old, he still did not have
a son. His wife was very concerned about this and gave
Hagar to Abraham to produce a son named Ishmael. God's
desire, however, was not with this son. Ishmael was born
when Abraham was eighty-six years old (Gen. 16:16). Thirteen

years later, when Abraham was ninety-nine, God appeared
to him again (Gen. 17:1), and Isaac, the child of God's promise, was born when Abraham was one hundred years old
(Gen. 21:5). Abraham returned again to the line of life.
Ishmael was produced according to the line of the knowledge
of good and evil. Isaac was produced according to the line of
life.

When the descendants of Abraham became the race of
Israel, God brought them to Mount Sinai. At Mount Sinai
God's intention was to train them to be His people to serve
Him with a tabernacle, with a priesthood, and with all kinds
of offerings. The tabernacle, the priesthood, and the offer-
ings are of the line of the tree of life. But the people of Israel
did not know themselves. Their thought was always with
Cain.

God, before the making of the tabernacle, decreed the law,
and the law is in the line of good and evil. We have seen
that the law was a side line. The main line is the line of
the tree of life with the tabernacle, with the priesthood, and
with the offerings. But the people of Israel desired to take
another way, the way of the law, the way of good and evil.
They promised God that they would do whatever He said
(Exo. 19:8; 24:3). God knew, of course, that they were talking
in a foolish way. While Moses was on the mountain with God
receiving the commandments of the law, they made a golden
calf to break the law. Later, Moses went up to the mountain
again. This time God gave him the pattern of the tabernacle.
He also showed Moses the priesthood with all the offerings.
The tabernacle, the priesthood, and all the offerings typify
Christ. This is the way of life. Throughout the entire history
of Israel in the Old Testament from Moses' time, we can see
these two lines—the line of the law and the line of the tabernacle, the priesthood, and the offerings, which are the line of
life.

David treasured the law and tried to keep it, but he failed
to the uttermost. He killed Uriah and robbed Uriah of his
wife. He needed the tabernacle, the priesthood, and the offerings. Through the tabernacle, the priesthood, and the offerings,
David was forgiven. Psalm 51 shows us that when David

repented, he was a strong "Abel." Psalm 51, a psalm of David's repentance and confession, is the most spiritual psalm. At the end of his confession, he asked God to do good to Zion and to build the walls of Jerusalem (v. 18). Later, however, when he was fleeing from Absalom, David turned back again to the group of Cain, as we saw in Psalms 3—7.

Now we can see that in the book of Psalms, as in the entire Bible, there are two lines. At the end of the Psalms, the psalmists are fully in the line of life. The concluding psalms are full of praises, full of "Hallelujahs." The psalmists by that time were not praising the law, but Christ. We have to see the two lines in the book of Psalms. In reading the Psalms, we should not agree with David when he is "Cain-David." We need to stay with "Abel-David." We need to stand with "Abel-David" in Psalm 51. We should treasure all the psalms concerning Christ in the line of life. We need to come out of the group of Cain and enter into and stay with the group of Abel.

When we study the book of Job, we can see many "Cains" there and also some "Abels." My burden is to help us know the two lines, the two ways, in the Bible. Among the Jews in the Old Testament, there was the wonderful way of the tabernacle, the priesthood, and all the offerings. There was also the way of the law. The people of Israel could not meet God by keeping the law; they met God in the tabernacle.

Whenever we try to accomplish something in ourselves like Cain, we do not have the inner anointing. We need to pray, "Lord, I can do nothing and I do not want to do anything. I just want to enjoy You, to partake of You, to experience You, to live You, and to express You." When we pray in this way, we are like Abel, and we are full of the inner anointing. Thus, we can see two sources, two lines, and two ways with two kinds of results. One result is the absence of God, and the other result is the presence of God.

B. The Main Line
as the Central Line of God's Economy
concerning Christ and the Church

The main line of the Bible is the central line of God's

economy concerning Christ and the church. This is the line of life. Christ is the centrality and universality of God's eternal economy. The church is the Body of Christ (Eph. 1:22-23), the counterpart of Christ, the complement of Christ, to be God's dwelling on the earth, typified by the tabernacle (Exo. 25:8-9; Josh. 18:1; 1 Sam. 1:3) and the temple (1 Kings 6:1), both of which are considered as the house of God (Judg. 18:31b; Psa. 5:7). The main line is of Mount Zion in the heavens (Psa. 2:6; Rev. 14:1), signified by Mount Zion on the earth (Psa. 3:4; 9:11, 14; 14:7; 15:1b); and the New Testament believers have come to Mount Zion in the heavens (Heb. 12:22) in the main line of God's economy.

C. The Side Line concerning the Law

The other line in the Scriptures is the side line concerning the law. This is the line of the knowledge of good and evil. The law was added alongside the main line of the economy of God (Rom. 5:20a). The side line is of Mount Sinai, where the law was given. The Old Testament saints, who were for the law, were slaves of this Mount Sinai (Gal. 4:24).

The psalmists, who were for the law, stayed ignorantly at Mount Sinai of this side line. Occasionally and unconsciously they turned to Mount Zion of the main line, as unveiled in Psalms 3:4; 9:11, 14; 14:7; and 15:1b. In Mount Zion they enjoyed the house, the temple of God, as unveiled in Psalms 5:7 and 11:4. This is an unconscious progression in the psalmists' seeking after God.

The psalmist in Psalm 15 was questioning as to who may sojourn in God's tent and who may dwell on God's holy mountain. The answer according to David's concept is the perfect man in the side line of the law (Psa. 15:2-5). But the answer according to the divine revelation is the God-man Christ (Psa. 16:1-11) as the firstborn Son of God with His many brothers as the many sons of God in the main line of God's economy (Rom. 6:14).

II. THE PRINCIPLES

There are many principles in the Bible and of the Bible which can help us to understand the Bible in a proper way. It is very difficult for many students of the Bible to understand the Bible because they do not know the principles of the Bible. In order to understand what these principles are, I want to present a few illustrations.

During Martin Luther's time, the Catholic Church taught that to be saved and justified by God, one had to do good works and keep the law. Then Luther stood up to say that justification is by faith. Faith is a principle in the New Testament. Genesis 15 says that Abraham believed God and it was accounted to him as righteousness (v. 6). God counted Abraham's faith as righteousness. This shows that we do not need to do anything to build up our own righteousness. We simply need to believe in Christ.

The book of Habakkuk talks about the Babylonians coming to devastate the entire country of Israel. In this book there is a verse which says, "The righteous one will live by his faith" (2:4). Faith is a big principle in the Bible. According to the entire Bible, faith is to stop our work, to stop our doing—on the negative side. Then on the positive side, faith is to trust in the Lord. Faith is to stop our doing and to trust in His doing.

The principle of faith is related to the principle of the Sabbath. The principle of the Sabbath is this: you have to cease your work because God is everything to you. If you need something to be worked out, God works for you. That is what it means to enjoy the Sabbath. The Sabbath is in the same principle as faith. The real believing, the real faith, means to stop your doing. Whatever you do is an insult to God. In the principle of the Sabbath and in the principle of faith, you do not need to work or to do anything, because God does everything and works out everything for your enjoyment. You just trust in Him and trust in His doing, in His working. This is faith.

Psalm 1 says that if you keep the law, you will be blessed (vv. 1-2), but Psalm 2 says that the one who takes refuge in the Son is blessed (v. 12). The only way that we can take refuge in the Son is to stop our doing. We need to take refuge in Jesus, to believe into Him. This is the principle of faith. According to the teaching of Catholicism, you have to work, to labor, and to suffer to be justified by God. Then Martin Luther found out that God's principle of His salvation is not by doing, not by working, but by believing in God and in all that He has done and is going to do. This is to take refuge in the working God and to stop our work. This principle of faith should govern our entire Christian life.

On the one hand, we need to stop our work. On the other hand, we still need to labor, but this labor is not in ourselves and by ourselves. Paul said, "I labored more abundantly than all of them, yet not I but the grace of God which is with me" (1 Cor. 15:10). The grace of God is Christ. Paul said, "Yet not I but the grace of God." This is similar to Galatians 2:20, where Paul said that he had been crucified with Christ and that it was no longer he who lived, but Christ lived in him. This is to rest, to keep the Sabbath, to take refuge in the Son, to believe into Him. Our entire Christian life should be according to this principle of the Sabbath and of faith.

Faith is one of the many principles in the Bible. Paul defined the principle of faith thoroughly in his Epistles. He said that no flesh can be justified by the works of the law (Rom. 3:20; Gal. 2:16; 3:11). There are many other principles of the Bible.

The Bible is in two testaments—the Old Testament and the New Testament. To understand the Old Testament, you need to keep one principle; and to understand the New Testament, you need to keep another principle. Today, the Pentecostals, like those in Catholicism, understand the Bible in a mixed-up way. They do not keep the principle of the Old Testament and of the New Testament. When you apply anything of the Old Testament, you must find out the principle of applying it in a spiritual way, not in a physical way.

This is the difference between the practice of Judaism and the practice of God's New Testament economy. The Torah, the first five books of the Old Testament, has become an idol to the religious Jews. They do not really care for God in reality but for the letter of their Torah. Even the ark became a superstitious thing to the children of Israel. When they were fighting the Philistines, they brought out the ark to go with them. Eventually, they were defeated and the ark was captured (1 Sam. 4:3-5, 10-11). The children of Israel also built the temple, and the temple eventually became an idol to them. They trusted in the temple rather than in God Himself. Later, the Babylonians came to destroy the temple.

The two lines of the Bible are the line of life and the line of the knowledge of good and evil. With these two lines, there are the principles of the Bible. As long as it is something other than God, whether good or evil, that is not life. Only God Himself is the tree of life.

Today people are claiming their rights, but they are violating the God-ordained principles. Paul spoke of the distinctions between male and female in his Epistles (1 Cor. 11:2-15; 1 Tim. 2:9-15). Deuteronomy 22:5 says, "A woman shall not put on a man's belongings, nor shall a man wear a woman's garment; for everyone who does these things is an abomination to Jehovah your God." For a woman to wear a man's clothing or for a man to wear a woman's clothing breaks God's principle. We have to keep the principles. Every part, chapter, paragraph, sentence, and clause of the Bible must be interpreted according to the proper principles.

According to the principle in the Old Testament, the Old Testament saints had to keep the Sabbath, the seventh day. But when the Lord Jesus came, He ended the Old Testament time. *To end* means to conclude and to consummate. Christ consummated, concluded, ended, the Old Testament. Now according to the book of Hebrews, Christ is everything. In the New Testament, Christ is our Sabbath (Mark 2:27-28; Col. 2:16-17).

Now that we are in the New Testament age, we have to keep this principle concerning Christ. The principle in the Old Testament was to keep the Sabbath day. The principle in the New Testament concerning the Sabbath is to believe in the Lord, to rest in the Lord, and to enjoy the Lord. The Seventh-Day Adventists mix up the Old Testament principle with that of the New Testament. They keep the Old Testament Sabbath in the New Testament age. They are wrong in principle. Their intention might be good, but their principle is wrong.

A. The Principles in the Old Testament

We need to see the principles of the Bible in both the Old and New Testaments. The tabernacle (Exo. 25:8-9; 40:1-2) as the precursor of the temple (1 Kings 6:1), the priesthood (Exo. 28:1), and the offerings (Lev. 1—7), all as types of Christ, were ordained by God to be the main line for God's chosen people to worship God, serve God, contact God, and partake of God until Christ as the fulfillment of all the types came (Heb. 9:8-12).

The law as the testimony of God (Psa. 78:5) was given by God to be the side line alongside the main line to guard the chosen people of God until Christ as the end of the law (Rom. 10:4a) came (Gal. 3:23-25).

B. The Principles in the New Testament

God has ordained Christ to be the centrality and universality of His economy to fulfill His good pleasure (Eph. 3:8-11; 1:9-11). The law as the alongside factor has been ended by Christ (Rom. 10:4a), and the believers are no longer under the law (Rom. 6:14).

III. THE SPIRIT OF THE BIBLE

Colossians 1:15-19 shows that the spirit of the Bible exalts Christ. These five verses are unique in the Bible in exalting Christ. Christ must have the first place; He must have the preeminence. Christ has the preeminence in the Godhead because in the Godhead, He is the image of God, the embodiment of God, and the expression of God. He is in the first place, even in the Godhead. Then in the old creation, He was the first creature, the Firstborn of all creation (Col. 1:15). In the new creation, in resurrection, He is also the first. He is the preeminent One. Furthermore, in the Body of Christ, in the church, Christ is the first. In the Godhead, Christ is the first; in the old creation, Christ is the first; in the new creation, Christ is the first; and in the church as the Body of Christ, Christ is the first. He is first in everything.

Since He has the first place in all things, we must give Him the first place in our being and in all that we do. He must be first in our marriage, in our spending of money, and in our demeanor. In the way that we dress, we must give Christ the preeminence. The spirit of the Bible is just to exalt Christ. When we come to study the Psalms, we must realize this. We must realize that we cannot exalt anything higher than Christ. If we exalt anyone or anything other than Christ, we break the spirit of the Bible. If we are going to interpret any types or explain any parables, we must take care of this spirit. The spirit of the Bible is to exalt Christ.

The spirit of the Bible exalts the Christ ordained by God to have the preeminence (the first place) in the old creation, in the new creation, in the Body of Christ, and in everything (Col. 1:15-19). Also the spirit of the Bible does not give any orthodox position to the law (Gal. 4:21-25) given by God alongside His economy (Rom. 5:20a).

Many teachings in Christianity today are off the mark because they do not take care of the lines, the principles, and the spirit of the Bible. We have to stay on the line of the tree of life. Whether or not we speak with the oracle of God depends upon what we speak. A prophet is one who has received the word from God. Then he speaks the word in the line of the tree of life, in the proper principles, and in the spirit of exalting Christ. In whatever we speak, we must have a spirit to exalt Christ.

In the past two years, we have released messages on Isaiah, Daniel, Zechariah, and Jeremiah. It is not easy to see Christ in these four books. How many people see God's economy in these four books with Christ as the centrality and universality? Whenever we study a book of the Bible, we must keep the lines, the principles, and the spirit of the Bible. Then the light comes. If we read the Bible without seeing the lines, the principles, and the spirit of the Bible, we will not know what it is talking about.

When we study the Psalms in the light of the lines, the principles, and the spirit of the Bible, we can see the human concept and the divine concept. We can see Christ in God's economy versus the law in man's appreciation. We may think that all of the psalms are good psalms, since they are psalms of prayer, psalms of thanksgiving, and psalms of praise. But when we see the lines, the principles, and the spirit of the Bible, we will see that many of the psalms may be good, but they are good in a wrong way.

David said that because of his righteousness, God heard him. This is not just wrong, but terribly wrong. This is against the principle of the Bible. How could God hear us because of our righteousness? The Bible says that even our best righteousness is as a soiled garment (Isa. 64:6). No flesh can be justified before God by the works of the law. This is the principle. We cannot be justified and please God by our righteousness.

Cain offered the fruit of his labor to God. It seemed that this was a kind of worship to God, but actually this was an insult to God. This was an insult to God because God does not need us to do something for Him. We need Him to do everything for us. He wants us to stop our doing, rest in Him, and take refuge in Him. By doing this, we honor God. This is the principle.

We may love people and help people, but our love and help can be an insult to God. Do we love people and help people by ourselves or by Christ? If it is by ourselves, this is the good of the tree of the knowledge of good and evil. If we hate people, this is the evil of the same tree. The fruits are different, but the source and the result are the same. We may say that we do everything with the best knowledge. This means that our doing is according to the tree of knowledge, not the tree of life.

We should have the attitude that even though we can do something by ourselves, we would not do it. We do not like to act by ourselves because God hates this. God hates anything out of us, anything by us, and anything through us. We need to stop our doing and rest in Him, trusting in His doing. This honors God and brings in His blessing.

Many times good things can be a real temptation, a snare, and a trap to us. When we are doing good things, we have to check who is doing them. Are we doing them or is Christ doing them? Even the best thing done merely by man is an insult to God. Only the things done by Christ as our life and only the things accomplished by God as our enjoyment are in the line of the tree of life. When we act in the line of the tree of life, this is in the proper line, in the keeping of the proper principle, and in the spirit of exalting Christ.

When we see the lines, the principles, and the spirit of the Bible, we have the boldness to say which psalms are of the tree of life and which psalms are not. Regardless of how good something is, God only cares for who does it. God wants us to live Him, but not by ourselves. God wants us to express Him, but not by ourselves. We have to stop our expression. We have to put our trust in Him and let Him live in us and out of us. Then whatever we do will be an honor and a glory to God. Otherwise, whatever we do, even though it may be good, is an insult to God.

LIFE-STUDY OF THE PSALMS

MESSAGE NINE

DAVID'S CONCEPT
CONCERNING A MAN AND
CONCERNING DAVID'S KINGSHIP
BEFORE GOD
BASED UPON THE KEEPING OF THE LAW
AND THE PRINCIPLE OF GOOD AND EVIL

Scripture Reading: Psa. 17—21

In this message we come to Psalms 17—21. We may say that these five psalms are five "birds of the same feather." The taste, the flavor, the spirit, and the attitude are all the same in these psalms.

In the previous message, we saw the lines, the principles, and the spirit of the Bible. The two lines of the Bible are the line of the tree of the knowledge of good and evil and the line of the tree of life. We saw that Cain was in the line of knowledge and that Abel was in the line of life. We can either be in the group of Cain or in the group of Abel.

In Psalm 1 there is not any hint that David was with Abel. In this psalm every aspect and every point indicate that David stayed with Cain in the line of knowledge. But there are also three stations in the first sixteen psalms in which David was with Abel in the line of life. These three stations are Psalm 2, Psalm 8, and Psalm 16. These psalms are extraordinary and great in unveiling the secret concerning the centrality and universality of Christ in God's economy. After the first sixteen psalms, we can see that David made some progress and improved in his concept.

In Psalms 17—21 David jumped out of the line of knowledge a number of times. David at least had a little taste in these psalms of the line of life. Psalms 22—24 are the fourth station of the line of life in the Psalms. These three psalms unveil Christ to us. Psalm 22 reveals Christ's death, Psalm 23 unveils Christ's shepherding in His resurrection, and Psalm 24 shows that Christ will be the overcoming and upcoming King in the age of restoration.

Psalms 17—21 show us David's concept concerning two things—concerning a man before God and concerning David's kingship before God. His concept was based upon the keeping of the law and the principle of good and evil. We can see this in light of the divine revelation in the Bible, particularly in the New Testament.

The divine revelation in the Bible is progressive. In Galatians 2:20 Paul said, "I am crucified with Christ; and it is no longer I who live, but it is Christ who lives in me." In Philippians 1:21a Paul said, "For to me, to live is Christ." These verses reveal a great step forward in the progression of the divine revelation. In the entire thirty-nine books of the Old Testament, we cannot find any word concerning Christ's living in us and our living Christ. David's concept in Psalm 1 was that the one who meditates in the law is blessed, but Paul said, "For to me, to live is Christ." If we desire the blessing in Psalm 1, we are very primitive and backward. Our understanding of the divine revelation of the Bible must be progressive.

In the Old Testament, we cannot find all the mysterious expressions by Paul. This is because Paul's ministry was to complete the word of God, the mystery concerning Christ and the church (Col. 1:25-26). If Paul's fourteen Epistles were taken away from the Bible, we would not know God's economy (1 Tim. 1:4), the mystery of God, Christ (Col. 2:2), and the mystery of Christ, the church (Eph. 3:4; 5:32). There is no word in the Old Testament which says, "To me, to live is Christ." When we come to the Psalms, we must see them in the light of the full revelation of God's New Testament economy.

I. DAVID'S CONCEPT CONCERNING A MAN BEFORE GOD

In Psalms 17—19 we see David's concept concerning a man before God.

A. The Improvement of David's Concept

Psalm 17 shows us the improvement of David's concept. David's concept improved from his righteousness (vv. 1-6) to God's wondrous lovingkindness and God's hiding him in the shadow of His wings (vv. 7-9).

In verse 3 David said, "You have tried me: You have found nothing. / My thoughts do not pass through my mouth." David said that his thoughts did not pass through his mouth and that his prayer was not made with "lips of deceit" (v. 1). James, in the New Testament, said that the hardest thing for us to control is our mouth (James 3:1-12). But in Psalm 17, David told God that he had success in controlling his mouth. In verse 5 David said, "My steps have held fast to Your tracks; / My footsteps have not slipped." David said that he was still on God's track, like a locomotive which is still on the rails.

In verses 7-9 David's concept turned from his righteousness to God's wondrous lovingkindness and God's hiding him in the shadow of His wings. In verse 8 he prayed, "Guard me like the apple of Your eye; / In the shadow of Your wings hide me." David enjoyed the shadow of God's wings, and he even enjoyed being guarded like the apple of God's eye.

In the first six verses he was in his righteousness. He was boasting of his righteousness. James said that no one can control his mouth, but David said that God examined him and found nothing. In verses 7-9, however, he came out of his righteousness. He entered into God's eye and came under God's wings to enjoy the shadow. His boasting in his righteousness was in the line of the tree of knowledge, but God's eye and God's wings are in the line of the tree of life. This shows an improvement in David's concept.

Right after this, however, David turned his attention to his enemies. Verses 10-14 are his accusation of his enemies. After the mentioning of his enjoyment in God's eye and under God's wings, he could not forget his enemies. To accuse our enemies and to ask God to bring them down (v. 13a) is not a prayer according to God's economy. In God's economy, God tells us to love our enemies (Matt. 5:44).

At the end of Psalm 17, we can see David's improvement in

the satisfaction with God's likeness (presence), yet he was still remaining in his righteousness before God (v. 15). How could David boast of his righteousness when he committed such a sinful act by taking Bathsheba and murdering her husband, Uriah? God forgave David of this great sin, but He did not forget what David did. First Kings 15:5 says that David did what was right in the eyes of the Lord all the days of his life, except in the case of Uriah the Hittite. Much later, in the New Testament, the genealogy of Christ in the book of Matthew says, "David begot Solomon of her who had been the wife of Uriah" (1:6).

The Bible tells us that in the new covenant, God forgives our sins and does not remember them (Heb. 8:12). Why then did God record David's failure in the genealogy of Christ? This shows us that the Bible is not easy to understand. Psalm 51 shows that God forgave David, but in Matthew 1 God still mentioned Uriah, meaning that God did not forget. Uriah was a Hittite, a heathen. Matthew 1:6 says that David begot Solomon "of her who had been the wife of Uriah" to emphasize David's great sin, thus showing that Christ as the kingly Savior is related not only to the heathen but also to sinners.

In spite of David's great sin, he said in Psalm 17:15, "As for me, in righteousness will I look into Your face." He still remained in his righteousness before God, but at least in one sense, he was not in righteousness. James said, "Whoever keeps the whole law yet stumbles in one point has become guilty of all" (James 2:10). We have seen previously that David, by his one transgression, directly broke the last five commandments because he murdered, committed adultery, stole, lied, and coveted (Exo. 20:13-17). David should have said that he would look into God's face because of God's mercy and lovingkindness. God's lovingkindness is versus David's righteousness. What is trustworthy—David's righteousness or God's lovingkindness? If God would examine us to the uttermost, how could we stand? We could not stand before God's face in our righteousness. We have to hide ourselves under the shadow of His wings.

In Psalm 17 we see David's human concept, but we also see

the improvement of his concept. We see his improving from being "Cain-David" to being "Abel-David."

B. A Psalm of David Expressing His Concept

Psalm 18 is a psalm of David expressing his concept. The title of this psalm says that David talked to Jehovah with the words of this song after God delivered him from all his enemies and from Saul. This psalm is not merely a prayer or praise but a talk with God.

I would like to ask if we have had times to talk with the Lord. To talk means to open yourself up and release all your opinions. Have we ever had such a talk with the Lord Jesus? Psalm 18 is a human talk with the divine God. This is wonderful. Just to have the opportunity and the privilege to talk to God is a very great blessing. To talk with someone implies intimacy. We must be face to face, having eye contact with the one to whom we are talking. We need such an intimate, human talk with the divine God. In David's talk to God, he begins by saying, "I love You, O Jehovah, my strength" (v. 1). This is a very sweet talk.

Psalm 18 reveals the improvement of David's concept in his enjoyment of the saving God as his strength, his crag, his fortress, his Deliverer, his God, his rock, his shield, his salvation's horn, and his high tower in whom he took refuge (vv. 1-5). A crag is a steep, rugged rock. David said that Jehovah was his crag and his rock, in whom he took refuge. David loved Jehovah because Jehovah was so much to him. He enjoyed Jehovah as his saving God.

In verse 6, David realized that God heard his voice from His temple, not because of his righteousness. This is an improvement from David's relying on what he was and what he had to what God is and what God has.

Even though David realized that God heard his voice from His temple, he portrayed God not as in His temple but as in His fury and His terrifying majesty (vv. 7-15). This shows that David improved in his concept, but then he went back to his natural concept.

In verses 16-28 David turned to his righteousness and cleanness because of which God delivered him from his enemies.

Do you believe that God delivered David from his enemies because of his righteousness and cleanness? David was wrong to think this. God is not good to us because of our righteousness. He is good to us because of His compassion. We need not only His mercy but also His far-reaching compassion to preserve us.

Anyhow, David recognized that God was the One who strengthened him, shielded him, supported him, and enabled him to war, who had made his feet like hinds' feet, and whose condescending gentleness had made him great (vv. 29-36). God is transcending, but God's gentleness is condescending. God is on the throne, but He shows us His gentleness by coming down to us. Thus, David testified that it was by such a God that he overtook his enemies and defeated those who hated him (vv. 27-42). This shows us again the mixture in David's concept.

Eventually, David praised God that God had rescued him from the strivings of the people and had made him the head of the nations, who served him, obeyed him, and came cringing to him; and he blessed God his rock and exalted the God of his salvation, who had exalted him above his enemies (vv. 43-49). On the one hand, we see much improvement in David's concept here. On the other hand, we see the mixture in his concept.

The conclusion of Psalm 18 is that God magnified salvation to David as God's king and executed lovingkindness to him as God's anointed and to his seed forever (v. 50). God's magnifying salvation to David was not just to save him but to save him for making him the king. He was not worthy by his righteousness to be God's anointed. But God anointed him because of His lovingkindness. Christ is the seed of David to inherit God's covenant made to David.

C. David's Praise of the Testimony of the Speaking of the Universe and His Appraisal of the Law Leading Him to a Deeper Seeking after Perfection before Jehovah

Psalm 19 is David's praise of the testimony of the speaking

of the universe and his appraisal of the law leading him to a deeper seeking after perfection before Jehovah.

Verses 1-6 are David's praise concerning the speaking of the universe created by God. No doubt, in these verses, David was in the line of life. The entire universe speaks every day and even every moment. "The heavens declare the glory of God, / And the firmament proclaims the work of His hands" (v. 1). In verses 4b-5, the sun signifies Christ as a bridegroom and as a mighty man. We know that Christ is typified by the sun because David refers to the sun as a bridegroom. Christ is the Bridegroom with the bride. Christ's rising, as typified by the sun, is a circuit around the globe, and nothing is hidden from His heat (v. 6). The word *circuit* here indicates that the earth is round.

After David's praise concerning the speaking of the universe in verses 1-6, he highly appraises the law in verses 7-11. In verses 1-6, he was "Abel"; in verses 7-11, he was "Cain." We have to give David the credit in the line of life and the debit in the line of the knowledge of good and evil.

David's appraisal of the law was very high. Verse 7 says, "The law of Jehovah is perfect, / Restoring the soul; / The testimony of Jehovah is faithful, / Making the simple wise." The law of God is God's testimony (Exo. 31:18; 32:15). In verse 11 David said there is much reward in the keeping of God's commandments. This concept is not according to the divine concept of the New Testament economy of God.

David said in Psalm 1 that the one who delighted in the law would be like a tree planted beside streams of water (vv. 2-3). But in the Gospels, John the Baptist said, "Already the axe is laid at the root of the trees. Every tree therefore that does not produce good fruit is cut down and cast into the fire" (Matt. 3:10). In Luke 13:6-9, the Lord told a parable indicating that God came in the Son to seek fruit from the Jewish people, who were likened to a fig tree. If they would not repent and produce fruit, they would be cut down. Israel was like a tree planted by the law as the waters, but God would cut them down if they did not repent and receive Christ. We have seen that the spirit of the Bible does not exalt the law. It only exalts Christ. In the whole Bible there is no other portion which uplifts the law as highly as Psalm 19:7-11.

After David's uplifting of the law, he offered a prayer to Jehovah as his rock and as his Redeemer (vv. 12-14). In verse 12 he asked God to deal with his secret faults. All of us have some secret faults which only we know. David also prayed to be kept from presumptuous sins (v. 13). To be presumptuous is to be too bold without consideration.

David prayed that he would be acceptable before Jehovah in his words outwardly and in his meditation inwardly (v. 14). Sometimes you may be acceptable outwardly just in your words, but what about your inward meditation? Such a prayer indicates that David was endeavoring to keep the law to such an extent that he would be dealt with in his secret faults, in his presumptuous sins, in the words of his mouth, and in the meditation of his heart. He wanted to be perfect and clean.

Whether or not David could arrive at such perfection is not the issue. Even if he could be perfect, would this make God happy? In considering this, we must take care of the entire principle of the Bible. The entire principle of the Bible tells us that God does not want anything from man. Regardless of how good it is, as long as it is human, God will put it aside. What God wants is not a good man, but a God-man. God's desire was to be incarnated as a man by the name of Jesus, to die on the cross, to be resurrected, and in resurrection to become a life-giving Spirit to indwell us, to live in us, and to live Himself out of us. When Christ lives through us, our conduct is not our goodness but Christ. "To me, to live is Christ." We have to interpret Psalm 19 in view of the entire principle of the Bible.

If David could have been a perfect person, he would have been highly exalted. But the Bible does not exalt anyone but Christ. Christ must have the preeminence in everything. This is why Paul said, "It is no longer I who live, but it is Christ who lives in me" (Gal. 2:20a). According to the divine concept, we can see that David was wrong. Abel was accepted by God, not because his secret faults and his presumptuous sins were dealt with, but because he realized that he was a sinner. He needed Christ to be his offering. He offered to God not what he was, but Christ. Thus, he was accepted in Christ. He was accepted by God, not in himself, in what he did, or in what he raised up, but altogether in Christ. At the end of Psalm 19, however, David was not in the line of Abel but in the line of Cain.

We may not have agreed with what Cain did in Genesis 4, but we surely have agreed with David's prayer at the end of Psalm 19. This is a very deep prayer. Over fifty years ago, I prayed David's prayer in Psalm 19 every morning over a long period of time. We can pray this prayer, but no one can attain the standard of this prayer. In verses 12-14, David prays, "Who can discern his errors? / Clear me of my secret faults. / Keep Your servant from presumptuous sins; / Do not let them have dominion over me; / Then I will be blameless and cleared / Of great transgression. / May the words of my mouth and the meditation of my heart / Be acceptable before You, / O Jehovah, my rock and my Redeemer." This prayer seems marvelous, but actually David was in the line of Cain here. Like Cain, he was trying his best to bring the produce of his harvest to God. In other words, he was bringing his doing, his working out, and his result to God, while putting Christ aside. In Psalm 51, however, David applied Christ to the uttermost because he realized that he had sinned greatly and that he needed Christ.

II. DAVID'S CONCEPT CONCERNING
HIS KINGSHIP BEFORE GOD

Psalms 20 and 21 reveal David's concept concerning his kingship before God.

A. David's Blessing in His Kingship

Psalm 20 shows us David's blessing in his kingship. In verses 1-9, David blessed his people. According to the principle of the Bible, the greater blesses the lesser (Heb. 7:7).

David blessed his people with Jehovah's answering, exalting, help from the sanctuary, strengthening from Zion, remembering all their meal offerings, and accepting their burnt offering (vv. 1-3). This was so that Jehovah might give them their heart's desire and fulfill their every intention and that they might shout victoriously in His salvation and raise the banner in the name of their God (vv. 4-5). David had the assurance that Jehovah saves His anointed (King David) and will answer him from His holy heaven with the mighty salvation from His right hand (v. 6).

David continues by saying that we boast in the name of Jehovah our God instead of in chariots and in horses, and we, not our enemies, are risen and stand upright (vv. 7-8). The conclusion of his blessing is verse 9, which says, "Save, O Jehovah! / May the king answer us when we call." The king in this verse refers to David.

Most of David's blessing is all right, but we can still see that he was somewhat remaining in his old concept. Psalm 20, however, still shows us that David has improved and progressed in his concept beyond the three foregoing psalms. To bless is higher than to pray. A person who blesses people needs a higher status, a higher stature in life. No small children can bless others. A little girl cannot say to her father, "Daddy, I will bless you," but she can say, "Daddy, I will pray for you." Children can pray and do pray for their parents. But a child cannot bless his or her parents, because blessing requires some stature in life.

We must grow in life to arrive at the stature of being able to bless others. The fact that David could bless his people means that he had the stature in life. After Jacob became Israel and was in his old age, he went down to Egypt and blessed people. His hands were not working hands but blessing hands (Gen. 47:7, 10; 48:15, 20). The older you are, the more you can bless others. But being able to bless others needs not only age but also the stature in life. Blessing is also higher than thanking or praising. A little boy can praise God, but he cannot bless others.

David's blessing in Psalm 20 involved himself, God, and his people. This means that in Psalm 20, he is higher, deeper, and richer than in the previous psalms. David's concept concerning his kingship has improved from his righteousness to God's sanctuary, Mount Zion, the meal offerings and the burnt offering to God, God's mighty salvation, and God's name. His blessing does not say anything about his righteousness. If we stand on our righteousness, we may be able to pray, but we cannot bless. To bless others, we must stand on all that God is. We cannot bless people with our righteousness. We have to bless people with what God is and has.

B. David's Praise to Jehovah for His Kingship and God's Furious Dealing with His Enemies

In Psalm 21, David praises Jehovah for his kingship and speaks of God's furious dealing with his enemies. David praised Jehovah for his kingship through His strengthening, salvation, blessings, crowning, lengthening of life, great glory, splendor and honor, and lovingkindness (vv. 1-7). David did not mention his righteousness here. If we depend upon our righteousness, our kingship can never be built up. Endeavoring to keep the law makes us slaves, not kings. According to Galatians 4, all the children brought forth by the law are slaves (vv. 24-25). But the children brought forth by grace become kings. To depend upon God's lovingkindness builds up the kingship.

In verses 8-12, David spoke of God's furious dealing with David's enemies by devouring them and destroying their descendants. This is David's concept. For his kingship he depended upon God's lovingkindness. For his enemies, however, he applied God's furious dealing.

In verse 13 David blessed Jehovah that He may be exalted in His strength that David as the king with his people will sing and psalm His might. This verse shows us a man who not only blesses his people but also blesses God. As a king, he blessed his people. As the one anointed by God, he blessed the anointing God. The conclusion of Psalm 21 is very good.

We can see much improvement with David in these five psalms. He has been improving gradually from Psalm 17 to the end of Psalm 21. This leads us to Psalm 22 concerning Christ's death, Psalm 23 concerning Christ's shepherding in His resurrection, and Psalm 24 concerning Christ's reigning as the coming King.

LIFE-STUDY OF THE PSALMS

MESSAGE TEN

THE CHRIST WHO HAS PASSED THROUGH THE REDEEMING DEATH AND ENTERED INTO THE CHURCH-PRODUCING RESURRECTION

Scripture Reading: Psa. 22

In the book of Psalms, there are certain highlight psalms. The top psalms we have seen thus far are Psalm 2, Psalm 8, and Psalm 16. Now we come to the fourth top psalm, Psalm 22.

Generally speaking, we love every psalm because every psalm is full of an aspiration to seek after God, to pray to Him, to contact Him, and to receive the spiritual help from Him. Even Psalm 1 does this. We have seen that Psalm 1 uplifts the law instead of Christ, but we should not condemn Psalm 1 to the extent that we give it up. That is wrong. We have to love every psalm because every psalm as the Word of God is eatable (Jer. 15:16; Matt. 4:4). If you are weak or down, you can read one psalm a number of times with some amount of prayer. Then you will be nourished. Every psalm can be a spiritual supply to us.

But often we receive this spiritual supply in a wrong way. Eating is not that simple. We need the proper groceries and the proper way to cook them. This is why we need to enter into the right way to understand all of the psalms one by one. My burden is mainly to show us that the book of Psalms, in the proper understanding, is centered on Christ. The Psalms are fully Christ-centered. Christ is not only the centrality but also the universality of the Psalms. I believe that the Lord has given us the proper and particular way to study, to know, and to interpret the Psalms. In this message we want to see that Christ is particularly revealed in Psalm 22.

I. THE HIND OF THE DAWN
BEING A TYPE OF CHRIST IN RESURRECTION

The title of Psalm 22 says, " To the choir director: according to the hind of the dawn." This title of the melody of this psalm is very meaningful. The hind of the dawn here refers to the Christ in resurrection. There was such a teaching in the church, in the Body of Christ, in the past. I received this light through Brother Watchman Nee. This title of Psalm 22 shows that it is a psalm concerning Christ in resurrection. Christ is a hind. He is a leaping, jumping, active, living deer. A hind is a fast animal. When a hind runs, it leaps; it jumps. Christ in resurrection is the leaping One (S. S. 2:8-9).

Our going to Russia for the spread of the Lord's recovery has been a "leaping" move. Even a year ago, we did not have the idea to go to Russia. The decision to follow the Lord to "leap" for His move in Russia was on Memorial Day of last year, 1991. This move is surely the move of the Christ in resurrection. Psalm 22 is on Christ as the hind of the dawn, the resurrected Christ in the early morning.

Of course, without death, there is no resurrection. The resurrection follows the crucifixion. The first twenty-one verses of Psalm 22 cover the death of Christ, the crucifixion of Christ, and the last ten verses cover His resurrection. Isaiah 53 is a particular chapter on Christ's death in detail. Psalm 22 is another chapter of the Bible in the Old Testament on the death of Christ which is full of details. We need these two chapters in order to see a thorough, detailed picture of Christ's death.

The subject of Psalm 22 is the Christ who has passed through the redeeming death and entered into the church-producing resurrection. His death is for redeeming, and His resurrection is for producing the church.

II. CHRIST PASSING THROUGH THE REDEEMING DEATH

Verses 1-21 show us Christ passing through the redeeming death.

A. David's Groaning Cry to God

Verses 1b-5 are David's groaning cry to God. David was

complaining to God. He asked God why He had forsaken him,
saying that he called out to God, but God did not answer
him. Our God is loving and is also very patient with us. David
was groaning before God. Have we ever groaned before God?
We all may have prayed, but not many of us have groaned
before God.

Our God is surely a loving God, but sometimes it seems
that He is not so loving. Instead of being promoted, a brother
may be laid off. Another brother may not be healed of his
illness, even though he has prayed for three months. God
surely hears our prayers, but many times He does not answer
our prayers which are not according to His desire, His economy, His plan. When our prayer does not work, we have to
learn to come to God to complain to Him. We should not be
those who merely praise or pray to God. We need to realize
that God likes to hear our complaints.

Verse 1 says, "My God, my God, why have You forsaken
me?" This word was spoken by David in his suffering.
Actually, it became a prophecy concerning Christ in His
suffering of His redeeming death. It was quoted by the Lord
Jesus while He was suffering the crucifixion (Matt. 27:46).

Verses 2-5 are the continuation of David's groaning prayer,
which turned from groaning to praising. After this, Christ
continued to speak. Beginning from verse six, the voice
changes to another person, to Christ. This is the way the
Psalms were written. While David was speaking, eventually
Christ came in to speak in his speaking.

B. The Suffering David Typifying Christ
Passing through His Death

In Psalm 22 we see the suffering David typifying Christ
passing through His death (vv. 1a, 6-21). David and Solomon
were both types of Christ. David typifies the suffering Christ,
and Solomon typifies the reigning and ruling Christ in His
kingship.

1. Through Men's Reproach, Despising,
Deriding, Sneering, Head Shaking, and Mocking

The suffering of Christ unto death was through men's

reproach, despising, deriding, sneering, head shaking, and mocking (vv. 6-8; Heb. 13:13b; Isa. 53:3; Luke 23:11; Mark 15:29-32; Matt. 27:39-44). I hope that some, especially the young people, would remember these words which describe the Lord's suffering. Each of them has a particular meaning to describe what the Lord suffered on the cross. We may have never considered the significance of each of these words. This shows that when we read the Bible, we have a tendency to take everything for granted.

The word *reproach* is also used in Hebrews 13:13, which says, "Let us therefore go forth unto Him outside the camp, bearing His reproach." This indicates that we need to come outside the camp of religion to follow the suffering Jesus. To bear the Lord's reproach is to bear His disgrace or shame. To despise is to look down on with contempt and scorn. To deride is to make fun of or laugh at in contempt. To sneer is to smile or laugh with facial contortions that express scorn or contempt. When Christ was on the cross, the ridiculers also shook, or wagged, their heads (Psa. 22:7b; Matt. 27:39; Mark 15:29), saying, "He committed himself to Jehovah; let Him rescue him" (Psa. 22:8a). To mock is to hold up to scorn or contempt and to imitate or mimic in derision. All these things were suffered by the Lord Jesus Christ while He was nailed on the cross. Groups of people reproached Him, despised Him, derided Him, sneered at Him, shook their heads at Him, and mocked Him.

2. Trusting in God for Deliverance

Psalm 22:9-11 shows that Christ trusted in God for deliverance. While people were mocking Him and deriding Him, He was trusting in God. Deliverance here is resurrection. He intended definitely to die and expected to be delivered from death, that is, to be resurrected from the dead.

3. Through the Suffering of Crucifixion

Psalm 22:12-18 shows how Christ passed through the suffering of crucifixion. The Jewish people did not have the practice of crucifying criminals. This was a practice of the heathen (Ezra 6:11) adopted by the Romans for the execution

of slaves and heinous criminals. As the Lamb of God, Christ
was crucified for our redemption (John 1:29; Heb. 9:12).

Years ago, I read an article describing how the children of
Israel slew the lamb during the Passover. They took two
wooden bars and formed a cross. They tied two legs of
the lamb at the foot of the cross and fastened the other out-
stretched legs to the crossbar. Then they slew the lamb so
that all its blood was shed, for they needed all of the blood
to sprinkle on their doorframes (Exo. 12:7). The way the
Passover lamb was killed is a picture of Christ's crucifixion
on the cross as the Lamb of God.

While Christ was being crucified on the cross, many fierce
men, signified by mighty bulls, encompassed Him (Psa.
22:12). They opened their mouth at Him like a ravening and
roaring lion (v. 13). Evil men, signified by dogs, surrounded
Him, and a congregation of evildoers enclosed Him (v. 16a-b).

Psalm 22:16c says that they pierced His hands and feet
(Zech. 12:10; John 19:37; Rev. 1:7). Charles Wesley in one of
his hymns spoke of the "five bleeding wounds" which Christ
received on Calvary (*Hymns,* #300). His two hands, His two
feet, and His side (John 19:34) were pierced by the Roman
soldiers who executed Him.

They divided His garments to themselves, and for His
clothing they cast lots (Psa. 22:18; John 19:23-24). In His
crucifixion, the Lord's right to be clothed was stripped from
Him, along with His life. They made the Lord Jesus altogether naked in order to have a public, shameful display.

Psalm 22:17b says that they looked, they stared at Him.
The evildoers were staring at the Lord Jesus with contempt
and hatred while He was on the cross.

On the cross, He was poured out like water (v. 14a). Isaiah
53:12 says that He poured out His soul. We cannot fully realize the tremendous amount of suffering which the Lord
experienced on the cross.

Psalm 22:14b says that all His bones were out of joint.
This was because He could not hold up the weight of His body
hanging on the cross. His bones being out of joint caused Him
great agony and pain.   ·

Also, He counted all His bones (v. 17a). His heart was like

wax melted within Him (v. 14c-d). His strength was dried up like a shard (v. 15a; John 19:28), a piece of broken pottery. His tongue was stuck to His jaws (Psa. 22:15b). God had put Him in the dust of death (v. 15c; Phil. 2:8b). He was put to death by God. On the one hand, it was man crucifying Him, killing Him, but eventually it was God who put Him into death. Actually, God killed Jesus. If Jesus had been killed only by man, He could never have been our Redeemer. He would have been merely a martyr. But God judged Him and put Him into death for our redemption (Isa. 53:4, 10).

4. Asking God to Deliver Him from Death

Christ asked God to deliver Him from death (Psa. 22:19-21). Hebrews 5:7 says that Christ cried to God for God's deliverance, that is, for God to raise Him up from the dead.

5. Forsaken by God

Psalm 22:1 shows that on the cross Christ was forsaken by God (v. 1a; Matt. 27:45-46). The beginning of Psalm 22 speaks of this, but in the sequence of events on the cross, Christ cried out "My God, My God, why have You forsaken Me?" at about the ninth hour, or 3:00 P.M. (Matt. 27:46). This was at the end of His crucifixion. Christ was hanging on the cross for six hours, from the third hour, 9:00 A.M. (Mark 15:25), to the ninth hour, 3:00 P.M. In the first three hours, He was persecuted by men for doing God's will; in the last three hours, He was judged by God to accomplish our redemption. It was during the last three hours that God counted Him as our Substitute who suffered for our sin (Isa. 53:10).

Darkness fell over all the land (Matt. 27:45) because our sin and sins and all negative things were being dealt with on the cross. Isaiah 53:6 says that God laid all of our sins upon Christ. He was forsaken by God for our sins (1 Cor. 15:3), becoming sin on our behalf (2 Cor. 5:21) to be judged by God as our Substitute.

While He was on the earth, God the Father was with Him all the time (John 8:29), but at a certain point in His crucifixion, God left Him. God's leaving Him was economical, not essential. Essentially speaking, God could never leave Christ.

But economically speaking, God did leave Him for a while. Thus, He cried out, "My God, My God, why have You forsaken Me?"

First Peter 3:18 reveals that He was forsaken by God in a vicarious death. This verse says that as the Righteous One, Christ died on behalf of the unrighteous. The modernists say that Christ's death was not for redemption but was merely a martyrdom for the good of the people. This is heresy. John 1:29 says, "Behold, the Lamb of God, who takes away the sin of the world." All the sin of the world was laid upon Christ on the cross. He died a vicarious death for us to redeem us from our sins, from God's judgment, and from eternal perdition.

III. CHRIST ENTERING INTO THE CHURCH-PRODUCING RESURRECTION

After passing through His redeeming death, Christ entered into the church-producing resurrection (Psa. 22:22-31).

A. In Resurrection, Christ Calling His Disciples His Brothers

It was in His resurrection that Christ called His disciples His brothers. Psalm 22:22 says, "I will declare Your name to my brothers; / In the midst of the assembly I will praise You." In this verse "I" is the resurrected Christ who declares the Father's name to His brothers. If He had remained in death, He could not have declared God the Father's name to His brothers.

Christ was on the earth with His disciples for the three and a half years of His earthly ministry, but He never called them His brothers until the morning of the day He resurrected. On that day, the Lord told Mary, "Go to My brothers and say to them, I ascend to My Father and your Father, and My God and your God" (John 20:17). This means that the disciples became God's sons in Christ's resurrection. Before His resurrection the disciples were not His brothers because they had not been regenerated. But when Christ was resurrected, all the believers, including you and me, were resurrected with Him and in Him (Eph. 2:6). Through His resurrection, we were regenerated (1 Pet. 1:3). Resurrection was a big delivery, a big birth. Acts 13:33 says that resurrection was a birth to Christ. Christ was the only begotten Son of God (John 3:16), but in resurrection He was begotten as the firstborn Son of God with many brothers (Rom. 8:29), many sons of God.

First Peter 1:3 says that through Christ's resurrection, God regenerated all of us believers. Some may think that they were regenerated at a certain point in time a few years ago. But actually we all were regenerated at the same time before we were born. I once read of a certain woman who brought forth seven children in one delivery, but this cannot compare with the great delivery of children through Christ's resurrection. The resurrection of Christ was a delivery of millions of sons of God at the same time. He was the firstborn Son of God in resurrection, and we followed Him to be the many sons of God. On the day of His resurrection, He could say that His Father is our Father because He and we were all born of the same Father. We, His believers, His disciples, became His brothers.

B. His Brothers Constituting the Church

The second half of Psalm 22:22 is very meaningful. It says, "In the midst of the assembly I will praise You." "The assembly" is the church, and "You" is the Father God. At the Lord's table we follow the Lord's pattern in praising the Father. After we remember the Lord by taking the bread and the wine, we follow the Lord to praise the Father, to worship the Father. According to logic, verse 22b should say, "In the midst of *them* I will praise You." But the Lord changed the pronoun *them* to *the assembly*. "My brothers" became the church, the assembly. The Lord's brothers constitute the church (Heb. 2:11-12).

C. Declaring the Father's Name to His Brothers and Praising the Father in the Church

In resurrection Christ declared the Father's name to His brothers and praised the Father in the church. His resurrection is the church-producing resurrection. Hebrews 2:11-12 says, "For both He who sanctifies and those who are being

sanctified are all of One, for which cause He is not ashamed
to call them brothers, saying, 'I will declare Your name to
My brothers; in the midst of the church I will sing hymns of
praise to You.'" He who sanctifies is Christ, and those who
are being sanctified are we believers. We are both of One,
that is, out of one Father. Hebrews 2:12 is a quotation of
Psalm 22:22.

D. His Church Ushering In His Kingdom
for Him to Rule over the Nations

Christ's church ushers in His kingdom for Him to rule
over the nations. Psalm 22:27-28 says, "All the ends of the
earth / Will remember and return to Jehovah, / And all families of the nations / Will worship before You; / For the
kingdom is Jehovah's, / And He rules among the nations."
Christ has the kingdom, and He will rule among the nations.

The church ushers in the kingdom. Actually, the church is
the reality of the kingdom and a precursor of the manifestation of the kingdom. Today the church is the kingdom.
Romans 14:17 says the church life is the kingdom life, the
kingdom of God. But this is a precursor of the coming kingdom, just as the tabernacle was a precursor of the temple.
Today's church life is a miniature, a precursor, of the coming
kingdom of one thousand years. The church is produced by
the resurrection of Christ, and the kingdom will be ushered in
by the church.

E. Following Christ's Praise to God in the Church,
David Advising God's People to Praise Jehovah
and All the Earth to Worship Him

Following Christ's praise to God in the church, David
advised God's people to praise Jehovah and all the earth to
worship Him (Psa. 22:23-26, 29-31). Psalm 22:23 says, "You
who fear Jehovah, praise Him! / All you seed of Jacob, glorify
Him! / And stand in awe of Him, all you seed of Israel!" This
means that Christ advised the Jews to learn of the church.
Christ took the lead in praising God in the church, and the
church follows Him to praise God. Now the seed of Jacob
should follow Christ and the church. Thus far, Israel has not

followed, but when Jesus comes back, all Israel will repent and be saved (Rom. 11:26-27; Zech. 12:10). Then they will join us to praise God. In David's advice at the end of Psalm 22, we see the church as the kingdom and all the people worshipping God and praising the Father.

LIFE-STUDY OF THE PSALMS

MESSAGE ELEVEN

CHRIST AS THE SHEPHERD IN HIS RESURRECTION
AND
CHRIST AS THE KING IN GOD'S KINGDOM

Scripture Reading: Psa. 23—24

Psalms 22—24 are a group of psalms revealing Christ from His crucifixion to His kingship in the coming age. In Psalm 22 we see Christ's death, His resurrection, and His many brothers produced in His resurrection to form His church. Psalm 23 is concerning Christ as the Shepherd. This Shepherd today is in His resurrection. Psalm 24 is concerning Christ as the coming King in God's kingdom. Thus, in these three psalms, we have Christ crucified, Christ resurrected, Christ producing the church, Christ being the Shepherd and shepherding His flock, the church, and Christ coming back to be the King.

I. CHRIST AS THE SHEPHERD IN HIS RESURRECTION

Psalm 23:1 says, "Jehovah is my Shepherd." Christ is our Shepherd and we are His flock. The church in the Bible is called a flock. In John 10 the Lord said that He was the good Shepherd who would collect the sheep from Israel and from the Gentiles to form them into one flock (vv. 14-16), which is the church (1 Pet. 5:2; Acts 20:28).

Jehovah, of course, is the divine God, and we are mere humans. How can God, the divine One, approach us human beings to be our Shepherd? If God would come to us in a direct way, that might frighten us to the uttermost. The Bible tells us that this happened when God appeared to various people (Rev. 1:17; Gen. 17:3; Dan. 8:17; Matt. 17:6). The Bible also tells us that no one can see God (1 Tim. 6:16; John 1:18; Exo. 33:20). How can the divine Triune God be so close to us, just as a shepherd is to his flock? Furthermore, how can we sinners, the fallen people, be the flock of the divine Shepherd? According to our fallen nature we are snakes, vipers (Matt. 23:33), and "scorpions."

Psalm 23 implies that this Shepherd is the One who became a man, who died for us to redeem us and wash away our sins, and who entered into resurrection to become a life-giving Spirit (1 Cor. 15:45b) to regenerate us. As such a One, He can change our nature. Since He has taken these three steps—1) incarnation; 2) crucifixion for redemption; and 3) resurrection for regenerating—He is altogether qualified, equipped, and suitable to be our Shepherd. He is not only God but also a man. He is not only divine but also human. He died for our sins, He was resurrected, and in His resurrection He became a life-giving Spirit.

The Lord Jesus today is the Spirit (2 Cor. 3:17). As the life-giving Spirit, He is our Shepherd inwardly. He is not only with us but also within us. We were snakes and scorpions, but we have been redeemed, we have been washed in His blood, and we have been resurrected (Eph. 2:6) and regenerated. As those who have been redeemed, washed, resurrected, and regenerated, we are the sheep of God's flock, the church. By Jehovah, the Triune God, being incarnated, crucified, and resurrected to become the life-giving Spirit, He is qualified to be our Shepherd. By His redeeming, washing, resurrecting, and regenerating us, we are qualified to be His flock. He is qualified to be our Shepherd, and we are also qualified to be His flock. Psalm 23 is altogether a psalm on Christ as the Shepherd in His resurrection.

We can also see Jehovah as the Triune God in this psalm. Verse 2 says, "He makes me lie down in green pastures." The color green signifies the riches of life. When we see the green trees and pastures, we see the riches of life. If the trees are yellow and dried up and the grass is brown, this indicates death.

The green pastures signify the Lord Jesus. The Lord Jesus spoke concerning this in John 10. He said that His sheep would hear His voice and follow Him out of the fold to enjoy the green pastures as the flock (vv. 9, 16). In John 10, Christ is the door (v. 9), the Shepherd (v. 11), and the pasture (v. 9).

Christ Himself is our pasture, our nourishment. He is the feeding place for all the sheep. In John 6 Christ said that He is the bread of life (v. 35) to nourish us (v. 57). The "bread" for the sheep is the green pasture, so the green pasture is Christ. Christ can be our green pasture through His incarnation, death, and resurrection. After His incarnation, death, and resurrection, He is growing here as the green pasture for our nourishment.

Psalm 23:2b says that Christ as our Shepherd leads us to waters of rest. The waters of rest are the Spirit. The Spirit is the water, and Christ is the pasture. Verse 5 says, "You anoint my head with oil." Hebrews 1:9 refers to the oil of exultant joy. This oil signifies the Spirit. John 7:39 says that before Christ's resurrection, the Spirit was not yet. This means that the Spirit was not yet consummated. The Spirit of God has been consummated through Christ's incarnation, crucifixion, and resurrection. In Christ's resurrection, the Spirit of God became the life-giving Spirit (1 Cor. 15:45b). Now He is available to us because He has been consummated. In Psalm 23, the Spirit as typified by the waters and the oil signifies the consummated Spirit after Christ's resurrection.

This psalm also tells us that Christ's shepherding of us is in five stages. The first stage is of the pastures and the waters of rest (v. 2). Pasture and waters are for our nourishment, including cherishing and enjoyment. The second stage is the stage of the paths of righteousness (v. 3). The paths of righteousness indicate our walk. After we enjoy Christ, are filled up with Christ, and are nourished by Christ, we walk on the paths of righteousness. The third stage is the valley of the shadow of death (v. 4). The valley, the shadow, and death are not pleasant. Christ's shepherding leads us through the valley of the shadow of death. The fourth stage is the battlefield (v. 5), where we are fighting against the adversaries. At the battlefield a table, a feast, is spread for us. Finally, the last stage is to dwell in the house of God all the days of our life (v. 6).

I would like us to consider what stage we are in among these five stages of Christ's shepherding. The first stage is the initial stage of enjoyment. This is just like elementary school.

In our educational system there are five stages—elementary, junior high, high school, college, and graduate school. This is comparable to the five stages of Christ's shepherding in Psalm 23. Many of us are in "elementary school" while others are in "high school" in their experience of Christ. A brother who is more mature in the Lord and who has been a seeking Christian for many years may have passed through all five stages of Christ's shepherding. Now in his present experience, he may say that he experiences all five stages at various times.

A. The Initial Stage of the Enjoyment in Green Pastures and at Waters of Rest

The resurrected Christ shepherds us first in the initial stage of enjoyment in green pastures and at waters of rest (Psa. 23:1-2). Because He is our Shepherd, we will lack nothing (Phil. 1:19b). Right after we were saved, we entered into this first stage of enjoyment. In John 21 the Lord Jesus asked Peter if he loved Him. When Peter said that he did love the Lord, the Lord charged him to feed His lambs (v. 15). We need to be like nursing mothers to cherish and feed the little ones under our care (1 Thes. 2:7). Right after a child is delivered, a mother feeds the child so he can grow.

In the initial stage of the enjoyment of Christ, the lambs, the infants, feed on Christ as the green pasture (John 10:9). Infants do not have table manners. All the little lambs lie down to eat the pasture without any thought of manners. Christ makes us to lie down, not sit down in a mannerly way, in green pastures. This kind of eating, without the thought for proper manners, is more enjoyable. The little lamb lying down in the pasture and eating the grass does not have to worry about proper table manners. This is just like an infant lying in the bosom of his nursing mother. No table manners are necessary.

We have been feeding the little lambs, the new ones in the Lord, for many years. They do not have any "manners" in their enjoyment of Christ. It seems that they can say everything. A new one may say, "Yes, I have been saved, but I don't feel much that the Lord is so good." This is not polite. We may be feeding this new one, but he is without "manners." This is because he is a lamb who is "lying down," not "sitting," to enjoy the Lord as the green pastures.

He also leads us to waters of rest (Psa. 23:2b; 1 Cor. 12:13b). The green pastures are Christ, and the waters of rest are the Spirit. The Spirit is the restful waters. When we go to take care of the new ones, we must not only feed them with Christ but also help them to drink of the Spirit. We must help them to call on the name of the Lord and to pray. This is to help them to drink the Spirit by exercising their spirit.

In partaking of a meal, drinking should always go along with eating. When I eat a meal I usually have two glasses of water. Then I have a comfortable and restful time of eating. The waters we drink are very restful. If someone served us food without anything to drink, this would not be so pleasant or restful. We would not have a comfortable feeling. This is why we need Christ as the pasture and the Spirit as the waters of rest. Actually, the pastures and the waters refer to the same person. In one aspect, He is our pasture, our food, to feed us. In another aspect, He is the life-giving Spirit as waters to bring us the proper rest. Both the pastures and the waters are the resurrected pneumatic Christ as the life-giving Spirit.

B. The Second Stage of Revival and Transformation on the Paths of Righteousness

Psalm 23:3 says, "He restores my soul; / He guides me on the paths of righteousness / For His name's sake." This is the second stage of revival and transformation on the paths of righteousness. To restore our soul is to revive us. Restoring also includes renewing and transforming. This corresponds with the New Testament teaching in Romans 12:2 which says that we need to be transformed by the renewing of the mind, which is the leading part of our soul. Christ in His shepherding restores—revives and transforms—our soul.

He restores us—revives and transforms us—in our soul to make us take His way, to walk on the paths of righteousness. Both the paths and righteousness are Christ. The resurrected

Christ today is our paths. In order to be a proper sister or a proper brother, we need Christ as our paths, as our way. A sister who does not behave and walk as a female does not have Christ as her paths. A brother who acts foolishly does not have Christ as his paths. Some brothers need a particular path to be an elder. Others need a path to be a co-worker. We also need a path to act as Christians and another path to work in God's economy. We need many paths, the paths of righteousness, in our Christian life and work.

John 7 says that when we drink of the life-giving Spirit as the living water, we will flow out, not just one river but many rivers (v. 38). There is a river of the proper humanity, a river of kindness, a river of love, a river of patience, etc. We need many rivers. In the same way, we need a path of humility, a path of loving, a path of patience, etc. These are the paths of righteousness.

Righteousness is to be right with people before God according to His righteous and strict requirements. We must admit that we are short of the paths to be right. We have to take the paths of righteousness by being restored—revived and transformed—in our soul, which comprises our mind, our emotion, and our will. We must be proper and balanced in our mind, our emotion, and our will. Otherwise, we cannot be righteous; we cannot be right with man and with God.

Christ shepherds us on the paths of righteousness. A shepherd has a staff to guide and instruct the sheep. Sheep have a tendency to go astray. The shepherd uses his staff to correct the sheep and keep them on the right way with the flock. Quite often our behavior goes astray, so we need Christ's correction.

To be a lady or a gentleman may be difficult, but to be a Christian is much more difficult. Christians should be the highest class of people. Sometimes the sisters do not cut their hair properly, so their hair is not right. If we do not buy the proper pair of shoes befitting a Christian, this shows that we are wrong in our person. We need to be right in everything. The brothers need to be right in the way that they cut their hair and in the kind of necktie they wear.

We have to be right not only ethically, morally, but also materially. Some young brothers who came into the church life in Los Angeles in the late sixties dressed in a wild way. After being in the church life for a period of time, however, the way in which they dressed became proper, and their long hair and beards were cut. One brother came to the meeting and sat on the front row with his bare feet. Within a short period of time, this brother began to wear shoes and later he wore shoes and socks. This was evidence of the Lord's transforming work from within him. These young people changed without any outward correction or adjustment from others.

This shows us that we have to be right not only ethically, morally, but also physically, materially. We Christians are high-class people. In order to minister the Word, the inner law of life requires me to dress in a proper way. Then I appear as a very ordinary, proper person. We all have to be under the Lord's shepherding in all that we do. His shepherding is a kind of balancing, correcting, and adjusting.

He guides us (to walk according to the spirit) on the paths of righteousness (to fulfill the requirement of righteousness—Rom. 8:4). Righteousness can be fulfilled only by those who walk according to their spirit. We have three parts—body, soul, and spirit (1 Thes. 5:23). We should not do things according to our body, because it is full of lusts. We should not do things according to our soul, because it is full of opinions. Instead, we should do things according to our spirit. When we walk according to the spirit, we fulfill the righteous requirement of the law.

Christ as our Shepherd leads us in the paths of righteousness for His name's sake—in the person of the resurrected pneumatic Christ. Matthew 28:19 says that we are to baptize people into the name of the Father, of the Son, and of the Holy Spirit. The name indicates the person. For His name's sake is for His person's sake. Today Jesus Christ as a living Person is the pneumatic Christ in His resurrection. He is life-giving Spirit. He leads us inwardly to walk in the paths of righteousness in Himself as the Person. He is such a Shepherd in us.

C. The Third Stage of the Experience of the Presence of the Resurrected Pneumatic Christ through the Valley of the Shadow of Death

The third stage is the stage of the experience of the presence of the resurrected pneumatic Christ through the valley of the shadow of death (Psa. 23:4). Even though we walk through the valley of the shadow of death, we do not fear evil, for the pneumatic Christ is with us (2 Tim. 4:22). This means that we experience His presence. For Him to be with us is for us to enjoy His presence. His presence is a comfort, a rescue, and a sustaining power to us when we are walking in the valley of the shadow of death.

We human beings cannot avoid having troubles as we live on this earth. A husband's wife who takes care of him and the children may suddenly become so ill that she is unable to walk. Then this brother gets into the valley, which is under a shadow and full of death. Some saints may have children who are crippled. This brings these saints into the valley. A brother may be an elder in a locality, and the Lord may suddenly bring in another elder, with whom it is difficult for this brother to coordinate. This other elder then becomes the valley of the shadow of death to the first elder. He cannot quarrel with this other elder, or he will offend his spirit. He has to keep the one accord with him. Also, his spirit will not allow him to withdraw. He has to stay in the valley to suffer. These are examples of the valley of the shadow of death.

About five years ago, I was put into a valley. In 1987 I was working in Taipei, laboring day and night on the Chinese Recovery Version of the New Testament. Then at the end of 1987, I returned to the United States and realized that there was turmoil present among us. During this rebellious turmoil, I was put into a valley. When we are in the valley, the best way for us to deal with it is to rest. The tests in the valley always tempt us to do something so that we can come out of the valley. But the more we do, the more the valley extends. We just need to be quiet, to rest.

Our resting in the Lord will shorten the valley, reduce the shadow, and remove the death. We should not talk about our being in the valley. The more we talk, the wider the valley becomes. The best way is for us to forget that we are in the valley, because we have the Lord with us. We do not fear evil, because He is with us. Second Timothy 4:22 says that the Lord is with our spirit. The Lord is not merely within us in a general way, but He is in our spirit in a particular way. If we have had the proper experience in the valley, we can testify that it was a place for us to enjoy the Lord's presence in such a close way.

In 1943 there was a big revival in the church in Chefoo, my hometown in mainland China. At that time we were under the invasion of the Japanese army. They were wondering how I could draw so many people. They studied me secretly for a few months, and then in May of 1943, they came to get me. They brought me to their military police headquarters, and I was put into prison for thirty days. That was a real valley to me. The Japanese invading army killed thousands of Chinese during the war, so I could have been killed by them at any time. I was under their threatening and torture for two three-hour sessions a day.

One day they put a young Greek man into the prison cell with me. He and I both spoke a little English, so we could communicate with each other. The Japanese did not know this. One day they purposely decided not to give me any food. One of them came to me and, not being able to speak Chinese, he pointed up to the heavens, indicating that I should ask my God to give me food. The young Greek man, however, insisted on sharing his food with me. He and I became intimate friends.

After a few weeks, he was taken away, and I was left alone in my imprisonment. One day when I was alone, as I was praying, I had a deep sense that the Lord was there with me in a special, intimate way. I was in the valley, and the Lord caused me not to fear any evil. Eventually, I was preserved and protected by the Lord from being harmed. After thirty days, the Japanese released me. That was a real experience and enjoyment of the Lord's presence in the deep valley of the shadow of death.

In the valley of the shadow of death, the Lord's rod and

His staff—His protection, His guidance, and His sustenance—comfort us. The rod is for protection. If a wolf comes,
the shepherd uses his rod to protect the flock. The staff is for
training, for direction, for guidance, and also for sustenance.
The Lord has the rod to protect us, and He has the staff to
train us, to instruct us, to guide us, and to sustain us. We
experience the Lord's protection and guiding in the valley of
the shadow of death.

D. The Fourth Stage of the Deeper and Higher Enjoyment of the Resurrected Christ

Now we come to the fourth stage of the deeper and higher
enjoyment of the resurrected Christ (Psa. 23:5). The Lord
spreads a table—a feast—before us in the presence of our
adversaries (1 Cor. 10:21). The Lord's table is a feast. Every
Lord's Day when we come to His table to take the feast, it is
always in the presence of our adversaries. Every day is a
fighting day to us. We Christians have to fight. Otherwise, we
will be defeated. There may be adversaries in our business, in
our home, and even in the church. On the one hand, we enjoy
the feast of the Lord, and on the other hand, we should fight
for the victory. If we are defeated during the week, it will be
difficult for us to enjoy the Lord's table that much. We need to
fight the battle in the Lord all week long before we come to
the Lord's table. Then we will be able to have a rich enjoyment of the Lord as our feast at His table.

In the fourth stage of the deeper and higher enjoyment of
the resurrected Christ, the Lord anoints our head with oil
(of exultant joy—Heb. 1:9); our cup (of blessing—1 Cor. 10:16a)
runs over. To anoint the head is to anoint the whole body.
Psalm 133 speaks of the ointment upon the head spreading
down to the skirts of the garments. No doubt, this is the
anointing of the compound, life-giving Spirit in Christ's resurrection. All the riches of Christ's being and doing are
compounded together in this anointing compound ointment.

The Bible uses the word *cup* to indicate blessing. The cup
of blessing runs over. Psalm 23:5 speaks of the table, the
feast, which is Christ with His riches for our enjoyment. Then
there is the anointing oil, which is the Spirit. Then there is

the cup of blessing, which refers to the Father. The Father is the blessing, even the source of blessing. Thus, in verse five there is the Triune God—the Son as the feast, the Spirit as the anointing oil, and the Father as the source of blessing.

E. The Fifth Stage of the Lifelong Enjoyment of the Divine Goodness and Kindness in the House of Jehovah

Psalm 23:6 speaks of the fifth stage of the lifelong enjoyment of the divine goodness and kindness in the house of Jehovah. Surely goodness and kindness will follow us (the grace of Christ and the love of God will be with us—2 Cor. 13:14) all the days of our life (in the present age). *Goodness* refers to the grace of Christ, *kindness* refers to the love of the Father, and *follow* refers to the fellowship of the Spirit. Second Corinthians 13:14 reveals the move of the Triune God for us to enjoy all His riches. The grace of the Son, the love of the Father, and the fellowship of the Spirit are with us. This is the fifth stage of our enjoyment of the Triune God in Psalm 23.

Eventually, this enjoyment will usher us into the house of God. We will dwell in the house of Jehovah (the church and the New Jerusalem—1 Tim. 3:15-16; Rev. 21:2-3, 22) for the length of our days (in the present age and in the coming age and in eternity). Our days are not only in the present age but also in the coming age and in eternity. We will live for eternity; our days will be that long. Today we are in the church. If we are overcomers, we will be in the kingdom of one thousand years in the New Jerusalem. Eventually, in eternity we will be in the New Jerusalem with all of the chosen and redeemed saints. God's house is our dwelling place where we enjoy the Triune God—the Son's grace, the Father's love, and the Spirit's fellowship. Today we enjoy the Triune God in the church, and in the future we will enjoy Him in the New Jerusalem.

If we are not in the church, we lose the shepherding of Christ. Outside of the church, without the church, there is no way for Christ to shepherd us. This is because He is the Shepherd of the flock, and the flock is the church. To get out of the church is to get out of the flock, and the Shepherd is always with the flock.

To be in the church is an enjoyment. Without the church, I would not like to live on this earth. Without the church, I would not have any enjoyment. Many people like sinful and worldly amusements, so they have parties and go to clubs. We do not do this because the church is our "club," the church is our "party," the church is our amusement. The best place for our amusement is the church life. If we decide to stay home in the evening instead of coming to the church meeting, we will suffer loss. To avoid this suffering, we need to come to the church meetings. In the church meetings, in God's house, we can enjoy the divine goodness (the grace of Christ) and the divine kindness (the love of God) following us (in the fellowship of the Holy Spirit) all the days of our life.

We human beings have to be social. If we are socializing in the wrong place, we will have trouble. The best place for us to be social is the church. The church is the proper society. Eventually, the church will consummate in the New Jerusalem where we will meet together for eternity.

II. CHRIST AS THE KING IN GOD'S KINGDOM

Psalm 24 reveals Christ as the King in God's kingdom. This will be in the coming age.

A. The Realization of the Earth and the Fullness Thereof as God's Kingdom

In Psalm 24:1-2 we see the realization of the earth and the fullness thereof, and the world and those who dwell in it, founded by God upon the seas and established by Him upon the streams, as God's kingdom. The thought in these two verses is very good.

B. The Mixtures of David's Concept

In verses 3-6 we again see the mixtures of David's concept. In these verses, his natural concept returns again. David said, "Who may ascend the mountain of Jehovah, / And who may stand in His holy place? / He who has clean hands and a pure heart, / Who has not engaged his soul in falsehood / Or sworn deceitfully. / He will receive blessing from Jehovah, / And righteousness from the God of his salvation. / This is the generation of those who seek Him; / Those who seek Your face are Jacob." These verses have nothing to do with the kingdom and are absolutely like Psalm 15.

We should not blame David too much for his natural concept because we are the same as he was. We have to remember that David was still living in the flesh. This is why there are two kinds of concepts in the Psalms—the human concept and the divine concept.

C. The Victorious Christ to Be the Coming King in God's Eternal Kingdom

Verses 7-10 are surely a proper continuation of verse 2. These verses show us the victorious Christ as the coming King in God's eternal kingdom. Verse 7 says, "Lift up your heads, O gates; / And be lifted up, O long enduring doors; / And the King of glory will come in." The gates are of the cities of the nations. The doors are of the houses of the people. The long enduring doors indicate waiting and expecting with long endurance (Phil. 3:20; 1 Cor. 1:7). This indicates that the people of the earth have been waiting and expecting Christ's second coming. In Haggai 2:7 we are told that Christ is the desire of all the nations. All the nations, in a general way, are expecting Christ to come, but Christ would not come that quickly according to our human concept. Thus, we need to wait and expect His coming with long endurance.

Because we must wait for His coming with long endurance, we have a tendency to drop our heads in discouragement. This is why the psalmist says, "Lift up your heads." If we expected someone dear to us to come and he does not come, we would drop our heads. But if we received a phone call from him, telling us that he is coming, we would lift up our heads, that is, we would be encouraged to expect his coming.

We have to lift up our heads, because the King of glory will come in (vv. 7, 9; Luke 21:27; Matt. 25:31). We must get ready to welcome Him. Psalm 24:8 asks, "Who is the King of glory?" The King of glory is "Jehovah strong and mighty! / Jehovah mighty in battle!" Jehovah is Jesus, and Jesus is the embodiment of the Triune God in resurrection. He is the One who is strong in fighting and victorious.

Verse 9 says, "Lift up your heads, O gates; / And lift up, O long enduring doors; / And the King of glory will come in." Verse 7 says, "Be lifted up," but verse 9 says, "Lift up." To be lifted up means that we are still weak, needing someone to move us. But to lift up means we have become stronger. We can act to lift up ourselves. The King of glory, whom we welcome, is Jehovah of hosts. *Hosts* means armies. He is Jehovah of the armies. Jehovah is the incarnated, crucified, and resurrected Triune God. He is the One in His resurrection coming back to possess the entire earth, to take it as His kingdom. The King of glory is Jehovah of hosts, the consummated Triune God embodied in the victorious and coming Christ (v. 10).

We have seen that Psalm 23 reveals Christ as the Shepherd in His resurrection, and that Psalm 24 reveals Christ as the King in God's kingdom. Hallelujah for the shepherding Christ, and hallelujah for the reigning Christ! Hallelujah for our Christ being our Shepherd today and our King in the future!

LIFE-STUDY OF THE PSALMS

MESSAGE TWELVE

THE ENJOYMENT OF GOD IN THE HOUSE OF GOD

Scripture Reading: Psa. 5:7; 11:4; 18:6; 20:2; 23:6; 26:8; 27:4-6; 34:8; 36:7-9

In this message we want to see the revelation of the enjoyment of God in the house of God in Book One of the Psalms, which includes Psalms 1—41. Thus far in our fellowship, we have seen four major stations concerning Christ—Psalms 2, 8, 16, and 22—24. We all need to see the particular aspects of Christ revealed in these psalms. Psalm 2 tells us that Christ is God's anointed One. Psalm 8 reveals Christ as the incarnated and crowned One, the excellent One in all the earth. Psalm 16 reveals Christ in His human living. It shows that Christ lived on this earth as a God-man, died on the cross, resurrected, and then ascended to the right hand of God. Psalm 22 shows us Christ crucified and resurrected to produce His brothers to constitute His Body, the church. Then in resurrection in Psalm 23, He became our Shepherd, shepherding us through five stages of enjoyment. Eventually, He will come back to be the King of glory, as revealed in Psalm 24. These psalms present us a completed Christ.

After these first four stations concerning Christ in the Psalms, Psalms 25—41 follow as a group of psalms showing us the mixed expressions in the psalmist's sentiment in his enjoyment of God in God's house. In these seventeen psalms, the main point, the major point, the crucial point, is the enjoyment of God in the house of God.

We have to realize that God is located! On the one hand, He is not a wandering God, but on the other hand, He is omnipresent. He is everywhere. Thus, He is the universal God, yet the universal God today is located! The house in which we live has an address, which indicates that we are located. People can write us letters if they know our street address and the city in which we live. Because we are located, people can contact us. Today our God is located. He has an address, and we can contact Him. In Psalms 25—41 we can see the location of God. This location is also mentioned in the foregoing psalms. The universal God is located in His house, His dwelling place.

I. THE REVELATION OF THE PSALMS BEGINNING WITH THE PSALMIST STRESSING THE LAW AND WITH THE SPIRIT TURNING THE PSALMIST TO CHRIST

The revelation of the Psalms begins with the psalmist stressing the law and with the Spirit turning the psalmist to Christ (Psa. 1—2). When the psalmist began in Psalm 1 by stressing the law, he was going in the wrong direction. In the first psalm, the psalmist seeking after God was driving on the wrong highway, so the Spirit came in to turn him to the right way.

In Psalm 2 the psalmist began to enjoy Christ—to take refuge in this Christ and to kiss this Christ (v. 12). The highest and best enjoyment of human life is kissing. When a child is born, the parents and grandparents enjoy kissing this child. If a person had no one whom he could kiss, he would surely be one of the most miserable people on earth. Psalm 2:12 commands us to "kiss the Son." Kissing Christ is the enjoyment of Christ.

Some may wonder where the word *enjoyment* is in the Bible concerning our relationship with Christ. Although this word is not in the Bible, the fact of the enjoyment of Christ is there. It is the same with the words *trinity* and *triune*. Although these words are not in the Bible, the early church fathers discovered the fact in the Bible that our God is triune, that He is the Divine Trinity. In like manner, the word *enjoyment* is not found in the Scriptures, but the fact is there. In Psalm 2 we are told to kiss the Son. *The Son* is a pleasant title. Kissing the Son is enjoying the Son.

The enjoyment of Christ in the Psalms begins with kissing the Son in Psalm 2. This enjoyment continues in Psalm 8, in which the psalmist declares, "How excellent is Your name / In all the earth!" (vv. 1, 9). Psalm 16 is also full of enjoyment. Verse 11 of this psalm says, "You will make known to Me the path of life; / In Your presence is fullness of joy; / In Your right hand there are pleasures forever." Psalm 22 gives us a very vivid picture of Christ's death on the cross. It also shows us His church-producing resurrection (v. 22). In Christ's resurrection His God is our God, His Father is our Father (John 20:17), and we are His brothers. The apostle Paul quoted Psalm 22:22 in Hebrews 2:12, pointing out that the Lord's brothers are the church.

Psalm 23 is full of the enjoyment of Christ as our Shepherd. Many Christians love Psalm 23, but not many have the realization that in this psalm they need to kiss Christ as the Shepherd. We saw in the previous message that Christ as the Shepherd leads us through five stages of enjoyment. The first stage is that of the green pastures and the waters of rest (v. 2). The second stage is the paths of righteousness (v. 3), and the third stage is the experience of Christ's presence through the valley of the shadow of death (v. 4). The fourth stage is the deeper and higher enjoyment of the resurrected Christ, in which we enjoy the Lord's table in the presence of our adversaries (v. 5). This implies that we are enjoying the Lord on the battlefield. The fifth and final stage is the lifelong enjoyment of the divine goodness and kindness in the house of Jehovah (v. 6). Psalm 24 goes on to show that the victorious Christ as the King of glory is coming to reign as the King in God's kingdom. All these points in the Psalms indicate that Christ is enjoyable.

II. THE ENJOYMENT OF CHRIST LEADING THE PSALMIST TO THE ENJOYMENT OF GOD IN THE HOUSE OF GOD

The enjoyment of Christ leads the psalmist to another state of enjoyment—the enjoyment of God in the house of God (Psa. 25—41). God Himself is enjoyable, and His dwelling place is also enjoyable. Psalm 27:4 says, "One thing I have asked from Jehovah; / That do I seek: / To dwell in the house of Jehovah / All the days of my life, / To behold the loveliness of Jehovah, / And to inquire in His temple." The one thing that David asked from God and sought was to dwell in the house of

God to behold His beauty. Psalm 27:4 shows us that our God is a lovable person with a lovely dwelling. Psalm 36 also tells us that we can be abundantly satisfied with the fatness, the abundance, of God's house (v. 8).

A. The Universal God Being Located in His House—His Dwelling Place

The universal God is located in His house—His dwelling place. The Scriptures reveal that God is located! Outside of Christ, we cannot find God (Col. 2:9). Christ is God's location, and the address of God is just one word—*Christ*. Christ is the street address and the city of God. If we say, "O God, where are You?" He will say, "I am in Christ." If we come to Christ, we will meet God. Whenever we call, "Lord Jesus," we have the sensation that God is present with us.

The revelation of God's house, His dwelling place, is not that simple. In the Old Testament time, God had His residence in the heavens (1 Kings 8:30b, 39a, 43a), and He also had a "retreat place" on Mount Zion in the center of Jerusalem in Palestine (Psa. 76:2b; 135:21; Isa. 8:18). In the center of Jerusalem, there was a temple, which could be considered as God's retreat place. A number of rich people have a residence and a retreat place. The residence is quite common, whereas the retreat place is very particular. If the weather is too hot or too cold, a person will go to his retreat place. The temple on Mount Zion within Jerusalem was God's retreat place.

It seems that our God did not feel satisfied with remaining in the heavens, so He came down to His temple on Mount Zion to have a retreat. He desired to leave the millions of angels in the heavens and come down to earth to stay with human beings for awhile. The end of Exodus tells us that when the tabernacle was raised up, the glory of God filled the tabernacle (40:33-35). Later, when Solomon built the temple, the glory of the Lord filled the temple (1 Kings 8:10-11). God was very happy when the tabernacle and temple were built. When a rich man gets his retreat place prepared, he is happy to go there. This retreat place may be a little smaller than his residence, but that smaller place is more pleasant to him. God felt pleasant when He came down to stay in the temple in Jerusalem.

1. The Incarnated Christ Being God's Tabernacle and God's Temple

In the Old Testament, both God's residence in the heavens and His retreat place on Mount Zion in Jerusalem were physical. But in the New Testament, God's residence is spiritual. In the New Testament, Christ is the tabernacle of God and the temple of God (John 1:14; 2:21).

2. The Church as the Enlargement of Christ Being God's Enlarged Temple—His Dwelling Place

Christ has been enlarged, and the enlarged Christ is the church as God's enlarged temple. The church as the enlargement of Christ is God's enlarged temple, His dwelling place. In 1 Corinthians 3:16 Paul said that the believers corporately are the temple of God; in Ephesians 2:22 he said that we are being built together into a spiritual dwelling place of God; and in 1 Timothy 3:15 he said that the church is the house of the living God. First, God is in Christ. When we call on the name of Christ, we get God. Furthermore, God is in the church. The church, of course, is not a physical building. We believers are the church.

When we are meeting together, we are the church in practicality, and God is dwelling in and among us. Often when I am in a meeting, I do not want to be dismissed. I am happy and feel so pleasant when I am with the saints in a meeting. When we are at home and not in the meetings, we may not feel that pleasant. There is no comparison between how we feel at home and how we feel in the meetings. Some of the saints have to drive a long distance to get to the meetings. Why do they do this? They are not crazy. They do this because they want to enjoy God in the house of God, the church. God is in Christ and in the church.

Sometimes we have problems and become puzzled, not knowing what to do. We may pray in our desire to know God's will, but it seems that our prayer is to no avail. Then we may come to the church meeting, and in the meeting we receive the light, and everything becomes clear to us. This is because God is in the church.

3. In the Ultimate Consummation, the New Jerusalem Being God's Redeemed People to Be the Tabernacle to God for Him to Enjoy His Redeemed People, and the Redeeming Triune God to Be the Temple to God's Redeemed People for Them to Enjoy Their Redeeming Triune God in Eternity

In the ultimate consummation, the New Jerusalem will be God's redeemed people to be the tabernacle to God for Him to enjoy His redeemed people, and the redeeming Triune God to be the temple to God's redeemed people for them to enjoy their redeeming Triune God in eternity. Revelation 21:2 and 3 tell us that in eternity future we, God's redeemed people, will be a tabernacle to God for God to enjoy us. Then verse 22 says that the Lord God the Almighty and the Lamb are the temple. This indicates that the Triune God will be the temple to us for us to enjoy Him as our redeeming Triune God in eternity. Therefore, the New Jerusalem is a mutual dwelling of both God and man for their mutual enjoyment. The New Jerusalem will be a composition of God and of us. To God, we will be the New Jerusalem as the tabernacle for Him to dwell in and enjoy. To us, God will be the New Jerusalem as the temple for us to dwell in and enjoy. The enjoyment in the New Jerusalem is both God's enjoyment and our enjoyment.

We need to see the enjoyment in the New Jerusalem. In the New Jerusalem there is a flowing river, which is the river of water of life. This river is bright as crystal (Rev. 22:1). In this crystal clear river, the tree of life grows and produces twelve fruits yearly (v. 2). In the New Jerusalem, there is new fruit every month. The fruits of the tree of life will be the food of God's redeemed for eternity. Eating the fruits of the tree of life will be our enjoyment.

Today God's location is in Christ and in the church. In the coming age and in eternity, God will be located in the New Jerusalem. Do we want to see God, to find God, to meet God, and to visit God? We need to go to Christ, the church, and the

New Jerusalem. To enjoy God in His house means that we must be in Christ, in the church, and eventually in the New Jerusalem. Otherwise, we will miss God.

B. The Psalmist's Initial Experience of the Enjoyment of God's House

At the beginning of the Psalms we see the psalmist's initial experience of the enjoyment of God's house.

1. Worshipping toward God's Holy Temple in Fear of Him

In Psalm 5:7, the psalmist said to God, "I will bow down toward Your holy temple / In fear of You." This was his experience outside of God's house.

2. Entering into God's House in the Abundance of His Lovingkindness

Then the psalmist spoke of entering into God's house in the abundance of His lovingkindness (Psa. 5:7). If someone had the privilege of entering into the temple on Mount Zion, he had to be under the abundance of God's lovingkindness. Actually, to enter into the temple in itself was an enjoyment of the abundance of God's lovingkindness. When we enter into God's house, we might say, "What love, what kindness, and what grace it is for me to be here in God's dwelling!" This is the enjoyment of God in His house.

3. Realizing That God Is in His Holy Temple on His Throne in Heaven

Psalm 11:4 says that God is in His holy temple on His throne in heaven discerning with His eyes and trying the sons of men. He tries the sons of men just as people put gold into the furnace to try it and purify it. The sufferings and trials of mankind are in God's sovereignty to try people. Psalm 11:4 says that His eyelids try the sons of men. When we are gazing at something, we are exercising our eyelids. God's gaze tries the sons of men.

4. Appreciating That God from His Temple
Heard His Cry in His Distress

In Psalm 18:6 the psalmist appreciated that God from His temple heard his cry in his distress. It is difficult to say whether the temple here refers to the residence of God in the heavens, or the physical temple on Mount Zion, His retreat place on earth. At any rate, this verse describes the initial, elementary, enjoyment of God related to His house.

5. Blessing Others with God's Sending Them
His Help from His Sanctuary and
His Strengthening from Zion

The psalmist enjoyed God in His house, so he blessed others with his experience. He blessed others with God's sending them His help from His sanctuary and His strengthening from Zion (Psa. 20:2). The word *Zion* here refers to the temple in Jerusalem. When God came and stayed in His retreat place, the temple on Mount Zion, He sent help and strength to those who trusted in Him.

6. With the Wrong Concept
concerning Who May Be in God's
Holy Sanctuary on His Holy Mountain

The psalmist as the one who enjoyed God in His temple, in His house, made a big mistake in understanding in Psalm 15:1-5 and Psalm 24:3-6. Both times he asked concerning who could be in God's holy sanctuary on His holy mountain. According to his concept, this one was the perfect man according to the law, who had clean hands and a pure heart. This is a wrong concept. This shows that David was like us in making mistakes.

C. The Psalmist's Improved Experience
of the Enjoyment of God's House
with the Enjoyment of God

Now we come to the psalmist's improved experience of the enjoyment of God's house with the enjoyment of God. We may illustrate the enjoyment of God in God's house by considering the enjoyment in a wedding room. In traditional Chinese weddings, a wedding room is decorated and prepared for the bride and groom in order to make that room a very pleasant place. However, that pleasant room without the bride would be vanity. The enjoyment of the wedding room must be with the enjoyment of the bride. In the same way, the enjoyment of God's house must be with the enjoyment of God.

1. Dwelling in the House of God for the Length of His Days

In Psalm 23:6 the psalmist spoke of dwelling in the house of God for the length of his days. We have seen that in Psalm 23 Christ as the Shepherd leads the church as His flock through five stages of enjoyment. Eventually, the sheep enjoy the Triune God as their goodness and kindness. Verse 6 says, "Surely goodness and kindness will follow me / All the days of my life, / And I will dwell in the house of Jehovah / For the length of my days." This includes the coming age, the age of the kingdom, and also eternity, the age of the new heaven and new earth.

2. Loving the Habitation of God's House and the Place Where God's Glory Abides (Is Manifested)

In Psalm 26:8 the psalmist said, "O Jehovah, I love the habitation of Your house, / And the place where Your glory abides." To abide means to remain for manifestation. When the people of Israel raised up the tabernacle and when they built up the temple, the glory of God descended upon the tabernacle and the temple to abide there, to remain there, to be manifested to the people. The psalmist told the Lord that he loved the habitation of His house and the place where His glory abode, remained, to be manifested to His people.

We have to say, "O Lord, I love Your church, and Your church is Your habitation. Your church is the place where Your glory abides to be manifested today." Psalm 84 expresses the psalmist's love for the house of God, which is the kind of love we should have for the church today. We have a hymn in our hymnal based on the psalmist's expression in Psalm 84 of his love for God's dwelling place (see *Hymns*, #851).

3. Seeking to Dwell in the House of God
All the Days of His Life

David said that he sought to dwell in the house of God all the days of his life (Psa. 27:4-6).

a. To Behold the Beauty
(Loveliness, Pleasantness, Delightfulness) of God

In Psalm 27:4 David said that he desired to behold the beauty of Jehovah in His house. The Hebrew word for *beauty* implies loveliness, pleasantness, and delightfulness. When we are beholding God's beauty, we are in a very pleasant atmosphere. Second Corinthians 3:18 says that we can have an unveiled face to behold the glorious face of the Lord in glory. In our time with the Lord in the morning, it is best to have short prayers with a number of "selahs" so that we can behold the Lord, look at the Lord.

b. To Inquire of God

The psalmist also inquired of God in His temple (Psa. 27:4b). This means that we can check with God about everything in our daily life.

c. To Be Concealed in God's Shelter

In Psalm 27:5 David said, "For He will conceal me in His shelter / In the evil day." God conceals His saints in His shelter in the evil day.

d. To Hide Himself in the Hiding Place of God's Tent

The psalmist also said that God would hide him in the hiding place of God's tent. We need to differentiate between the notions of concealing and hiding. When evils, calamities, are taking place, we can be concealed in God's shelter, and the evils cannot "see" us, cannot affect us. When someone is trying to capture us, there is a hiding place in God's tent where no one can find us. To be concealed is for getting away from the damage of calamities. To hide is for getting away from the ones who want to get us. The house of God is both a shelter and a hiding place.

I can testify that throughout the years, I have been concealed in God's shelter in the evil day and hidden in the hiding place of God's tent. According to my experience, I should have died at least three times. But on the one hand, the Lord concealed me, and on the other hand, the Lord hid me from the ones who were trying to get me.

e. To Be Raised Up and Have His Head Lifted Up by God

David also said that God would raise him up upon a rock and that he would have his head lifted up by God (27:5c, 6a). Most of the time, we drop our heads. We do not have our heads lifted up. When we walk, we mostly walk with our heads down. We need to be raised up and have our heads uplifted. We are earthly people, always looking upon the earth. It seems that we have lost something valuable and that we are looking on the ground for it. But when Abraham heard God's promise in the night, God told him to look toward heaven at the stars. Then God told Abraham that his descendants would be as numerous as the stars (Gen. 15:5). We need to forget about all of the earthly things. Instead, we need to look up. We need to lift up our heads and say, "Praise the Lord! Hallelujah!" This is a glory to Him.

Psalm 24:7 says, "Lift up your heads, O gates; / And be lifted up, O long enduring doors; / And the King of glory will come in." The gates are of the cities of the nations. The doors are of the houses of the people. We need to lift up our heads because our King is coming. We lift up our heads when we dwell in Christ and in the church, praising God and enjoying Him. Then we are raised up persons, and we have our heads lifted up by God.

f. To Offer Sacrifices of Shouts of Joy with Singing and Psalming to God

Psalm 27:6b says, "And I will offer in His tent / Sacrifices of shouts of joy; / I will sing and psalm to Jehovah." This all should be experienced by us in the house of God—in Christ and in the church. Surely we will also be like this in the New Jerusalem. We will behold God's beauty in the New Jerusalem. The New Jerusalem will be our shelter for us to be concealed and our hiding place for us to be hid. We will be raised up with our heads lifted up, praising, singing, psalming, and offering Christ to God. This is the enjoyment of God in the house of God.

4. Lifting Up His Hands
unto the Innermost Sanctuary

In Psalm 28:2 the psalmist said that he lifted up his hands unto the innermost sanctuary.

5. Praising God in His Temple by Saying, "Glory"

The psalmist also said that in Jehovah's temple all say, "Glory!" (29:9).

6. Tasting and Seeing That God Is Good

Psalm 34:8 says, "Taste and see that Jehovah is good." I did not see before that this verse is in the portion of the Psalms which reveals the enjoyment of God in God's house. This kind of tasting and seeing must be in the house of God. God is in His house. If we are not in His house, how can we taste Him and see Him? We taste and see that God is good in His house, that is, in Christ, in the church, and eventually in the New Jerusalem.

7. Enjoying the Riches in God's House

Psalm 36:7-9 reveals the psalmist's enjoyment of the riches in God's house.

a. Taking Refuge in the Shadow of God's Wings
under His Lovingkindness

The psalmist took refuge in the shadow of God's wings under His lovingkindness (36:7). I experienced taking refuge in the shadow of God's wings in 1938, after Japan had invaded China. I was arrested by the Japanese and placed in prison for one night, and the Lord did a marvelous thing to rescue me. Then five years later, in 1943, they arrested me again and put me into prison for thirty days. When I was in prison at that time, I took refuge in the shadow of God's wings.

b. Saturated with the Fatness
(the Abundance, the Riches) of God's House

Psalm 36:8 says that those who enjoy the riches in God's house are saturated with the fatness (the abundance, the riches) of God's house. God's house is full of the riches of God, the fatness. I have been in this house for over sixty years, and I have enjoyed many riches.

c. Drinking of the River of God's Pleasures

Psalm 36:8 also says that we can drink of the river of God's pleasures—not just one kind of pleasure, but many pleasures. In God's house, there is a river. The end of the Bible reveals that there is a river flowing in the New Jerusalem, the holy city, and that river spirals from the throne of God and of the Lamb through the whole city (Rev. 22:1).

d. Sharing of the Fountain of the Life of God

In God's house, we also share of the fountain of the life of God (Psa. 36:9a). Psalm 36 speaks of the river of God's pleasures and of the fountain of life. In the New Jerusalem, the tree of life is growing in the river of water of life. Thus, the fountain of life in Psalm 36 implies the tree of life growing in the river of the life of God.

e. Seeing Light in God's Light

Psalm 36:9b says, "In Your light we see light." Thus, in the house of God, we enjoy the river of life, the tree of life, and the light of life. These three things are strongly stressed in the New Jerusalem. Revelation 21 and 22 reveal that the light of the New Jerusalem is God in Christ. Christ is the lamp (Rev. 21:23), and God is the light in the lamp (22:5). The lamp with the light is in the New Jerusalem. This shows us again that God is located. God is located in Christ, and Christ is located in the New Jerusalem, where the Triune God will be the light. In that light, we see light.

It is amazing that in the ancient time, the psalmist, David, could utter such wonderful things in Psalm 36 according to the revelation of the Spirit, not according to his human, natural concept. Psalm 36 reveals the fatness for us to be saturated, the river of life for us to drink, the tree of life for us to share, and the light of life for our living and walking.

This is the enjoyment of God in His house, which is Christ, the church, and the New Jerusalem. Our God is located in these three persons: in Christ, in the church as a corporate person, and in the New Jerusalem as a corporate person. In these three persons, we can enjoy the located God as the fatness to saturate us, the river of life to quench our thirst, to satisfy us; the tree of life to feed us; and the light of life to enlighten us.

LIFE-STUDY OF THE PSALMS

MESSAGE THIRTEEN

THE MIXED EXPRESSIONS
OF THE PSALMIST'S SENTIMENT
IN HIS ENJOYMENT OF GOD
IN GOD'S HOUSE

(1)

Scripture Reading: Psa. 25—27

Thus far, we have seen four stations concerning Christ in the Psalms. These four stations are Psalm 2, Psalm 8, Psalm 16, and Psalms 22—24. Now we have come to the final part of Book One of the Psalms, Psalms 25—41. The general title of Psalms 25—41 is "The Mixed Expressions of the Psalmist's Sentiment in His Enjoyment of God in God's House." We need to consider the meaning of the word *sentiment.* A person's sentiment is the condition of his inward situation. When David was writing these psalms, there was a certain inward situation with him. He wrote these psalms according to an "inward scenery."

David was not a superficial, shallow person. He was extremely thoughtful. When he was writing these psalms, there was much feeling, thought, and consideration within him. Psalms 25—41 are David's mixed expressions of his inward sentiment, his inward situation, his inward scenery, in his enjoyment of God in God's house. Expressions are outward; sentiment is inward. In David's enjoyment of God in God's house, he had many inward feelings and thoughts, so he expressed them.

These seventeen psalms contain many mixed expressions. Some are spiritual, some are divine, some are very natural, and some should be condemned. Some of his expressions should be put under our feet, whereas others should be uplifted to the uttermost. The expressions in these psalms are either divine, good, or bad. We need the proper discernment concerning whether these expressions belong to the tree of life or to the tree of the knowledge of good and evil.

I. IN SEEKING GOD'S GUIDANCE AND TEACHING IN HIS WAYS AND PATHS

In Psalm 25, David expressed his sentiment in seeking God's guidance and teaching in His ways and paths. A way is a main road, and a path is a lane or a trail, a small road. In the divine things of God, in His divine revelation, there are ways, main roads, and there are paths. We need to seek God's guidance and teaching in His ways and in His paths.

A. Begging God Not to Let Him Be Put to Shame and Not to Let His Enemies Exult over Him, but to Let the Treacherous Ones Be Ashamed because of His Lifting Up His Soul to God, His Trusting (Confiding) in God, and His Waiting on God

David begged God not to let him be put to shame and not to let his enemies exult over him. To exult is to rejoice greatly in a jubilant way. David also wanted the treacherous ones to be ashamed because of his lifting up his soul to God, his trusting (confiding) in God, and his waiting on God (vv. 1-3). David's soul was down, so he lifted his soul upward to God. That means he looked to God.

David's begging God not to let him be put to shame and not to let his enemies exult over him belongs to the tree of the knowledge of good and evil, not to the tree of life. His asking God to let the treacherous ones be ashamed also belongs to the tree of the knowledge of good and evil.

Now we need to consider David's lifting up his soul to God, his trusting in God, and his waiting on God according to the context of Psalm 25. Does this belong to the tree of life or to the tree of the knowledge of good and evil? We cannot answer this question in a definite way because David sought God according to and in the age of the old covenant under the law. Today we are in the new covenant under grace.

In the old covenant age, David's lifting up his soul to God, trusting in God, and waiting on God were very good, but they are not up to the standard of the new covenant. The standard of the new covenant is much higher than that of the old covenant.

B. Asking God, as the God of His Salvation, to Teach and Guide Him through His Compassions and Acts of Kindness

David also asked God, as the God of his salvation, to teach and guide him through His compassions and acts of kindness (vv. 4-6).

C. Asking God Not to Remember but to Forgive His Sins, Transgressions, and Great Iniquity

David asked God not to remember but to forgive his sins, transgressions, and great iniquity (vv. 7, 11, 18b). This surely belongs to the tree of life because at the beginning of the New Testament there was a man telling people to repent (Matt. 3:1-2). The way for us to enter into the New Testament age is by our confession of sins plus God's forgiveness of our sins. This is the threshold of the New Testament age. We confessed and God forgave; then we entered into the New Testament age.

D. Being Assured That God, Being Good and Upright, Instructs Sinners concerning the Way

David was assured that God, being good and upright, instructs sinners concerning the way (Psa. 25:8). David does not say what "the way" is. I believe that this refers to God's instructing sinners concerning the way of confessing their sins and concerning the way of God's forgiveness. Be assured that God, being good and upright, instructs us sinners concerning how to confess and how to receive His forgiveness.

David also said that God guides and teaches the lowly His way in justice and treats those who observe His covenant and testimonies in lovingkindness and truth (vv. 9-10). The word *testimonies* in the Psalms refers to the law with the Ten

Commandments, the statutes, and the ordinances. In addition to the Ten Commandments, the law of Moses has many statutes. Then when the statutes are accompanied by judgments, they become ordinances. Ordinances are statutes with judgments. These are the three categories of the law—the Ten Commandments, the statutes, and the ordinances. In total, the law is God's testimony. In David's expressions we can see that he was in the sphere, the atmosphere, and even the element of the law, because he was born and living in the age of the law.

In the New Testament, the Lord Jesus did not teach people to keep the Old Testament law. According to the teaching of the Lord Jesus in Matthew 5—7, His inner law, the law of the kingdom of the heavens, is much higher and much deeper than the Ten Commandments. The law of the old covenant deals with the act of murder (Matt. 5:21), but the new law of the kingdom deals with anger, the motive of murder (v. 22). Anger produces murder, so in the New Testament, anger is equal to murder.

David goes on to say that God instructs the man who fears Him concerning the way that he should choose (Psa. 25:12). If you are such a person, David says that you will be one whose soul will dwell in prosperity and whose seed will possess the land (v. 13). This concept is according to the tree of the knowledge of good and evil. To follow the Lord in the New Testament, we must forsake everything. Did the apostle Paul enjoy any kind of outward prosperity? He did not even have a family. He forsook all and lost everything in his pursuit of Christ.

David also said that God makes known to those who fear Him His intimate counsel and His covenant. Verse 14 says, "The intimate counsel of Jehovah belongs to those who fear Him, / And His covenant will He make known to them." David put the covenant, the law, together with God's intimate counsel. This is a mixed expression.

I would like us to consider whether we have ever experienced God's intimate counsel. Many Christians love the Psalms because it is filled with sweet terms such as *intimate counsel*. I experienced God's intimate counsel in a very real way when I was imprisoned by the Japanese invading army about fifty years ago in mainland China. The Japanese military police put me into prison twice, the second time for thirty days. I passed through many sufferings during that time, but God preserved me. Furthermore, through a dream God gave me the assurance that my life would be preserved. Even today this dream is still being fulfilled. The Lord also gave me other dreams during this period of imprisonment. All of these dreams were the very intimate counsel of God to me in my time of suffering. In one sense, I was suffering in prison, but the Lord was within me in an intimate way to give me His intimate counsel. I can also testify that I have enjoyed God's intimate counsel throughout the many years of my Christian life.

David speaks of God's intimate counsel, but he mixes this up with the old covenant, the law. The divine concept according to the tree of life and the human concept according to the tree of the knowledge of good and evil are seen in David's mixed expressions.

E. Turning His Eyes Continually to God

David said that he turned his eyes continually to God that God might bring his feet out of the net and would turn toward him, be gracious to him, relieve the troubles of his heart, bring him out of his distresses, and look on his affliction and suffering (vv. 15-18a). There is also a mixture here of the divine concept according to the tree of life and the human concept according to the tree of the knowledge of good and evil.

F. Asking God to Look on His Many Enemies, Who Hate Him with a Violent Hatred

David asked God to look on his many enemies, who hated him with a violent hatred (v. 19). This belongs to the tree of the knowledge of good and evil. Surely David returned hatred to his enemies. This is completely against the principle of the New Testament, which tells us to love our enemies and pray for them (Matt. 5:43-44).

David also asked God to deliver him by keeping his soul

and not letting him be put to shame, for he took refuge in God (Psa. 25:20). Then he asked God to preserve him, not because of God's redemption and compassions but because of his integrity and uprightness, for he waited on God (v. 21). He said that he walked in integrity, walked in uprightness, and waited on God. This is also a mixed expression. During his age, there was nothing wrong with waiting on God, but for him to ask God to preserve him because of his integrity is according to the human concept. *Integrity* means absolute purity plus absolute perfection. David surely was not absolutely pure, perfect, or upright. He should not have asked God to preserve him because of his integrity and uprightness. This kind of thought belongs with the tree of the knowledge of good and evil.

G. Asking God to Redeem Israel out of All His Troubles

In verse 22 David asked God to redeem Israel out of all his troubles.

II. IN ASKING GOD TO JUDGE HIM, EXAMINE HIM, TRY HIM, AND TEST HIM

Psalm 26 reveals the mixed expressions of David's sentiment in his asking God to judge him, examine him, try him, and test him. Asking God to examine us, is like asking someone to come and examine a corpse. What is within us worthwhile for God to examine? We are like a corpse full of rottenness, corruption, and filthiness. But many readers of the Psalms love David's expressions in asking God to judge him, examine him, try him, and test him. The New Testament term is this—"I am crucified with Christ; and it is no longer I who live, but it is Christ who lives in me" (Gal. 2:20a). This means that we have been terminated. In this sense we are a corpse, unworthy of any kind of examination. Who has the boldness to ask God to come and examine him? I dare not do this.

When I was imprisoned by the invading Japanese army, I did not ask God, as David did, to judge me to see that I had walked in integrity or to examine me because I conducted myself in His truth (Psa. 26:1-3). Instead, I confessed my sins, shortcomings, wrongdoings, and defects to Him every day. We should tell the Lord, "Lord, I am good for nothing but death. But thank You that You have crucified me on the cross, and in baptism I have been buried. Now it should not be I who live, but You who live in me." What a great difference there is between this expression according to the revelation of the New Testament and David's expressions in Psalm 26!

Who dares to pray, "God, come and judge me, examine me, try me, and test me"? Are we worthy for God to try us? Within us are defects, shortcomings, wrongdoings, offenses, transgressions, trespasses, evils, iniquity, sin, sins, and defilement. Many times we are not right in our inward attitude toward others. For this reason, each day I have to make confession to the Lord. Even before I speak in the meeting, I frequently pray, "Lord, forgive us and cleanse us with Your precious blood." If I do not confess my sins and my defilement, I cannot have a pure conscience with a strong spirit to speak for the Lord.

A. Standing on His Walk in Integrity and in Truth to Be in the Favor of God's Lovingkindness

David was standing on his walk in integrity and in truth to be in the favor of God's lovingkindness (Psa. 26:1, 3, 11a). This concept belongs to the tree of the knowledge of good and evil.

B. Standing on His Not Being in Company with the Wicked

David stood on his not being in company with the wicked (vv. 4-5, 9-10). In Psalm 26 David spoke of his adversaries within and his enemies without. He felt that he was holy, separated, and that they were wicked. In the eyes of God, however, he and his adversaries and enemies were the same. What is better about us than others? All men are sinful.

We need to be delivered from our human concept and be filled with the divine concept of the New Testament. According to the divine concept, we have been crucified and buried with Christ (Gal. 2:20a; Rom. 6:4). Now it should not be we who live but Christ who lives in us. This is according to the tree of life.

C. Washing His Hands in Innocence to Go around God's Altar, Giving Thanks to God and Telling Out His Wonderful Deeds

David said that he washed his hands in innocence to go around God's altar (Psa. 26:6). As he went around the altar, he made himself heard with the voice of thanksgiving and the telling out of God's wonderful deeds (v. 7). David felt that he was innocent and clean. This is a wrong concept. I respect David very much, and I believe that he was a great man in the hand of God. He was very spiritual in a sense, but not in all senses. We can see that many times he was not that much up to the standard of God's economy.

The standard of the law is not the standard of God's economy. The standard of God's economy is the standard of the New Testament. God's economy is not for making us a good man but a God-man. Regardless of how good a person is, as long as he is not a God-man, he is not up to the standard of God's economy. Regretfully, however, nearly all the Christian readers of the Psalms keep the standard of being a good man. They have not seen the standard of being a God-man. God wants us to be a God-man, not merely a good man. We should have only one *o* as in *God,* not two *o*'s as in *good.*

D. Walking in His Integrity and Asking God to Redeem Him and Be Gracious to Him

David indicated that God should redeem him and be gracious to him because of his integrity (v. 11). This is an insult to God. If we are walking in integrity, being absolutely pure and absolutely perfect, we do not need redemption. God would surely not redeem us because of our integrity. Instead, a man should pray, "O God, redeem me because I am a great sinner." Paul said that Christ came into the world to save sinners and that he was the foremost sinner among all the sinners (1 Tim. 1:15). The proper prayer is: "Lord Jesus, I need Your redemption because I am a sinful person."

This is the right attitude. Surely this is according to the tree of life.

In verse 12 David said, "My foot stands on level ground; / In the assemblies I will bless Jehovah." To say that we walk in our integrity and that our foot stands on level ground is being too boastful and proud.

III. IN TRUSTING IN GOD FOR HIS PROTECTION AND DELIVERANCE FROM HIS ENEMIES

Psalm 27 is the mixed expressions of David's sentiment in his trusting in God for His protection and deliverance from his enemies. He spoke much in this psalm about his enemies, and he believed that he would be delivered because he trusted in God.

A. Taking God as His Light, His Salvation, and the Strength and Stronghold of His Life, So That He Does Not Dread His Adversaries and Enemies

David took God as his light, as his salvation, and the strength and stronghold of his life, so that he would not dread his adversaries and enemies (vv. 1-3). The thought in these verses belongs to the tree of the knowledge of good and evil. In them we again see David's pride.

B. Seeking the Face of God and Asking God Not to Abandon or Forsake Him

David also said that he sought the face of God and asked God, the God of his salvation, not to abandon or forsake him, but to take him up more than his father and his mother (vv. 7-10).

C. Asking God to Teach Him His Way and Lead Him on a Level Path because of His Enemies Who Lie in Wait for Him

David asked God to teach him His way and lead him on a level path because of his enemies who lay in wait for him, having believed that he would see the goodness of God in the land of the living (vv. 11-13).

We need to see that God did not preserve and deliver David because of his integrity. Instead, God preserved David and delivered him for God's purpose. In the Old Testament economy, God needed a man like David, but David was not a great man of integrity. He was not that pure. God said in 1 Kings 15:5 that David did what was right in the eyes of the Lord except in the matter of Uriah the Hittite. David murdered Uriah and robbed him of his wife, Bathsheba. Even the genealogy of Christ in Matthew 1 records that David begot a son of the wife of Uriah (v. 6). This is not a nice expression. To say that a man begot a son of someone else's wife is a black spot on his record. This shows that David was not absolutely pure and absolutely perfect. He did not have this qualification, and none among us has this qualification. No one except the Lord Jesus has ever walked in an absolutely pure and perfect way. Eventually, due to David's failure, his family became a corrupted mess. Among his children there was also fornication and murder (2 Sam. 13).

D. Advising and Encouraging Others to Wait on God and to Be Strong and Encouraged in Their Heart

At the end of Psalm 27, David advised and encouraged others to wait on God and to be strong and encouraged in their heart (v. 14). This is good, but it is altogether human activity which is not according to the standard of God's economy. According to Paul's word in Galatians 2:20 and Philippians 1:21a, every one of God's elect should confess, "I have been crucified with Christ. It is no more I who live but Christ lives within me. Even now I live not by my faith but by the faith of Jesus Christ. I live by Him as my faith. I am altogether finished. I am nothing but a dead and buried corpse. I do not know what it is to be encouraged and strong. I only know that I have been crucified and that Christ now lives in me. For me to live is Christ." If we Christians had such a view, such a revelation, held within us, our attitude toward and our appreciation of the Psalms would be absolutely different.

The chorus of #539 in *Hymns* says: "O Lord, Thou art the Spirit! / How dear and near to me! / How I admire Thy marvelous / Availability!" The Lord today is not only approachable but also available. If food is only approachable to us, this is not sufficient. The food has to be available for us to eat so that we can become one with the food. Approachability is not so good as availability. Today in God's New Testament economy, God is not only approachable but also available to us. The Lord said, "I am the bread of life....he who eats Me, he also shall live because of Me" (John 6:35, 57). To eat is to take Him, the available One, as our food. He also said that we need to drink of Him as the living water (John 4:10, 14). In the book of John, all the items concerning Christ are not just approachable. All of them are available—good for us to enjoy, that is, good for us to eat and drink.

A FURTHER WORD ON THE ENJOYMENT OF GOD IN THE HOUSE OF GOD

Now I would like to say a further word on the enjoyment of God in the house of God as seen in Book One of the Psalms, comprising Psalms 1—41. A number of items of David's enjoyment are good, but many of them are objective and not available. David said that he lifted up his hands unto the innermost sanctuary (Psa. 28:2). This is altogether objective. David also said that those in God's temple all said, "Glory!" (29:9). If God is merely the glory outside of us, He has nothing to do with us. Objective glory does not help us, but our being subjectively mingled with the Triune God works. The chorus of *Hymns,* #1199 says, "Mingle, mingle, hallelujah...Yes, mingling is the way!" In God's New Testament economy, subjective mingling is the way.

In Psalm 36:7-9, David's enjoyment of God in God's house is very subjective. These verses show us the subjective enjoyment of the available riches in God's house. The psalmist said that we could be saturated with the fatness, the abundance, the riches, of God's house (v. 8a). We can be saturated with all the fullness of God within God's house by eating Him. I want to say again that we should pay attention to the revelation in the Gospel of John. In this Gospel, the two crucial words are *eat* and *drink*. As the bread from heaven, Jesus is eatable. He is also drinkable as the living water. If we drink of the living water, it will become in us a spring of water, gushing up into eternal life. Eating and drinking the Lord to enjoy Him as our spiritual life supply is so crucial, but this is missed in today's Christianity.

In God's house we can drink of the river of God's pleasures (Psa. 36:8b). This is not just one pleasure but many pleasures. We Christians do not need worldly amusements, entertainment, parties, or clubs. Our "club" is the church life. The church is the best club on this earth. We have our pleasures here in the church. Our amusement is the river of God's pleasures. We can see a picture of this flowing river in Genesis 2, and this river, the river of water of life in Revelation 22, will be flowing forever.

Psalm 36:9a says that we can be those sharing of the fountain of the life of God. In the book of Jeremiah, God condemned Israel because Israel forsook Him as the fountain of living waters (2:13). But in God's house we can share of the fountain of the life of God. Eventually, we can see light in God's light (Psa. 36:9b).

In God's house we have the food, the river, the fountain of life, and the light. These four things are altogether not objective. Food is for eating, the river is for drinking, the fountain is for sharing of, and the light is for us to participate in by seeing. What an enjoyment this is! This enjoyment in Psalm 36 is much deeper, much higher, and much more profound than the enjoyment of God's house in Psalm 27. In Psalm 36 everything is available. The food is available, the river is available, the fountain of life is available, and the light is available. We have the availability of the riches in God's house for our enjoyment.

This enjoyment will eventually lead us to the New Jerusalem. In the New Jerusalem, we will be saturated with the fruit of the tree of life; we will drink of the river of the water of life; we will share of the fountain of God's life; and we will also see light in God's divine light (Rev. 22:1-2, 5). This is the consummate enjoyment of God in the house of God.

LIFE-STUDY OF THE PSALMS

MESSAGE FOURTEEN

THE MIXED EXPRESSIONS
OF THE PSALMIST'S SENTIMENT
IN HIS ENJOYMENT OF GOD
IN GOD'S HOUSE

(2)

Scripture Reading: Psa. 28—30

In this message we want to see the mixed expressions of the psalmist's sentiment in his enjoyment of God in God's house in Psalms 28—30. When we put these three psalms under the "microscope" of God's New Testament economy, it is difficult to find anything in them that is up to the divine standard. The only point that might be worthwhile for us New Testament believers to consider is that David said his heart trusted in God (Psa. 28:7). Of course, when David said this, he did not have the realization that we have today in the New Testament.

It is somewhat easy to understand what is written in many of the psalms. In the New Testament, however, there are sayings which are very mysterious and difficult to understand. The Lord Jesus said, "Abide in Me and I in you" (John 15:4a). This is a very simple word, but who can fully understand it? When I was a young Christian, I tried to find a book to help me understand what it meant to abide in Christ. Eventually, I found a book by Andrew Murray concerning abiding in Christ, but all he said was that consecrating ourselves is to abide in Christ. This book did not help me understand what it means to abide in Christ. The truth concerning abiding in Christ is very mysterious and deep.

There are many things in the New Testament that are simple in terminology but deep and mysterious in their significance. The New Testament frequently uses the expression *in Christ* or *in the Lord*. When some missionaries translated the Bible into Chinese, they thought that the Chinese would not be able to understand the usage of the preposition *in*. Therefore, they translated "in the Lord" as "trust in the Lord" or "rely upon the Lord." This translation, however, brings in a wrong concept. Noah and his family had to get into the ark in order to be saved by the ark from God's judgment. In order to be saved they could not merely rely upon the ark; they had to be in the ark.

The New Testament terms are deep because the New Testament was written based upon the principle of the New Testament economy, which is the manifestation of God in the flesh. The great mystery of godliness is the manifestation of God in the flesh (1 Tim. 3:16). No one can fully comprehend this. No one can understand what Paul meant when he said, "I am crucified with Christ; and it is no longer I who live, but it is Christ who lives in me" (Gal. 2:20a). Who can understand what Paul meant when he said, "For to me, to live is Christ" (Phil. 1:21a)? He also said that he labored more abundantly than all the apostles, yet it was not he but the grace of God which was with him (1 Cor. 15:10). He spoke of the grace of Christ, the love of God, and the fellowship of the Holy Spirit being with us all (2 Cor. 13:14). In Philippians he spoke of the bountiful supply of the Spirit of Jesus Christ being our salvation (1:19). We may read these expressions in the Bible, but who can understand them? It is easy for us to understand many of the psalms because they were written according to our human concept. The New Testament, however, was written altogether according to another concept on another "planet." This is why it is so difficult to understand.

The New Testament charges us to believe *into* Christ, the Son. Many will not translate this Greek word as *into*, because they say that this is not good English. They maintain that *into* should be translated as *in*. In other words, we are to believe in Christ. The word *in*, however, should actually be translated as *into*. We do not merely believe in Christ; we believe *into* Christ. To believe *into* Christ is to receive Him and be united with Him as one. The word *into* conveys this divine revelation.

The writer of a book entitled *Bone of His Bone* quotes Jessie Penn-Lewis as saying that the Greek text of John 3:16 conveys a different meaning from our English versions. It is not he who believes *in* Christ but he who believes *into* Him who shall have eternal life. Then the author goes on to say that the Christian life is not an imitation of Christ but a participation in Christ. To believe into Christ is to be united with Christ as one. This shows that in speaking of the divine things in God's economy, we should not be bound by language. Language should be managed by us to serve our purpose in the culture.

The New Testament says that we should believe *into* Christ. Noah and his family could not have been saved if they had merely relied upon the ark outwardly. They had to enter into the ark. This is a picture of our believing into Christ. We were once outside of Christ. We were born in Adam, but we were outside of Christ. We needed to take a step to get into Him. The first step was our believing into Christ, and the following step was our being baptized into Christ. Through our believing and being baptized, we have been transferred out of Adam into Christ. Now we are in Christ.

This brief fellowship should help us to see the standard of God's New Testament economy in comparison with the mixed expressions of the psalmist's sentiment in Psalms 25—41. While the psalmist was enjoying God in God's house, he expressed his sentiment, and his expressions were a mixture. In this message we want to see these mixed expressions in Psalms 28—30.

IV. IN CALLING GOD TO HEAR THE VOICE OF HIS SUPPLICATIONS

Psalm 28 shows us the mixed expressions of the psalmist's sentiment in calling God to hear the voice of his supplications.

A. Asking God, His Rock, Not to Be Deaf and Silent to Him When He Cried Out to Him

The psalmist asked God, his rock, not to be deaf and silent

to him when he cried out to Him (vv. 1-2). We cannot say that
this belongs to the tree of life, because there is no indication
of life here. Is it proper to ask God not to be deaf to us? If we
asked someone not to be deaf to us, he might not be happy
with us.

We have seen that many portions of the Psalms contain
David's words according to his human concept, not God's
words according to the divine concept. We believe that all of
the Scripture is God's breath and each book of the Bible is
God's revelation with every line and word coming from the
inspiration of the Holy Spirit (2 Tim. 3:16; 2 Pet. 1:21). Every
line and word of the Scripture is inspired by God, but there
are many words in the Bible that are not God's words. The
Bible even contains the words of Satan. Genesis 3 records the
serpent's words to Eve (vv. 1, 4-5). These words are a part of
the Bible, but they are Satan's words, not God's words. This
shows that although the entire Bible is God-breathed, not all
of the words in the Bible are God's words.

B. Asking God Not to Drag Him Away
with the Wicked, but to Repay Them
according to Their Evildoings

David asked God not to drag him away with the wicked
but to repay them according to their evildoings because they
did not regard the deeds and the works of God. Then he said
that God would tear them down and not rebuild them
(vv. 3-5). Surely this speaking is according to the tree of the
knowledge of good and evil. As those in the New Testament
age, we cannot ask God to repay the wicked ones. In the New
Testament, we are charged to love our enemies and to pray
for those who persecute us (Matt. 5:44).

C. Blessing God as His Strength and His Shield

David blessed God as his strength and his shield, for God
had heard the voice of his supplications (v. 6). Furthermore,
his heart trusted in God and exulted with songs and thanks
to Him (v. 7). He was blessing God, considering God as his
strength within and also as his shield without.

D. Asking God, as the Strength of His People and the Stronghold of Salvation to His Anointed, to Save His People, Bless His Inheritance, Shepherd Them, and Carry Them Forever

David also asked God, as the strength of His people and as the stronghold of salvation to His anointed, to save His people, bless His inheritance, shepherd them, and carry them forever (vv. 8-9). Psalm 28 does not reveal anything that is up to the standard of God's New Testament economy.

V. IN PRAISING GOD FOR HIS GLORY AND MAJESTY

Psalm 29 reveals the mixed expressions of David's sentiment in his praising God for His glory and majesty.

A. Exhorting the Sons of God, the Mighty One, to Ascribe to God Glory and Strength and Worship Him in Holy Splendor

David exhorted the sons of God, the Mighty One, to ascribe to God glory and strength and worship Him in holy splendor (vv. 1-2).

B. The Powerful and Majestic Voice of God— the Thunder of the God of Glory

In verses 3-9 David speaks of the powerful and majestic voice of God—the thunder of the God of glory. According to David, God's powerful and majestic voice is like thunder. He said that the voice of Jehovah was over the waters (v. 3), breaking the cedars of Lebanon, making them to skip like a calf, like a young wild ox (vv. 5-6). He also said the voice of Jehovah cleaves out flames of fire (v. 7) and shakes the wilderness, even the wilderness of Kadesh (v. 8). Furthermore, according to David, Jehovah's voice causes the hinds to calve and strips the forests bare, and "in His temple all say, Glory!" (v. 9).

As God's people in the New Testament, do we need this kind of prayer and praise to the Lord? We should be able to see that the standard, the level, on which this psalm was written is low. There is no comparison between David's praise and blessing in this psalm and the utterance in Paul's prayers in Ephesians 1 and 3. The New Testament does not have any prayer or praise according to David's way in Psalm 29. This psalm is too much in the material and physical realm.

C. Admiring God as the One Enthroned at the Flood and Sitting as King Forever

David also admired God as the One enthroned at the Flood and sitting as King forever (v. 10).

D. Blessing the People of God with God's Giving Strength to Them and His Blessing Them in Peace

At the end of Psalm 29, David blessed the people of God with God's giving strength to them and His blessing them in peace (v. 11).

VI. IN HIS SONG AT THE DEDICATION OF THE HOUSE OF GOD

Psalm 30 shows us the mixed expressions of David's sentiment in his song at the dedication of the house of God. The house of God, the temple, was built and dedicated after David's death.

A. Extolling God for His Lifting Him Up over His Enemies, for His Healing, and for His Deliverance of His Soul from Sheol

David extolled God for His lifting him up over his enemies, for His healing, and for His deliverance of his soul from Sheol (vv. 1-3).

B. Exhorting God's Saints to Psalm to Him and Praise His Holy Name

David also exhorted God's saints to psalm to God and to praise God's holy name (v. 4). God's holy name is His memorial. Then he said that God's anger lasts but a moment, but His favor lasts a lifetime; weeping may linger in the evening, but a ringing shout goes up in the morning (v. 5).

C. Prospering and Never Being Shaken

In verse 6 David said, "As for me, I said in my prosperity, / I will never be shaken." Although David said this in Psalm 30, he surely was not prospering when he was being chased by his rebellious son, Absalom. In verse 7 David said that God made his mountain strong. His mountain refers to his empire, his kingdom.

D. Calling Out to God
and Making Supplication to Him

David called out to God and made supplication to Him (v. 8). He said that there was no profit to God if he went down into the pit. He also said that there was no praise and no declaring of God's faithfulness from the dust (v. 9). David was calling out to God, making prayers to God, and reminding God that if he died and went into the pit, there would be no praise to God and no declaration of God's faithfulness. For this reason he said that God should keep him alive. According to David's concept, it seemed that God owed him something.

E. Asking God to Hear Him and
Be Gracious to Him to Be His Help

David asked God to hear him and be gracious to him to be his help. He also thanked God for turning his mourning into dancing and loosening his sackcloth to gird him with rejoicing, that his glory (spirit) might sing psalms to God without silence and praise God forever (vv. 10-12).

I hope that by reading these psalms we can see that there is no comparison between the Old Testament economy and God's New Testament economy. The Old Testament is the old covenant, and the old covenant was based upon the law. The psalmists were very pious. They loved the law, uplifted the law, and treasured the keeping of the law to the uttermost. Many of the psalms were based upon the principle of keeping the law. The keeping of the law was the basic factor and structure of their composition.

But in Jeremiah 31 God told His fallen, degraded elect, the children of Israel, that He would make another covenant, a new covenant, which would not be based upon the law of letters, but upon a living law which God would write into their being (vv. 31-34). We are enjoying this new covenant today. The living law, the law of life, being written into the New Testament believers is to have God imparted into them. Thus, God in them is the law of life. In the new covenant, we who were once dead have been enlivened, resurrected from the dead, and regenerated to become a new person. After our regeneration, God continues to renew us, to sanctify us, to transform us, to conform us, and eventually to glorify us at the second coming of Christ.

There is no comparison between the old covenant of the Old Testament and the new covenant of the New Testament. The Psalms, therefore, are full of expressions that are not uttered in the New Testament, especially in the apostle Paul's Epistles. In 1 Corinthians 1:9, Paul said that God called us into the fellowship, the participation, of His Son. We have been called by God to partake of Christ, to enjoy Him. Thus, Christ becomes our life, our nature, and even our person. By God's salvation in the New Testament, we have been made one with Christ. According to the Lord's speaking in John 15, we believers and Christ are one tree. He is the vine tree, and we are the branches. Thus, all of us are one with Him, and we grow together with Him. Christ and we are all one person because He is the Head and we are the Body. The Head and the Body are not separate but are one person. We Christians are one with Christ.

Stanza four of *Hymns,* #152 says:

> What from Thee can separate me?
>   Thou wilt love me to the end!
> Oh! Thy love is so prevailing,
>   E'en Thyself with me to blend!
> We two one will be for ever;
>   I am Thine and Thou art mine!
> This will be my testimony:
>   In Thy love we'll ever twine!

This hymn says that the Lord's love has blended us with Him and made us one with Him. This is the highest plane of love.

The real blessing in God's New Testament economy is that Christ has made Himself one with us and has made us one with Him. First Timothy 3:16 speaks of the great mystery of godliness, which is the manifestation of God in the flesh. We are the flesh, yet God made us, the flesh, His expression. The church is the Body of Christ, and the Body of Christ is the fullness of the One who fills all in all (Eph. 1:22b-23). This fullness is Christ's expression. What a wonder it is that God made us men of flesh His expression!

We have to remember that the Word who was God became flesh (John 1:14) and lived in this flesh for thirty-three and a half years. He died in the flesh (1 Pet. 3:18; Col. 1:22). If He had not died in the flesh, we would have no share in His death. Because He died in the flesh, that indicates He died with us (Gal. 2:20a). He died in union with us. We are the flesh, and He became flesh. This is a part of the history of Christ. His history has become our story. God became a man, and by dispensing Himself into us He made us God-men, men who are one with God, having God within us as our life and nature (Col. 3:4a; 2 Pet. 1:4).

I thank God that we live in such an age, the age of the great mystery of godliness, the age of God manifesting Himself in our flesh. In this age we do not need to keep the law. We have Christ, the embodiment of the Triune God, and Christ today is realized as the life-giving Spirit, the consummated, compounded Spirit (1 Cor. 15:45b). Today we are one with this compound Spirit (1 Cor. 6:17). Many in today's Christianity still remain in the Old Testament economy. They do not understand the Lord's words in John 14—17, and they do not understand Paul's fourteen Epistles. Furthermore, they do not understand the significance of our being in Christ. We have believed and have been baptized into Christ, and now we are in Him. In Christ everything is okay; outside of Him everything is a mess. We all need to be turned from the human concept of uplifting the law to the divine concept of exalting Christ according to the divine revelation.

LIFE-STUDY OF THE PSALMS

MESSAGE FIFTEEN

THE MIXED EXPRESSIONS
OF THE PSALMIST'S SENTIMENT
IN HIS ENJOYMENT OF GOD
IN GOD'S HOUSE

(3)

Scripture Reading: Psa. 31—33

When we come to the Psalms with a clear view concerning the entire Bible with its principles, we can realize that the book of Psalms bears two burdens. It takes care of two responsibilities. First, it shows us Christ. Second, it shows us Christ in comparison with the law.

Beginning in the book of Genesis, Christ is revealed as the tree of life. One Bible teacher has said that the tree of life is over today, but the tree of life in Genesis 2 is a central item. If the tree of life is taken away from Genesis 2, Genesis 2 means nothing and becomes nothing. It is wrong to say that the tree of life is over today. In Revelation 2:7 the Lord Jesus said that to the overcomer He would give to eat of the tree of life. Jesus came to feed us with Himself as the tree of life. The first responsibility the written word of God bears is to show us Christ.

God's desire in eternity past was not concerning the law. The law came in at Mount Sinai. Mount Sinai is mentioned by Paul in Galatians 4, not in a positive sense but in a negative sense (vv. 24-25). In the eyes of both God and the apostle Paul, Mount Sinai is a very negative term. Sinai produces slaves, and is signified by a concubine, Hagar. The proper wife was Sarah. The concubine was Hagar. Whatever comes out of this concubine is a slave. All the Jews who treasure, uplift, and try to obey the law are slaves under the law.

Besides Mount Sinai there is another mount, Mount Zion. Hebrews 12 says that in the New Testament we have come, not to Mount Sinai but to Mount Zion (v. 22). Here we are not slaves, but we are sons of the free woman. That means we are sons of grace. The grace of God is signified by the free woman, Sarah. The law is signified by a concubine. We are not for the law, but as the sons of the free woman, we are exalting Christ. The first responsibility of the Psalms is to show us Christ.

The second responsibility of the Psalms is to give us a comparison between Christ and the law. In message eight we saw the lines, the principles, and the spirit of the Bible. In the Bible God shows us only two lines. One is the proper line and the other is the negative line. The proper line is of Christ from God, and the negative line is of Satan. This is why there are two trees in Genesis 2, and those two trees signify two sources. The tree of life signifies God as the source of life. The tree of the knowledge of good and evil signifies Satan as the source of death. Then out of these two sources there are two lines. One line is the line of the day, and the other line is the line of the night. The negative line of darkness is the line of satanic chaos. The positive line of the day is the line of the divine economy.

In addition to these two lines, there is also the line of the law. Christ is the main line, and the law is a side line. If you do not handle the side line properly, the side line becomes a part of the negative line, which is the line of chaos, the line of death, the line of the knowledge of good and evil. Since the day the law was given, God's people have very rarely handled the law properly. I believe that Moses knew something about the position of the law because when he became old he wrote Psalm 90. In verse 1 he said, "Lord, thou hast been our dwelling place in all generations." According to Moses' realization, God is our dwelling place, and we are living in God. This is absolutely not according to the law.

The Psalms' second responsibility is to show us the difference between Christ and the law. However, most of the readers of the Psalms do not understand this. They think that

everything in the Psalms is positive. But we have seen that
many expressions in the Psalms are according to the human
concept of uplifting the law, not according to the divine concept of exalting Christ. We saw in the previous message that
it is difficult to find anything in Psalms 28—30 that is up to
the divine standard of God's New Testament economy.

In this message we want to see the mixed expressions of
the psalmist's sentiment in Psalms 31—33. Much of David's
speaking in these psalms is according to the natural concept.
Regretfully, when most readers of the Bible come to the
Psalms, they do not see much of Christ. They may see the
good points in the Psalms which are according to the human
concept. The Psalms exhort and advise us to fear God. Then
they tell us to take refuge in God. As persons under all kinds
of attack, we need a refuge, a place to hide. We can take
refuge in our God. The Psalms also speak of trusting in God,
waiting on God, and hoping in God. Then the Psalms speak of
praising God, thanking God, and worshipping God. These are
the points based upon which all the psalms are composed: to
fear God, to take refuge in God, to trust in God, to wait on
God, to hope in God, to praise God, to thank God, and to worship God. These are the main points in many of the psalms,
especially in Psalms 31—33.

VII. IN EXPERIENCING AND ENJOYING
GOD'S SALVATION FROM HIS DISTRESS

Psalm 31 shows us the mixed expressions of the psalmist's
sentiment in experiencing and enjoying God's salvation from
his distress. In Psalm 31 David does not speak of God's salvation from eternal perdition and from God's judgment but of
salvation from his distress. In Psalm 31 he lists the items of
his distress.

A. Taking Refuge in God as a Rock of Protection
and a Fortress to Save Him out of the Net
Secretly Laid for Him by His Enemies

David said that he took refuge in God as a rock of protection and a fortress to save him out of the net secretly laid for
him by his enemies (vv. 1-4). The Lord Jesus said that He as

the rock is for building the church (Matt. 16:18), but David said that God as the rock was for his protection to save him from his distress. God's desire is to save people mainly from eternal perdition and judgment, not from their distress. Once we are saved from eternal perdition, God wants to continue to be our salvation so that we can live and magnify Christ (Phil. 1:19-21a). Perhaps the wife wants to be saved from her husband's bad temper, and the husband wants to be saved from his wife's disapproval. In other words, they want to be saved from their distress. But God's salvation for the New Testament believers is for them to be sustained and strengthened to live and magnify Christ.

David also exulted in God's kindness that He had not delivered him into the hand of his enemies but had made his feet stand in a place broad and free (vv. 5-8). These expressions indicate that David was too self-centered even in seeking God's salvation.

B. Enumerating to God
His Afflictions and Distresses

In verses 9-13 David enumerated to God his afflictions and distresses: "Be gracious to me, O Jehovah, for I am in distress. / My eye is wasted with grief, / Indeed my soul and body" (v. 9). It is very good for David to ask God to be gracious to him, that is, to have grace upon him. This sounds somewhat like the New Testament. David also said that his eye was wasted with grief, even his soul and his body. To be wasted means to be dried up. David said that he had become a dried up person through his grief, which to him was distress.

In verses 10-13 he said, "For my life has been consumed in sorrow, / And my years, in sighing. / My strength fails because of my iniquity, / And my bones have wasted away. / Because of all my adversaries, / I have become a reproach, / And especially so to my neighbors, / And something dreaded to my acquaintances; / Those who see me on the street flee from me. / I am forgotten, like a dead man out of mind; / I am like a destroyed vessel. / For I hear the slander of many; / Terror is on every side. / When they take counsel together

against me, / They scheme to take my life." All of these items
in these verses were considered by David as his distresses.
David's word concerning others' taking counsel against him
and scheming to take his life was actually the experience of
the Lord Jesus (Matt. 27:1). In this point, David bore the
responsibility to show Jesus to us.

David's distresses included his grief, sorrow, and the
reproach of his opposers. We Christians today who follow the
Lord also suffer much distress, including persecution. The
New Testament, however, shows us that the apostle Paul did
not complain about this. In the book of Romans, Paul said
that all things worked together for his good that he could be
transformed as one of God's many sons into the image of
the firstborn Son of God (8:28-29). Paul did not complain
about his distress. Instead, he realized that all things worked
together for his good that he could be transformed and
conformed to the image of Christ.

C. Trusting in God for His Saving and Shining upon Him

David said, "But I trust in You, O Jehovah; / I say, You are
my God. / My times are in Your hand" (vv. 14-15a). This is a
very good word, but the New Testament revelation is higher
than this. David's times were in the hand of God, but our
entire being is in Jesus. David's times were in God's hand, but
we are now in Christ, the embodiment of God (1 Cor. 1:30a;
2 Cor. 5:17). It is much higher to be in Christ.

Verse 16a says, "Cause Your face to shine upon Your
servant." David was seeking God's face to shine upon him. He
wanted to be pleasant to God, and he wanted God to be happy
with him. This verse is in the context of his desire to be delivered from his enemies and for them to be put to shame
(vv. 15b, 17). Thus, the shining which David sought in Psalm 31
is not the kind of shining for which we are seeking. The kind
of shining which we need to seek is the shining that exposes
us. When we are under God's shining, we will see that we are
ugly, not pleasant. When we get into the shining of God, we
will prostrate ourselves on the ground to confess.

D. Blessing God and Exhorting His Godly Ones to Love Him and to Be Strong and Encouraged

In verses 21-24 David blessed God and exhorted His godly ones to love God and to be strong and encouraged.

VIII. IN EXPERIENCING GOD'S FORGIVENESS

In Psalm 32 David expressed his sentiment in his experience of God's forgiveness.

A. Experiencing His Confession and God's Forgiveness of Sin

Verses 1-2a say, "Blessed is he whose transgression is forgiven; / Whose sin is covered. / Blessed is the man to whom / Jehovah does not impute iniquity." This implies a lot. If there were no Redeemer, how could the righteous God not impute our iniquity to us? If God did this without a Redeemer, God would be unrighteous. God's not imputing our iniquity to us is based upon Christ's redemption.

David said that the blessed man is the one to whom Jehovah does not impute iniquity and "in whose spirit there is no deceit" (v. 2b). On the one hand, David indicated that he had been forgiven of his sins, yet on the other hand, he indicated that in his spirit there was no deceit. This is altogether unscriptural. If there were no deceit within man, he would not be a sinner in need of God's forgiveness. Since you need God's forgiveness, you must realize that you are full of deceit. Who is the one that does not have any deceit in his spirit yet should confess his sins? This is not logical.

Verses 3-4a say, "When I kept silent, my bones wasted away / Through my groaning all day long. / For day and night Your hand / Was heavy upon me." David's expression here is good in showing us that God was dealing with him concerning his sins. He continued by saying, "My life sap was dried up / As in the drought of summer. Selah. / I acknowledged my sin to You, / And I did not cover my iniquity. / I said, I will confess my transgressions to Jehovah. / Then You forgave the iniquity of my sin. Selah" (vv. 4b-5). The iniquity of his sin refers to the effectiveness of sin. God forgave not only our sin but also the effectiveness of our sin which was deserving of His punishment.

B. Exhorting the Godly Ones to Pray with Confession at a Time When God May Be Found

Verse 6 says, "Because of this let everyone who is godly / Pray to You at a time when You may be found; / Surely when great waters overflow, / They will not reach him." This shows that although David confessed his sin and realized the iniquity of his sin, he considered himself as a godly one. Is he sinful or is he godly? This is a psalm on confession, but in this confession there is self-justification. He confessed his sin, but he also indicated that he did not have any deceit in his spirit, that he was a godly one, and that he was seeking God at the time when God might be found.

In verse 7 David said, "You are my hiding place; / You preserve me from trouble; / You surround me with the ringing shouts of deliverance. Selah."

C. God's Instruction and Teaching

Then God came in to instruct and teach David. Verses 8-10 say, "I will instruct you and teach you concerning the way you should go; / I will counsel you; My eye is upon you. / Do not be like a horse or like a mule, without understanding; / Whose trappings consist of bit and bridle to constrain them, / Else they do not come near you. / Many are the sorrows that the wicked have; / But he who trusts in Jehovah is encompassed by lovingkindness." David said that the wicked have many sorrows, but that the one who trusts in Jehovah is encompassed by lovingkindness. Was David a person with many sorrows, or was he the one trusting in Jehovah? It is difficult to say which category David was in. This shows that his speaking here is according to the natural concept.

Verse 11 says, "Rejoice in Jehovah and exult, O righteous ones; / And give a ringing shout, all you who are upright in heart." Who are the righteous ones and who is upright in heart? We do not have the boldness to say that we are such ones. Thus, this is a psalm with a good beginning but a poor ending. The beginning is confessing, and the ending is self-justification. Basically speaking, Psalms 31 and 32 show us a person trying to keep the law without Christ.

IX. IN PRAISING AND GIVING THANKS TO GOD

Psalm 33 is the mixed expressions of the psalmist's sentiment in praising and giving thanks to God.

A. Encouraging the Righteous to Praise God and Give Thanks to God

The psalmist encouraged the righteous to praise God and give thanks to God (vv. 1-5).

B. Praising God in His Restoring of the Heavens and the Earth

In verses 6-9 the psalmist praised God in His restoring of the heavens and the earth. Verse 9 says, "For He spoke, and it was; / He commanded, and it stood." When God said, "Let there be light," there was light (Gen. 1:3). When God commanded, something came out and stood. This is good, but we need to see that Paul's teaching is not concerning the restoration of the chaotic universe, but of the resurrection of Christ from the dead.

We were once dead, but one day the Lord made us alive and raised us from the dead (Eph. 2:1, 5-6). Today we are living in resurrection. We are not restored people but resurrected people! We may be impressed with God's restoring of the heavens and of the earth, but the New Testament is concerning the new creation in resurrection. Paul's prayer in Ephesians 1 refers to the resurrection (v. 20). Regardless of how much restoration the heavens and the earth undergo, they are still the old creation, but we are the new creation. We are not merely restored; we are resurrected. There is nothing in the New Testament which asks us to praise God for the restoration of the heavens and the earth. Instead, Paul spoke of his desire to know Christ and the power of His resurrection (Phil. 3:10).

I want to point out again that the Psalms show us the inferiority of the law and the superiority of Christ. It is good to praise God for His restoration of the heavens and the earth, but this is not as high as praising Him for the resurrection of Christ. In His resurrection, Christ raised us from the dead (Eph. 2:6). This is much higher than the restoration of the heavens and the earth.

C. Praising God in His Relationship with the Sons of Men on Earth

In verses 10-15 the psalmist praised God in His relationship with the sons of men on earth.

D. Praising God in His Deliverance and Preservation

The psalmist praised God in His deliverance and preservation, which are stronger than those by a great army, by a mighty man of great strength, and by a horse with its great power (vv. 16-19). He compared God's saving power and God's preserving strength to a great army, a mighty man, and a horse. When I was a young Christian, I felt that this was wonderful, but today I do not feel the same. The New Testament does not compare our God with a horse. This shows again that we should not trust in our natural understanding when we read the Psalms. We need to have a change from our natural concept to the divine concept.

E. Waiting on God as His Help and His Shield, Trusting in His Holy Name, and Having Hoped in Him

At the conclusion of Psalm 33, the psalmist said that he was waiting on God as his help and his shield and trusting in His holy name, having hoped in Him (vv. 20-22).

THE DIFFERENCE BETWEEN CHRIST AND THE LAW

Now I would like to speak a word concerning the difference between Christ and the law. The difference between Christ and the law is the difference between the Old Testament economy and the New Testament economy. Under the law in the Old Testament, man was always striving to arrive at the standard of the law. Man realized that he was weak and sinful, so he asked for God's mercy, God's lovingkindness, and he put his trust in God. He also took refuge in God, waited on God, hoped in God, praised God, thanked God, and worshipped God. This was all man's doing because in the Old Testament God was apart from man, and man was apart from God. Man and God were separate.

Then in the New Testament economy, God came into man to become incarnated and be born as a God-man. When Christ lived on this earth, that was God living on this earth in man. Through His redemption, He solved all the problems for man and paved the way so that He could enter into man. In His incarnation He entered into the womb of a virgin, but through His death and resurrection He entered into thousands of men. In order to enter into man, He was resurrected. In resurrection He became the life-giving Spirit (1 Cor. 15:45b) and the firstborn Son of God (Rom. 8:29) who brought men into God. In His incarnation He brought God into man; in His resurrection He brought man into God. By this He accomplished the mingling of God and man. He mingled God and man into one.

Now we believers are in Him and He is in us. He and we have become one person. He has the divine life and the divine nature, and so do we. We have the human life and the human nature, and so does He. He has become us, and we have become Him. We need to recognize that we have been crucified with Him. Now it is no more we who live, but it is Christ who lives in us (Gal. 2:20).

In the New Testament economy, we have to do something, but not the things done by the Old Testament saints. In the New Testament economy, we have to believe into Christ (John 3:16, 36). Then we have to love Him (John 14:21, 23). We also have to live Him that we may magnify Him (Phil. 1:19-21a). In the New Testament, we are not doing something out of ourselves in our natural strength. We are enjoying Him. To believe into Him is to receive Him; to love Him is to enjoy Him; and to live Him is to magnify Him. This is not our doing in ourselves. Whatever we are doing in the New Testament is an enjoyment.

God does not want us to do good. He wants us only to live Christ. To live Christ implies many things. To live Christ implies being holy and overcoming. To live Christ implies not losing our temper and being enduring and full of patience. We just need to live Christ, and this living implies everything in the Christian life. It implies our faithfulness and our honesty. To live Christ means everything. This is why the New Testament charges us to live Christ that we may magnify Christ. We need to live, move, and walk by the spirit, having our entire being according to the mingled spirit (Rom. 8:4). This is the New Testament economy.

Much of the terminology in the Old Testament psalms is good, but it is good in a natural realm. It has nothing to do with the Spirit. The New Testament is altogether in another field, in another world. It is altogether in the Spirit, who is the consummation of the Triune God. Thus, everything in the New Testament is altogether a matter in the Triune God. Our honesty, faithfulness, patience, endurance, kindness, and everything we are and do involves the Triune God. All of our virtues should be the expression of the Triune God, not of ourselves. The Christian life in the New Testament is not our doing, but is altogether a matter of our living Christ. To live Him in order to magnify Him is to enjoy Him. Thus, every day we should not do anything but enjoy Christ. Christ is our enjoyment.

This thought is in *Hymns,* #499, #501, and #841. These three songs were written absolutely according to the New Testament economy. Hymn #841 is concerning the building up of the church. Many Christians, however, still exalt the law, remaining in the Old Testament economy.

We need to have the proper discernment to see the difference between the Old Testament economy and the New Testament economy. On the one hand, the psalms are lovely because they are the aspiration of the sentiment of the ones who were seeking after God. On the other hand, many portions of the Psalms are not according to the New Testament economy. The New Testament economy includes first, incarnation; second, resurrection; and third, mingling. God came into us and He brought us into Him. He has accomplished a mingling of divinity and humanity. We and He are living as one person in the same one life and with the same one nature.

We should not endeavor to keep the law. Instead, we live only one person—Christ. We live Christ that He may be magnified.

I hope we can see this revelation. When we come to any psalm, we have to weigh it with this scale of God's New Testament economy. Then we can realize what belongs to Mount Sinai and what belongs to Mount Zion. We are here on Mount Zion where we have the church, the Body of Christ, and God's economy for God's testimony.

LIFE-STUDY OF THE PSALMS

MESSAGE SIXTEEN

THE MIXED EXPRESSIONS
OF THE PSALMIST'S SENTIMENT
IN HIS ENJOYMENT OF GOD
IN GOD'S HOUSE

(4)

Scripture Reading: Psa. 34—36

In this message we want to continue our fellowship on the mixed expressions of the psalmist's sentiment in his enjoyment of God in God's house. If we do not have a deep hunger to seek after the Lord with His Word, these messages may disappoint us. This is because what we may like according to our natural concept is exposed. What we see in the Bible and what the Bible is to us depend upon what kind of person we are. Our understanding of the Bible is always according to what we are. This is why we need to be adjusted and brought into the divine concept.

In this message we want to see the mixed expressions of the psalmist's sentiment in Psalms 34—36. The title of Psalm 34 says that this was a psalm of David "when he disguised his sanity before Abimelech, who drove him out, and he departed." We can see from this that the situation in which Psalm 34 was written was not an honorable one. David was not normal; he disguised himself as being insane because he was before a king who had the power to kill him. As a result of disguising himself, David was delivered from Abimelech (1 Sam. 21:10—22:1a). Afterward, he wrote Psalm 34. In this psalm he gave all the credit to God, but actually he delivered himself by disguising himself. To disguise oneself is a kind of falsehood.

In Psalm 35 David asked God to fight against his enemies

with weapons (vv. 1-8). Then in Psalm 36 he asked God to deal with the wicked (vv. 1-4) and even gave God instructions as to how to deal with them (vv. 11-12).

We need to remember that the book of Psalms needs to be interpreted according to the divine concept of the divine revelation in the entire Bible. The Psalms is the longest book of the Bible, but it is not the only book. It must be interpreted in the light of the divine concept of God as the divine revelation concerning His eternal economy in Christ, taking Christ as its centrality and universality.

We need to be adjusted from our human concept to the divine concept. At the beginning of my Christian life, I came to the Bible with much of my own thought. Throughout the years I have been adjusted, and the adjustment which I have received in studying the Bible has taken away layer upon layer of my human concept.

Our understanding of the Bible depends upon the measure of our growth in the spiritual life. Even today in our human life, our knowledge depends upon the measure of our growth in the human life. When someone is a child, we cannot expect him to understand that much. As this child grows, he is able to understand more and more. Eventually, when he becomes a full-grown man, he can understand things properly. It is difficult to understand the book of Psalms properly according to the divine concept. We have seen that at times David spoke things in the Psalms which were very wonderful. Then he spoke something which was altogether according to the human, natural concept.

In order to understand the Bible, we must exercise one principle. This principle is that God planned in His economy to make Himself one with man. The basic principle, the main principle, of Christ's birth is that God came to join Himself to man, to be a man, and to be one with man. This is the basic principle of the Bible.

When we read the Bible, we need to keep the principle of God's being one with man. We should keep the principle that the Word of God as the divine revelation shows us that God's main purpose is to make Himself one with man and to make man one with Him. In John 15 the Lord said, "I am the vine;

you are the branches.... abide in Me and I in you" (vv. 5, 4). This shows us that God and the believers in Christ are one. We and God were once separate, but one day we, the wild branches, were grafted into Him in Christ (Rom. 11:24). We have been grafted into Christ as the tree, and this grafting has made us one with Him. What is needed now is for us to abide in Him that He may abide in us. Then He and we will be one, having one life, one nature, and one living.

If we see this, we will be fully adjusted in our understanding of the Bible. We need to hold the divine concept in John 15 where the Lord said that He is the vine, that we are His branches, and that we should abide in Him that He may abide in us. In Psalms 34—36, we can see that David was not acting as a branch who was one with God.

In our understanding of the Bible, we have to pick up the proper principles. The main principle is that God desires to be one with His chosen people. Eventually, the oneness between God and man will be completed, consummated. All of God's chosen people will be consummated to be fully one with God to become the constituents of the holy city, the New Jerusalem. Whenever we come to the Psalms, we need to hold this concept; otherwise, we can be misled.

X. IN BLESSING AND PRAISING GOD

Psalm 34 shows us the mixed expressions of the psalmist's sentiment in his enjoyment of God in God's house in blessing and praising God. To bless God is to speak well about God, to talk about God in a good way. To praise God is to give the honor and the glory to God.

A. Written After David Disguised Himself as Being Insane before Abimelech

It is good to bless and praise God, but we should not forget that such a wonderful psalm was written after David put on a "mask." He wrote this psalm after he disguised himself as being insane before Abimelech. This story is recorded in 1 Samuel 21:10-15. There David disguised himself before this Philistine king in order to escape from being killed.

B. Because of God's Answer and Deliverance

David blessed and praised God because of God's answer and deliverance (vv. 1-6). In verse 1 he said, "I will bless Jehovah at all times; / His praise will continually be in my mouth." This is good, but we have to remember the situation in which David said this. When he disguised himself before Abimelech, he surely was not blessing God at that time. Instead, 1 Samuel 21:13 says that David scrabbled on the doors of the gate and let his spittle fall down upon his beard to make Abimelech think that he was insane.

Verses 2-6 say, "My soul makes its boast in Jehovah; / The lowly hear and they rejoice. / Magnify Jehovah with me, / And let us exalt His name together. / I sought Jehovah, and He answered me; / And He delivered me from all that terrified me. / They looked to Him and were radiant; / And their faces will never be abashed. / This poor man called out, and Jehovah heard; / And He saved him out of all his troubles."

David said that Jehovah delivered him. But I would like to ask whether he was delivered out of the hand of Abimelech by Jehovah or whether he delivered himself. People may pray for a number of things, and then give all the credit to God when they are done. Actually, however, God did not do any one of them. Instead, they prayed according to their own desire, and they did it on their own. Sometimes they might have even done something in a way to cheat people, but God surely did not cheat people for them. We may pray for something, get what we prayed for, and then give the credit to God. This is an insult to God. In this case the credit should not go to God but to us to become a debit.

C. Advising and Teaching Others to Fear God and Take Refuge in Him

Verses 7-22 show us David's advising and teaching others to fear God and take refuge in Him. In verse 8 David said, "Blessed is the man who takes refuge in Him." However, when David disguised himself in front of that king, he did not take refuge in Jehovah but in his "mask," in his disguising himself. In verse 11 David said, "Come, children; hear me. / I will teach you the fear of Jehovah." Do we want David to teach us to disguise ourselves, to put on a mask? This shows that on the one hand, we may trust in the Lord; on the other hand, we may put on a mask to deliver ourselves. Eventually, who saved us—the Lord or our mask?

1. The Goodness of Fearing God and Taking Refuge in Him

In Psalm 34 David spoke of the goodness of fearing God and taking refuge in Him (vv. 7-10, 17-22). Verse 10 says, "The young lions hunger and starve, / But those who seek Jehovah will not lack any good thing." People may quote these verses for their personal benefit but eventually end up lacking the material things they desire. Second Corinthians tells us that Paul passed through much suffering and deprivation, even to the extent that he was lacking food and clothing (11:27).

2. The Way to Fear God

In Psalm 34 David spoke of the way to fear God (vv. 11-16; 1 Pet. 3:10-12). Verses 12-16 say, "Who is the man who desires life, / Who loves having days in order to see good? / Guard your tongue from evil, / And your lips from speaking deceit. / Turn away from evil and do good; / Seek peace and pursue it. / The eyes of Jehovah are set toward the righteous, / And His ears, toward their cry. / The face of Jehovah is against those who do evil, / To cut off the memory of them from the earth." These verses were quoted by Peter in 1 Peter 3:10-12, but Paul did not quote such a word. Paul's vision of the New Testament economy was clearer than that of all the other apostles.

When David asked, "Who is the man who desires life, / Who loves having days in order to see good?" he was not talking about the eternal life but about the physical life. David was a great saint in the Old Testament, and Peter was one of the great apostles in the New Testament, but I do not believe that what David said here is spiritual. Even among us, who dares ask the Lord to give him long days that he may enjoy many good things?

David said that if we love having days in order to see good, we should guard our tongue from evil and our lips from speaking deceit. But who has ever succeeded in guarding his tongue from evil? What David spoke here was according to the tree of the knowledge of good and evil.

Verse 15 says, "The eyes of Jehovah are set toward the righteous, / And His ears, toward their cry." But who is righteous on this earth? Paul said that not one is righteous (Rom. 3:10), and Isaiah said that our righteousnesses are like filthy rags (Isa. 64:6). If we depend upon our righteousness to enjoy God's eyes and ears being set toward us, we will enjoy nothing, because we have no righteousness of our own.

Concerning the righteous man, David said, "He keeps all his bones; / Not one of them is broken" (v. 20). This is a verse concerning Christ because David was a type of the suffering Christ. When Christ was on the cross, the soldiers did not break His legs when they saw that He had already died (John 19:33). John said, "These things happened that the Scripture might be fulfilled: 'No bone of His shall be broken'" (v. 36). There were times in describing his sufferings that David typified Christ.

When we look at Psalm 34, we can see the mixed expressions of David's sentiment. Verse 20 refers to Christ, but most of this psalm is not according to the tree of life. Our concept needs to be changed to the divine concept according to the tree of life. As we grow in Christ, our concept will be changed.

XI. IN ASKING GOD TO DEAL WITH HIS ENEMIES

In Psalm 35 David asked God to deal with his enemies.

A. Begging God to Fight
His Enemies with Weapons

First, he begged God to fight his enemies with weapons (vv. 1-8). Verse 1 says, "Strive, O Jehovah, with those who strive with me; / Battle against those who battle against me." Do you believe that God desires such a prayer? This is not according to the Lord's teaching in the New Testament, which tells us to love our enemies and pray for those who persecute us (Matt. 5:44).

Verses 2-3 say, "Take hold of shield and buckler, / And rise up as my help. / Draw out also the spear, and close up the way / Against those who pursue me; / Say to my soul, / I am your salvation." Instead of asking God for something, David here is teaching God how to deliver him by fighting against his enemies with weapons.

Verses 4-8 say, "Let those who seek my life / Be put to shame and humiliated; / Let those who devise evil for me / Be turned back and confounded. / Let them be like chaff before the wind, / With the angel of Jehovah driving them on. / Let their way be darkness and slipperiness itself, / With the angel of Jehovah pursuing them. / For without cause they hid their net for me in a pit; / Without cause they dug a hole for me. / Let destruction come upon them unawares, / And let his net, which he hid, catch him; / Let him fall into it, into destruction." Is this a spiritual prayer? Surely this prayer comes out of a man who is fully in himself. In the New Testament economy, a spiritual person could never ask God to come with a shield, with a buckler, and with a spear to fight against his enemies.

B. Boasting in His Trusting in God and in His Well-dealing with Those Who Mistreated Him

In verses 9-16 David boasted in his trusting in God and in his well-dealing with those who mistreated him. These verses say, "Then my soul will exult in Jehovah; / It will rejoice in His salvation. / All my bones will say, / Jehovah, who is like You, / Who delivers an afflicted one from him who is too strong for him, / And an afflicted and needy one from him who robs him? / Malicious witnesses rise up; / They ask me about things I know nothing of. / They repay me evil for good; / I am bereaved in soul. / But I, when they were sick, / Had sackcloth as my clothing; / I afflicted my soul with fasting, / And my prayer returned to my own bosom. / I conducted myself as if it had been my friend or my brother; / Like one mourning for his mother, I bowed down gloomily. / But at my stumbling they rejoice and gather together; / The dregs whom I had not known / Gather together against me; /

They tear at me and do not cease. / As profane mocking para-sites, / They gnash their teeth at me."

The above verses show that in David's consideration his ene-mies were very bad, whereas he was very good. His expressions in these verses display too much self-righteousness.

C. Urging God to Deliver Him
by Instructing God according to
His Natural Knowledge of Good and Evil

In verses 17-28 David urged God to deliver him by instructing God according to his natural knowledge of good and evil.

XII. IN ASKING GOD TO DEAL WITH THE WICKED

In Psalm 35 David asked God to deal with his enemies, and in Psalm 36 he asked God to deal with the wicked.

A. His Accusation of the Wicked

Verses 1-4 are his accusation of the wicked: "Transgres-sion speaks to the wicked / Within his heart; / There is no dread of God / Before his eyes. / For he flatters himself in his own eyes, / Until his iniquity is found out and hated. / The words of his mouth are wickedness and deceit; / He has ceased being wise and doing good. / He plans iniquity on his bed; / He sets himself on a path that is not good; / He does not reject evil." Here David did not have the heart or the inten-tion to ask God to be merciful to the wicked. Instead, he accused them.

B. His Praising of God's Lovingkindness,
Faithfulness, and Righteousness
Mixed with the Enjoyment of God in His House

Verses 5-10 are his praising of God's lovingkindness, faith-fulness, and righteousness mixed with the enjoyment of God in His house. Verses 7-9 are a top portion of the Psalms concerning the enjoyment of God in His house, but such a portion is in a psalm in which David asked God to deal with the wicked. This again shows us the mixed expressions of David's sentiment.

C. Entreating God to Deal with the Wicked according to His Way

Verses 11-12 say, "Do not let the foot of the arrogant come upon me, / Nor let the hand of the wicked drive me away. / There those who do iniquity are fallen; / They are cast down and unable to rise." In these verses David entreated God to deal with the wicked not according to God's way but according to his way.

OUR NEED TO BE RELEASED FROM OUR HUMAN CONCEPT AND TO BE BROUGHT INTO THE CENTRAL LINE OF GOD'S ECONOMY

In reading the Psalms, we should see the contrast between the human concept and the divine concept. Most of the saints do not see such a contrast. Instead, they highly appraise everything in the Psalms. In a sense, it seems that they received the help from reading the Psalms, but actually they did not receive the real help. Instead, they were misled.

I am burdened for us to see the contrast between the human concept in the Psalms and the divine concept in the New Testament. According to our concept, we may feel that the Bible, in both the Old and New Testaments, tells us mainly that we have to fear God, to take refuge in Him, to trust in Him, to wait on Him, to hope in Him, to praise Him, to thank Him, and to worship Him. This concept, however, is not the divine concept in the New Testament. What the New Testament shows us is God's economy.

In God's economy, God has only one intention—to gain an organism for Himself. In eternity past God decided to do one thing in His economy—to create for Himself an organism, the Body of Christ. He created the universe and man for this purpose. Then man became fallen, but God promised man that He would come through a woman to be a man, to join Himself with man, and to become one with man (Gen. 3:15). Eventually, He became a man and lived a life on this earth to show people the life of a God-man. Afterward, He went to the cross and died not only for our sins but also to deal with every problem in the universe. Then He was resurrected. In His incarnation He brought God into man, and in His resurrection He brought man into God so that God and man could be one.

Although this is the revelation of the New Testament, not many see this revelation. Instead, most Christians still hold a natural and religious concept of trying to do good. Most Christians would say that they need to improve their conduct. Because they know that they are weak and the temptations are strong, they ask God to help them and try to trust in God. But they do not see the central line of God's economy to make God and man, man and God, one entity, with the two having one living by one life with one nature. Such a revelation is missing among Christians today.

Many do not have an ear to hear this central teaching of God's economy. Paul solemnly charged Timothy before God and before Christ by His appearing and His kingdom to proclaim the word (2 Tim. 4:1-2). Paul was being poured out as a drink offering (v. 6), so he charged Timothy to be faithful to proclaim the healthy word. Then he said, "For the time will come when they will not tolerate the healthy teaching; but according to their own lusts they will heap up to themselves teachers, having itching ears" (v. 3). People who have itching ears are those who seek pleasant speaking for their own pleasure. According to Paul's word to Timothy, the itching and turned-away ear is the main factor in the worsening decline in the churches. We have to be faithful to speak the healthy words of God's economy, not the words that satisfy people's itching ears.

In the Lord's recovery, we have been enlightened to see what God wants. God wants us to be one with Him. God lives in us, and He wants us to live Him. The writings of the apostle Paul are crystal clear on this point, with no ambiguity. The main item in Paul's fourteen Epistles is stated in Galatians 2:20: "I am crucified with Christ; and it is no longer I who live, but it is Christ who lives in me; and the life which I now live in the flesh I live in faith, the faith in the Son of God, who loved me and gave Himself up for me." These words are divine. They have nothing to do with anything natural, religious, or superstitious.

God created Adam almost six thousand years ago. From

Adam to Abraham was two thousand years, from Abraham to Christ was two thousand years, and from the time of Christ until now has been also almost two thousand years. In the first two thousand years, God visited people to help them to realize that they needed Him. In the second two thousand years, God told Abraham that in his seed all of the nations would be blessed (Gen. 22:18; 26:4). They would be blessed by God's being one with them and by their being one with God. This is altogether mysterious and divine.

Christ as the seed of Abraham came to fulfill God's promise. When Christ came, the Jews had their religious way of worshipping God according to their kind of thought. Later, the apostles had to encounter two problems—the Jewish religion and Greek philosophy. This earth today is full of different philosophies from different cultures and religions. In addition to all of these philosophies, there is the philosophy and the logic in today's Christianity. Many Christians today understand the Bible according to their natural concept, not the divine concept.

In the Lord's ministry we have spoken concerning God's economy, God's dispensing, and the life-giving Spirit, the processed, consummated Spirit. We have seen that this Spirit is the compound Spirit, and this compound Spirit is the consummation of the processed Triune God. These things cannot be heard in the theology of today's Christianity.

Because of the opposition, I published an article in 1977 entitled *What a Heresy—Two Divine Fathers, Two Life-giving Spirits, and Three Gods!* Many of those opposing us teach that there are three Gods. This is the teaching of tritheism. They also teach that there are two divine Fathers. One is the Father in the Godhead and the other is the Father in Isaiah 9:6, whom they say is the Father of eternity. They also mistakenly say that there are two life-giving Spirits. One is the Holy Spirit in the Trinity, and the other is the life-giving Spirit mentioned in 1 Corinthians 15:45b. All of these teachings, of course, are heretical.

I have been speaking in the United States for thirty years with the burden to release the central line of the divine revelation according to God's economy. But according to my realization, not many of us appreciate this central line. Before I came to the United States, I had not seen that the Spirit was the consummation of the Triune God. I began to say mainly in Hong Kong in the summer of 1954 that the death and resurrection of Christ are in the Spirit. From that year the light concerning the all-inclusive Spirit came in and has been shining brighter and brighter.

Eventually, we saw the type of the compound ointment in Exodus 30:23-25. The compound ointment takes olive oil as a base compounded with four kinds of spices—myrrh, cinnamon, calamus, and cassia. These five elements compounded together become one ointment. The one hin of olive oil refers to God as the Spirit, and this divine Spirit is compounded with Christ's death, with the effectiveness of Christ's death, with Christ's resurrection, and with the power of Christ's resurrection. This compound Spirit is the consummation of the Triune God. The Father is embodied in the Son, and the Son is realized as the Spirit. In other words, the Spirit is the realization of the Son, and the Son is the embodiment of the Father. Thus, the Three of the Godhead are not three Gods; they are just one divine being.

The Bible reveals all of these things to let us know how God can be one with man and how man can be one with God. Eventually, we Christians should live a life of God and man, the life of a God-man. Today we live as a man, yet we also live as God in His life and in His nature but not in His Godhead. His Godhead is unique. We have His life and His nature, just as the children of a father have their father's life and nature. But none of the children have the fatherhood. Only the father of a family has the fatherhood. In the same way, God is unique and His Godhead is unique. We cannot share in His Godhead, but we do have the divine life and the divine nature. We are participating in this divine life and divine nature so that we can live God, live Christ. If we see this, our view concerning the Psalms will be changed.

My burden is to try the best to help the saints in the Lord's recovery come out of the misled concept concerning the Psalms. We need to be released from being misled and be brought into the central line of God's economy, which is to live

Christ as the embodiment of God by the realization of the Spirit. Today we are here as a man, but we are living the Triune God in our manhood. Many today, however, would oppose us for saying that we live God. But Paul said, "For to me, to live is Christ" (Phil. 1:21a). Paul was a man, but he told us that he lived Christ, and Christ is God. To live Christ is to live God. We all have to see this. The Christian life is not a kind of improvement of our human life. The Christian life is a transformed life, a life that transforms us into a God-man. I hope that this fellowship helps us to seek after God according to the proper revelation in the holy Word.

LIFE-STUDY OF THE PSALMS

MESSAGE SEVENTEEN

THE MIXED EXPRESSIONS
OF THE PSALMIST'S SENTIMENT
IN HIS ENJOYMENT OF GOD
IN GOD'S HOUSE

(5)

Scripture Reading: Psa. 37—39

In this message we want to see the mixed expressions of the psalmist's sentiment in Psalms 37—39. Psalm 37 reveals the psalmist's sentiment in his logic concerning God's dealing with the righteous and with the wicked based upon the principle of law-keeping. David could not stay away from the principle of keeping the law. Psalm 37 is essentially a lengthened repetition of Psalm 1. We may say that it is the enlarged, lengthened, and expounded Psalm 1. Psalm 38 reveals the psalmist's sentiment in his suffering of God's dealing, and Psalm 39 shows us that the psalmist realized the vanity of his life.

XIII. IN HIS LOGIC CONCERNING
GOD'S DEALING WITH THE RIGHTEOUS
AND WITH THE WICKED BASED UPON
THE PRINCIPLE OF LAW-KEEPING

A. Not Being Incensed because of Evildoers,
for They Soon Wither like Grass and
Fade Away like Green Herbage

In Psalm 37:1-2 David said, "Do not be incensed because of evildoers....For they soon wither like grass / And fade away like green herbage." Verses 7 and 8 say, "Be still before Jehovah, and wait on Him; / Do not be incensed because of him who enjoys prosperity on his way, / Because of the man who performs his evil schemes. / Cease from anger and forsake wrath; / Do not be incensed; it only leads to evil."

B. Trusting in Jehovah, Doing Good, Feeding on His Faithfulness, Delighting Yourself in Jehovah, and Committing Your Way to Jehovah

David also said that you should trust in Jehovah, do good, feed on His faithfulness, delight yourself in Jehovah, and commit your way to Jehovah. Then He will give you the requests of your heart and cause your righteousness to go forth like light and your justness like noonday (vv. 3-6).

C. The Evildoers Being Cut Off but Those Who Wait on Jehovah Possessing the Land

Verses 9-40 point out that according to David's concept, the evildoers will be cut off, but those who wait on Jehovah will possess the land. David said, "For the evildoers will be cut off; / But those who wait on Jehovah, / They will possess the land. / And in a little while longer there will be no wicked man; / Indeed, you will look diligently for his place, and he will not be there" (vv. 9-10). According to David's logic, in a little while there would be no wicked man. If there were no wicked man, we would not need the police, the law courts, or the government. But there is not such a thing on this earth today.

Again and again throughout Psalm 37, David said that the righteous would inherit the land and the wicked would be cut off. This is a principle set up by David's logic according to the principle of law-keeping. This logic, however, is altogether wrong. Such good logic belongs to the tree of the knowledge of good and evil.

In the following message we will be on Psalms 40 and 41. Psalm 40 says that Christ will come to do the will of God (vv. 6-8), and the will of God is that Christ has to replace everyone, everything, and every matter. In the whole universe, God does not want anything except Christ. God wants only one person—Christ. He wants Christ to replace all the offerings, to replace all things, to replace all matters, and to replace all men.

Paul said in Galatians 2:20a, "I am crucified with Christ; and it is no longer I who live, but it is Christ who lives in me." Paul said that he had been terminated and that there was someone else to replace him—Christ. He had been crucified and replaced by Christ. Christ lived in him. Paul spoke Galatians 2:20 in the context of his speaking concerning Christ replacing the law (vv. 11-21). He told the Galatians that they were foolish for trying to keep the law (3:1-3). David encouraged people to keep the law, but Christ crucifies, terminates, every law-keeper. Christ does not want to see anyone endeavoring to keep the law. He wants to see every law-keeper terminated by the cross.

XIV. IN HIS SUFFERING OF GOD'S DEALING

A. David's Concept in This Psalm Contradicting His Logic in Psalm 37

The concept in Psalm 37 is on one pole, and the concept in Psalm 38 is on the other pole. David's concept in Psalm 38 contradicts his logic in Psalm 37.

B. God's Chastening Forcing Him to Confess His Sins and Iniquities

In Psalm 38:1-8 we see that God's chastening forced David to confess his sins and iniquities. David said that in his flesh there was no soundness because of God's indignation, and there was no wholeness in his bones due to his sin (v. 3). There was indignation on God's side, and sin on David's side.

Verse 4 says, "For my iniquities have passed over my head; / Like a heavy burden, they are too heavy for me." If we do not like this verse, we are wrong. We have to love this verse to the uttermost.

Verses 5-8 say, "My wounds are odious and festering / Due to my foolishness. / I am bent down and bowed utterly; / I go about all day long mourning. / For my loins are filled with burning, / And there is no soundness in my flesh. / I am benumbed and crushed utterly; / I cry out due to the groaning of my heart." Groaning indicates that you have a burden to pray, yet you do not know what to say. In Psalm 37 it seems that David was so clear about everything and had the utterance to pray for everything. But in Psalm 38 all he could do was cry out due to the groaning of his heart. At times we may have some burden and some feeling, but we do not know how to utter them. We have no knowledge about how to utter our prayer. Thus, all we can do is groan and say, "O Lord Jesus. O Lord Jesus."

In Romans 8:26 Paul said, "Moreover, in like manner the Spirit also joins in to help us in our weakness, for we do not know for what we should pray as is fitting, but the Spirit Himself intercedes for us with groanings which cannot be uttered." The weakness here is our ignorance of how we should pray. We do not know the kind of prayer God desires, and we are not clear how to pray, according to the burden we feel, for our being conformed to the image of God's Son; hence, we groan (v. 23). In our groaning the Spirit groans also, interceding for us. His interceding is mainly that we may experience the transformation in life for growth into the maturity of sonship that we may be fully conformed to the image of God's Son (v. 29).

C. His Environment Compelling Him to Groan before God and Declare His Iniquity and Sin

Psalm 38:9-20 shows that David's environment compelled him to groan before God and declare his iniquity and sin. In verse 18 David said, "For I declare my iniquity; / I am anxious because of my sin." This is a good verse, which we all should love. We always have to say, "I declare my iniquity; / I am anxious because of my sin." This thought is altogether in contrast with David's logic in Psalm 37. Psalm 37 says that as long as you are righteous, not wicked, you will be all right. But in Psalm 38 David said that he was suffering, and he declared his iniquity. Psalm 38 is much higher than Psalm 37. It would be good to read Psalm 38 in a prayerful way again and again, even on our knees.

D. Begging God Not to Abandon Him but to Hasten to Help and Save Him

In Psalm 38:21-22 David said, "Do not abandon me, O

Jehovah; / O my God, do not be far from me. / Hasten to help
me, / O Lord, my salvation." In Psalm 37 it seems that David
did not need God to come to save him. He thought that he was
righteous and that because of this he would be all right. But
in Psalm 38 all he could do was cry out due to the groaning of
his heart. At the end he cried out for the Lord's help as his
salvation. He begged God not to abandon him but to hasten to
help and save him.

I would like to ask how God would answer David's cry to
help him. When the apostle Paul asked the Lord to remove
the thorn from his flesh, the Lord's response was, "My grace
is sufficient for you" (2 Cor. 12:9). The Lord might tell David,
"I will not answer your prayer for help in your way. Instead, I
will allow you to suffer because the more you suffer, the more
you know your sin. The more you are under suffering, the
more you will declare your iniquity, not your righteousness as
you did in Psalm 37."

Which psalm would you take for your prayer—Psalm 37 or
Psalm 38? We all have to learn not to pray in our natural way.
David's logic in Psalm 37 is very natural. We should abandon
our natural logic. Instead, we must learn to pray in the revelation of God. We must learn to pray when we are under God's
dealing, under God's compelling, in a kind of odious situation
(Psa. 38:5). Then we will be blessed, and we will become a
blessing.

XV. IN HIS REALIZING THE VANITY
OF HIS LIFE

We may say that the title of Psalm 38 could be "Sin and
Iniquity," and the title of Psalm 39 could be "Nothing and
Vanity." Psalm 39 reveals the psalmist's sentiment in his
realizing the vanity of his life. This psalm shows us that we
are nothing and vanity.

A. Keeping His Ways
by Muzzling His Mouth

In verses 1-3 David said that he kept his ways by muzzling
his mouth.

B. Realizing the Nothingness and
Vanity of His Life

David realized the nothingness and vanity of his life and asked God to remove His chastening (for his transgressions) from him and look away from him as a stranger and sojourner (vv. 4-13). We always think that we are something and somebody, but David was brought by the Lord into a situation to realize that actually he was nothing and vanity. David said that every man at his best is altogether vanity (v. 5). He said that his days were as handbreadths. A handbreadth is very short, that is, only about four inches. David said that man goes about as a semblance, an empty show, and that people are bustling about in vain. They heap up riches, but they do not know who will come to gather them (v. 6).

At the end of Psalm 39, David asked Jehovah to hearken to his cry (v. 12). But I do not believe that God would answer him right away. God would keep David in his situation for a while so that David would be compelled to realize his real situation and his real condition. We need to realize that our condition is sinful, and our situation is one of vanity.

In Psalm 37 David had much to say. It seems that in this psalm he knew everything and could say everything. But in Psalm 38 he realized that his condition was sinful, and in Psalm 39 he realized that his situation was full of vanity. Many of us are still remaining in Psalm 37. In one meeting a brother prayed a long prayer. It seemed that in his prayer he knew everything, understood everything, and could say everything. Such a long prayer, however, kills everyone. Instead, we should be those who pray, "O Lord, I don't know what to say, and I don't know what to do. I even don't know what I am. My lifetime is as nothing before You. Lord, have mercy upon me."

David eventually said that he was a stranger with God, a sojourner, just as all of his fathers were (Psa. 39:12). A stranger is one who does not know anything about the place where he is. In the New Testament, all the believers should be heavenly strangers and sojourners (1 Pet. 1:1; 2:11), sojourning as foreigners on this earth. This means that we all have been replaced by Christ. We all have been crucified with Him.

Then it is a fact that it is no longer we who live, but it is Christ who lives in us. We need to see the human concept in the Psalms so that we can jump out of this concept into the divine concept in Paul's Epistles.

The Bible tells us that the word of the Lord is the truth, the reality (John 17:17), and also the light (Psa. 119:105). Through the truth and light released in these messages, I hope that we can see what God wants us to be. God wants us to be nothing. God wants us to be replaced by Christ. Therefore, what God wants was expressed by Paul when he said, "I am crucified with Christ; and it is no longer I who live, but it is Christ who lives in me" (Gal. 2:20a). Christ has crucified me, and Christ has come into me to replace me. Now I have an organic union with Him. He lives and works, and I live and work with Him. Christ replaces me to live Himself through me. This is the divine concept of God according to the divine revelation of the New Testament.

LIFE-STUDY OF THE PSALMS

THE MIXED EXPRESSIONS
OF THE PSALMIST'S SENTIMENT
IN HIS ENJOYMENT OF GOD
IN GOD'S HOUSE

(6)

Scripture Reading: Psa. 40—41

In this message we have come to Psalms 40 and 41, the final two psalms in Book One of the Psalms. In these psalms we can again see the mixed expressions of the psalmist's sentiment in his enjoyment of God in God's house.

XVI. IN HIS SUFFERING OF HIS ENEMIES
AND THE RECOMPENSE
WHICH HE EXPECTED FOR THEM

Psalms 40 and 41 show us the mixed expressions of the psalmist's sentiment in his suffering of his enemies and the recompense which he expected for them. No doubt, when David wrote these two psalms he was under the persecution and mistreatment of his enemies. Because of his suffering, he wanted to see his enemies recompensed. In the New Testament, however, the Lord Jesus told us that we should love our enemies and pray for those who persecute us (Matt. 5:44). This shows that David's prayer to recompense his enemies is not according to the divine concept.

A. Waiting on Jehovah for His Deliverance

David waited on Jehovah for His deliverance (Psa. 40:1-5, 11, 13, 16-17; 41:1-2, 10-12). In 41:10 David said, "But You, O Jehovah, be gracious to me and raise me up / That I may recompense them." David was praising God for God's deliverance and looking to God for His salvation. This is not

wrong, but it was wrong to ask Jehovah to raise him up that
he might recompense his enemies. I hope that all of us can
see this. Do you believe God is happy to see His children ask
Him to raise them up that they might recompense their enemies? This is absolutely wrong. This is why we say that what
is written in many of the psalms is a mixture.

In verses 11-12 David said, "By this I know that You
delight in me, / That my enemy has not shouted in triumph
over me. / And as for me, You uphold me in my integrity, /
And You set me before Your face forever." David indicated
that he would know that Jehovah delighted in him if
Jehovah raised him up so that he could recompense his
enemies. He also asked God not to let his enemies shout
over him triumphantly. In the light of the New Testament
revelation, we can see that this is absolutely according to the
flesh. David also said that God upheld him in his integrity.
He should have said that he was upheld in God's mercy,
in God's compassions. Actually, we do not have any integrity
before God.

B. Appreciating God's Care for Him—
Sustaining Him on His Sickbed
and Making All His Bed in His Illness

David also appreciated God's care for him—sustaining
him on his sickbed and making all his bed in his illness (41:3).
Of course, this is poetic writing. But do you believe that
when David was sick, God came to take care of him just like
a nurse, making all his bed? Surely God takes care of us,
but the apostle Paul did not write anything in his Epistles to
tell us that God took care of him like a nurse to sustain
him on his sickbed and to make his bed in every way. For
David to speak in this way indicates that he was too much in
the self.

C. Referring to His Righteousness
and Integrity Again

David referred to his righteousness and integrity again in
40:9-10 and 41:12.

D. Realizing and Confessing
His Iniquities and Sins

David realized and confessed his iniquities and sins. Psalm 40:12 says, "For evils encompass me until they cannot be counted; / My iniquities have so overtaken me / That I cannot see; / They are more numerous than the hairs of my head; / Thus my heart fails me." Psalm 41:4 says, "I said, O Jehovah, be gracious to me; / Heal my soul, for I have sinned against You." To make confession of our sins is very good.

When David was writing Psalms 40 and 41, he was surrounded by his enemies. He indicated that all his enemies encompassing him were evils which had become so numerous that they could not be counted. Furthermore, his iniquities were so numerous that he could not see. He was overtaken and bent over by the weight of his iniquities, and the number of his iniquities surpassed the number of the hairs on his head. This shows us that he was altogether in a very desperate situation. Enemies were surrounding him, and iniquities were suppressing him.

E. Referring to God the Mistreatment
of His Enemies

David referred to God the mistreatment of his enemies. Psalm 41:5-9 says, "My enemies speak evil against me: / When will he die and his name perish? / And if he comes to see me, he speaks falsehood. / His heart gathers iniquity to itself; / When he goes out, he speaks it. / All who hate me whisper together against me; / Against me they devise my misfortune. / Some evil illness, they say, is cast upon him; / And when he lies down, he will not rise again. / Even my familiar friend, in whom I trusted, / Who ate my bread, has lifted his heel against me." David told God in detail concerning how his enemies had mistreated him.

David's enemies pretended that they were his friends. This is why they could come to see him and speak falsehood. Today many people are like this. They are so nice to a person in a way of pretense when they are with him, but when they leave his presence, they speak what they really feel about him. This is falsehood. David's enemies even said that some evil illness was cast upon him.

In the midst of these mixed expressions of David's sentiment, David spoke a word which became a prophecy concerning Judas Iscariot, who betrayed the Lord Jesus. Verse 9 says, "Even my familiar friend, in whom I trusted, / Who ate my bread, has lifted his heel against me." This word was quoted by the Lord in John 13:18 in reference to Judas.

F. Expecting That His Enemies Would Be Desolate and Put to Shame

David expected his enemies to be desolate and put to shame (Psa. 40:14-15; 41:10-11).

G. Prophesying concerning Christ in Such Mixed Expressions of His Sentiment

In such mixed expressions of his sentiment, David prophesied concerning Christ. The prophecy in Psalm 40:6-8 is a great prophecy concerning Christ, and the prophecy in Psalm 41:9 is a small prophecy concerning Judas betraying Christ.

1. In Psalm 40:6-8

Seemingly Psalm 40:6-8 was the word of David, but actually it is the word of Christ. Christ said to God, "You do not delight in sacrifice and offering; / You have bored My ears; / You do not require burnt offering and sin offering. / Then I said, / Behold, I have come; / In the scroll of the book / It is written concerning Me. / I delight in doing Your will, O My God; / Indeed Your law is within My inward parts" (lit.).

This prophecy was fully quoted and defined by the apostle Paul in Hebrews 10. Christ delighted in doing God's will, which was the will of God to replace the Old Testament sacrifices and offerings (vv. 5-10). Many Christians apply the doing of God's will in Hebrews 10 to their daily affairs. Actually, however, the doing of God's will in Hebrews 10 refers to Christ coming to replace the Old Testament sacrifices and offerings. In the old dispensation, God commanded His people to offer to Him sacrifices and offerings. But when Jesus came and lived on this earth, God no longer delighted in those Old Testament offerings. Instead, it was God's will to replace them with Christ Himself. Christ came to be the real sacrifice, the real offering, the living sacrifice, the living offering, who offered Himself on the cross as the reality of all the offerings. He is the reality of the sin offering, the trespass offering, the burnt offering, the meal offering, and the peace offering.

Actually, Christ came to replace all the Old Testament types. In other words, by Christ's first coming, the entire Old Testament has been terminated and replaced. Now our offering and sacrifice are Christ. Day and night we offer Christ to God as all kinds of offerings. Whenever we sin, we ask God to forgive us, taking Christ, God's Son, as our sin offering and trespass offering. He is the real offering for our sin and transgressions. When we need peace toward God, we can take Christ as our peace offering. We can also take Him as our burnt offering and meal offering. Christ is everything to us because He fulfilled all the Old Testament types and has taken them away. Today He is the reality of all the types in the Old Testament.

The revelation in Psalm 40:6-8 is one of the greatest revelations concerning Christ in His commission of His incarnation. Verse 6 says, "You do not delight in sacrifice and offering," and again, "You do not require burnt offering and sin offering." This indicates that God was intending to give up His Old Testament economy. Just by reading Psalm 40:6-8 alone, we cannot understand this much. But this portion was quoted and expounded by the apostle Paul in Hebrews 10. He indicated that to stop the sacrifices and offerings of the Old Testament is to replace the Old Testament for the establishment of the New Testament.

Sacrifice (for sin and sins before God) and offering (for fellowship with God) were the elements based upon which the old testament (covenant) was established, and the old testament (covenant) was the centrality and universality of God's economy in the Old Testament. God not delighting in and not requiring the sacrifice and offering means to terminate His economy in the Old Testament. This is the importance and the greatness of this prophecy in Psalm 40.

Verse 6 also says, "You have bored My ears." This was quoted by the apostle Paul in Hebrews 10:5 as "a body You have prepared for Me," from the Septuagint, a Greek version of the Old Testament translated about three hundred years before Christ. To bore the ears of a slave's body indicates the master's requirement of the slave's obedience (Exo. 21:6). This signifies that God required obedience of Christ as His Slave in Christ's humanity. This obedience was spoken of by Paul in Philippians 2:8, which says that Christ became "obedient even unto death, and that the death of a cross." This obedience was for Him to do the will of God by being the sacrifice and offering in His crucifixion in the flesh, the body (Col. 1:22). Based upon this the Septuagint interprets the boring of the ears into the preparing of a body, in which Christ offered Himself to God as the sacrifice and the offering to replace the sacrifice and the offering of the animals in the Old Testament.

I believe that the translators of the Septuagint realized that to bore the ears was to require the obedience of Christ, and Christ's obedience was mainly for Him to die on the cross. For Him to die on the cross, He needed a human body. Hebrews 2:14 says that because Christ was going to destroy Satan, He needed to partake of blood and flesh, that is, He needed a body. I believe that the Septuagint translators may have realized that "You have bored My ears" in Psalm 40:6 would not be understood by most readers so they translated it as "a body You have prepared for Me." To bore the ears was for Christ's obedience to die on the cross, and to prepare a body was also for His dying on the cross. Thus, both translations are with the same purpose. God prepared a body for Christ to come to do God's will to be God's unique sacrifice on the cross.

Psalm 40:7 says, "Behold, I have come," indicating Christ's first coming through His incarnation for the establishment of the new testament by Himself as the enacting sacrifice and offering.

Verse 7 also says, "In the scroll of the book / It is written concerning Me." This indicates that Christ was prophesied in the Scriptures of the Old Testament and that Christ will do

God's will for the accomplishment of God's New Testament economy according to the Old Testament prophecies concerning Him.

When the Lord appeared to His disciples in resurrection, He told them all the things that were written concerning Him in the Scriptures (Luke 24:27). In Luke 24:44-45 He told the disciples, "These are My words which I spoke to you while I was still with you, that all the things written in the Law of Moses and the Prophets and Psalms concerning Me must be fulfilled. Then He opened their mind to understand the Scriptures." The Lord's word here unveils that the entire Old Testament is a revelation of Him and that He is its center and content. Our life-study of the Old Testament is full of interpretations and definitions of the types concerning Christ.

Psalm 40:8 says, "I delight in doing Your will." This indicates that Christ was willing to do God's will in His commission of His incarnation to fulfill and replace all the sacrifices and offerings of the Old Testament for the termination of God's Old Testament economy, so that He could initiate and establish God's New Testament economy (Matt. 26:26-28) for the producing and building of the church to be His organic Body, which will consummate in the New Jerusalem. When the Lord established His table, He indicated that His blood shed through His death was the enacting factor of the new covenant.

In Hebrews 10:5-9, after quoting this prophecy concerning Christ in Psalm 40:6-8, Paul commented that Christ coming to do God's will is to take away the first that He may establish the second (Heb. 10:9). "The first" in Paul's comment refers to the sacrifices and offerings of the first covenant, the old covenant; and "the second" refers to the sacrifice of the second covenant, the new covenant, which sacrifice is Christ. The commission which God committed to Christ in His first coming through incarnation was to put away the animal sacrifices of the old covenant and to establish Himself, in His body, as the sacrifice of the new covenant. This is to terminate God's Old Testament economy and to initiate God's New Testament economy, thus making the prophecy in Psalm

40:6-8 one of the greatest prophecies concerning the all-inclusive Christ.

The prophecy in Psalm 40 concerning Christ should be considered the fifth station of all the prophecies concerning Christ in Book One of the Psalms. Psalms 2, 8, 16, and 22—24 are the first four stations. In the fifth station, Christ came through His incarnation to terminate God's old economy and initiate God's new economy, His New Testament economy, by replacing the animal sacrifices and establishing Himself as the unique sacrifice of the new covenant. As the unique sacrifice of the new covenant, Christ was the enacting factor of the New Testament economy to be the centrality and universality of God's New Testament economy. Hence, Christ is great in the prophecy in Psalm 40:6-8. He has changed the age for the consummation of God's new creation out of God's old creation. His changing of the age is greater than the creation of the universe mentioned in Genesis 1.

The prophecy concerning Christ in Psalm 40:6-8 is the goal and the destination of the revelation of Christ in Psalm 2, Psalm 8, Psalm 16, and Psalms 22—24. All Christians know that Christ came in His incarnation, but if we want to know what kind of Christ came, we have to know Psalm 2, Psalm 8, Psalm 16, and Psalms 22—24. These psalms are descriptions of the very Christ who came in His incarnation to carry out God's will as God's commission to turn the age, to terminate everything old and to replace the old things with Himself as everything new. We all were included in the old creation, but the old creation was terminated and replaced by Christ. Today in Christ we are no longer old; we are new (2 Cor. 5:17).

The prophecy concerning Christ in Psalm 40:6-8 was spoken in the context of the mixed expressions of David's sentiment. David's speaking in the Psalms reminds me to a certain extent of Peter's speaking in the Gospels. Peter frequently said the wrong thing, but one day he told the Lord that He was the Christ, the Son of the living God (Matt. 16:16). Then the Lord Jesus told Peter that he was blessed because flesh and blood did not reveal this to him, but the

Father in the heavens (v. 17). The Lord went further to tell the disciples that He was going to the cross (v. 21), but Peter began to rebuke Him, telling Him, "God be merciful to You, Lord! This shall by no means happen to You!" (v. 22). When Peter said this, the Lord said to him, "Get behind Me, Satan!" (v. 23). At one moment Peter was blessed to receive a heavenly revelation of Christ from the Father, but in the next moment he was one with Satan. At one moment he was Peter; in the next moment he was Satan.

Peter's situation may be compared to David's situation in the Psalms. In the Psalms, David's speaking is according to two concepts—the human concept and the divine concept. At one time David is speaking, but suddenly his mouth becomes the mouth which reveals the divine revelation concerning Christ. Peter's case in the Gospels was similar to this.

Matthew 17 says that the Lord Jesus brought Peter, James, and John with Him to the mount of His transfiguration. When Peter saw the Lord transfigured and speaking with Moses and Elijah, he became very excited. He spoke foolishly by saying, "Lord, it is good for us to be here; if You are willing, I will make three tents here, one for You and one for Moses and one for Elijah" (v. 4). In his absurd proposal, Peter put Moses and Elijah on the same level as Christ. He was on the mount of Christ's transfiguration, but he spoke nonsense. David's speaking in the Psalms was in the same principle. In his speaking we can see both the divine concept and the human concept. In the Old Testament, there is a talkative David. In the New Testament, there is a talkative Peter.

David wrote many psalms, and in these psalms we can see both his natural concept and the divine concept of God according to the divine revelation. In Psalms 40 and 41, the only portions which are according to the divine concept are 40:6-8 and 41:9. These portions speak concerning Christ. However, we need all the verses in the psalms so that we can have a comparison to show us the divine revelation and the human expressions of the human sentiment.

2. In Psalm 41:9

As we have pointed out, Psalm 41:9 is a prophecy concerning Judas Iscariot betraying Christ. This verse says, "Even my familiar friend, in whom I trusted, / Who ate my bread, has lifted his heel against me." The familiar friend in this verse is Judas Iscariot (John 6:70-71). Judas Iscariot was one who ate with the Lord (John 13:18, 23-27; Luke 22:21-22) and lifted up his heel against Christ, betraying Christ. However, Judas did not partake of the Lord's table (Mark 14:17-25; John 13:26-30).

H. Blessing God for Eternity

In Psalm 41:13 David blessed God for eternity—"Blessed be Jehovah, the God of Israel, / From eternity to eternity! / Amen and Amen!"

XVII. ANOTHER THREE POINTS
OF THE PROPHECIES CONCERNING CHRIST

Psalms 25—41 are a section of psalms showing us the mixed expressions of the psalmist's sentiment in his enjoyment of God in God's house. In this long section, we have seen that there is one of the greatest prophecies concerning Christ in His coming to replace the Old Testament sacrifices and offerings. In this section there are another three points of the prophecies concerning Christ.

A. Taking Counsel Together against Him
and Scheming to Take His Life

Psalm 31:13b says, "When they take counsel together against me, / They scheme to take my life." This prophecy was fulfilled in the New Testament with the Lord Jesus. Matthew 26:4 says that the chief priests and the elders took counsel together to seize Jesus by craftiness and kill Him.

B. Committing His Spirit
into God's Hand

Psalm 31:5a says, "Into Your [God's] hand I [Christ] commit my spirit." This was quoted by Christ when He was crucified on the cross. At the end of His crucifixion, He said, "Father, into Your hands I commit My spirit" (Luke 23:46; cf. John 19:30).

C. God Keeping All His Bones and Not One of Them Being Broken

Psalm 34:20 says, "He [God] keeps all his [Christ's] bones; / Not one of them is broken." This verse was fulfilled at the time of the Lord's death. When the Roman soldiers who crucified Him saw that He had already died, they did not break His legs. John 19:36 says, "For these things happened that the Scripture might be fulfilled: 'No bone of His shall be broken.'" Christ was also typified in Exodus by the Passover lamb, whose bones were not to be broken (12:46).

These are the minor prophecies concerning Christ unveiled in Psalms 25—41.

XVIII. A CONCLUDING WORD CONCERNING CHRIST IN THE DIVINE REVELATION IN THE FIRST BOOK OF THE PSALMS

The first book of the Psalms comprises Psalms 1—41. We should not forget that in this first book there are seven psalms which speak concerning Christ: Psalm 2, Psalm 8, Psalm 16, Psalms 22—24, and Psalm 40.

A. In the Mixed Expressions of the Sentiment of God's Lovers and Seekers, Christ Being Revealed as the Centrality and Universality of God's Economy

In the mixed expressions of the sentiment of God's lovers and seekers, Christ is revealed as the centrality and universality of God's economy. David was surely a lover of God and a seeker of God just as Peter was in the New Testament. Peter made mistakes, but he loved the Lord and sought after the Lord. This is why the Lord came to him and asked him, "Simon...do you love Me?" (John 21:17). Christ would not ask someone this question if he did not love Him. For Christ to ask Peter if he loved Him is precious. David was also a lover and a seeker of God. In the mixed expressions of his sentiment, Christ is revealed as the centrality and universality of God's economy.

1. Having Been Anointed to Be God's Messiah

Psalm 2 reveals that Christ has been anointed to be God's Messiah, resurrected to be the firstborn Son of God, and installed to be God's King; He has also been given the nations as His inheritance and the earth as His possession for His kingdom.

2. Bringing God into Man in His Incarnation and Man into God in His Resurrection

Psalm 8 reveals that as the embodiment of God, Christ has brought God into man in His incarnation and man into God in His resurrection, thus bringing heaven to the earth and joining the earth to heaven to be the excellent One in all the earth.

3. As the God-man, Mingled with Divinity and Humanity

Psalm 16 reveals that as the God-man, mingled with divinity and humanity, Christ took God as His portion, being obedient to God unto death, resurrecting into glory, ascending to His heavenly attainments and obtainments, and sitting at the right hand of God for the accomplishment of God's eternal economy concerning the church, the Body of Christ.

4. Dying an All-inclusive Vicarious Death and Entering into the Church-producing Resurrection

Psalms 22—24 reveal that Christ died an all-inclusive vicarious death and entered into the church-producing resurrection. In resurrection He became the Shepherd of God's flock, leading the sheep of God to participate in the church as the house of God in this age, consummating in the New Jerusalem in the coming age and in the eternal age; and He will be God's triumphant King of glory to reign in God's eternal kingdom.

5. Coming to Do the Will of God
to Fulfill and Replace All the Old Testament
Sacrifices and Offerings

Psalm 40:6-8 reveals that Christ came to do the will of God to fulfill and replace all the Old Testament sacrifices and offerings according to what is written in the Old Testament concerning Him.

B. Bringing God's Chosen People into
the Enjoyment of God Firstly in the Church and
Ultimately in the New Jerusalem

Such a Christ brings God's chosen people into the enjoyment of God firstly in the church in this age and ultimately in the New Jerusalem in the millennium and in eternity (Psa. 27; 36).

LIFE-STUDY OF THE PSALMS

MESSAGE NINETEEN

THE PSALMISTS' INTENSIFIED ENJOYMENT OF GOD IN HIS HOUSE AND CITY THROUGH THE SUFFERING, EXALTED, AND REIGNING CHRIST

(1)

THE PSALMISTS PANTING AFTER GOD

Scripture Reading: Psa. 42—44

The Psalms are composed of five books. Thus far in our fellowship, we have covered Book One of the Psalms, composed of the first forty-one psalms. In this message we will begin our fellowship on Book Two of the Psalms. In this book we see the psalmists' intensified enjoyment of God in His house and city through the suffering, exalted, and reigning Christ.

The psalms in Book One were written mainly by David. Book Two, however, contains eight psalms that were composed by the sons of Korah, Psalms 42—49. David is a glorious name among the nation of Israel, but Korah is an infamous name because Korah rebelled against Moses and God (Num. 16:1-3). In spite of this, some of the descendants of Korah became composers of the Psalms. This indicates that among the five books of the Psalms, the revelation is progressive. The five books of the Psalms are not on the same level. The Psalms is like a stairway with five steps, that takes us higher in its revelation in a progressive way.

Book Two of the Psalms begins in Psalm 42:1 in a very good way. The psalmist said, "As the hart pants / After the streams of water, / So my soul pants / For You, O God." We can sense the Lord's freshness in the desire and aspiration of the psalmist here. This is much different from what is expressed by the psalmist in Psalm 1. The human concept of

Psalm 1 is that the man who delights in the law of God prospers in everything. The psalmist said that the one who delighted and meditated in the law would be like a tree transplanted beside streams of water (vv. 2-3). A tree drinks water by absorbing it.

In Psalm 42, however, the psalmist said that his soul panted for God, just as the hart pants after the streams of water. Then he said, "My soul thirsts for God, / For the living God. / When will I come and appear / Before God?" (v. 2). Psalm 1, the opening word of Book One, begins with the law. But Book Two begins with God. What do we prefer—the law or God? Do we want to be like a tree transplanted by the streams of water by delighting in the law or like a hart panting after God? Surely there is no comparison between God and the law. This shows us that Book Two of the Psalms is higher than Book One.

Thus, we have to realize that the psalms progressively become higher in their revelation from Book One through Book Five. Book Five is the high peak of the Psalms. The high peak of this book is expressed in the word *Hallelujah! Hallelujah* means praise Jehovah, praise God. Thus, Book Two begins with God, and Book Five ends with "Praise God."

When we get into the New Jerusalem, we will all say, "Hallelujah! Hallelujah!" Some have asked me what language we will use in the New Jerusalem. I do not know what language we will speak, but we will probably say—"Hallelujah! Hallelujah!"—all the time. What other things will we need to talk about by that time? When we study the book of Psalms, we should reach some points where we sing "hallelujah" spontaneously. Even when we read Psalm 1 we can say, "Hallelujah! Hallelujah! I don't need to love the law anymore."

It is very striking that Book Two begins with the psalmist's panting after God. Panting after God is different from worshipping God in a formal, religious way. God is our living water for us to drink. Do we need to bow down to worship the water? We need to pant after this water and then drink it. In verse 1 the word *pants* is used. In verse 2 the word *thirsts* is used. My soul *pants* for God and *thirsts* for God. I love these

predicates. We need to have times with the Lord in which we
pant after Him and thirst for Him.

I. BOOK TWO OF THE PSALMS UNVEILING
THE PSALMISTS' INTENSIFIED ENJOYMENT
OF GOD IN HIS HOUSE, AND EVEN THE MORE
IN HIS CITY, THROUGH THE SUFFERING,
EXALTED, AND REIGNING CHRIST

Book One of the Psalms has turned the psalmists from the
law to Christ, and Christ has brought them to the enjoyment
of God in His house and in His city. We should come to God
through Christ. Christ is the real stairway to God. Christ told
us that He is the way. Thomas said, "Lord, we do not know
where You are going; how can we know the way?" (John 14:5).
Then Jesus said, "I am the way" (v. 6). He is the real stairway
to God.

Thus, Book One of the Psalms turned the psalmists to the
right direction, to Christ. Then Christ brought them to the
enjoyment of God in His house and in His city. I say this
because of the first two verses of Book Two, which say, "As the
hart pants / After the streams of water, / So my soul pants /
For You, O God. / My soul thirsts for God, / For the living God"
(42:1-2). This is the enjoyment of God. Book Two begins with
the direct enjoyment of God.

Book Two unveils the psalmists' intensified enjoyment of
God in His house, and even the more in His city, through the
suffering, exalted, and reigning Christ. Book One does not
speak of the enjoyment of God in the house of God and the
city of God as strongly as Book Two does. We may say, in a
sense, that God was homeless at the beginning of Book One.
The law is not God's home. Who is God's home? We have seen
that God's home is firstly Christ as the tabernacle and the
temple (John 1:14; 2:21). The first part of the New Testament,
the Gospels, tells us clearly that God's home was Christ. He
was the tabernacle of God. Actually, this tabernacle was a
portable home. Christ was God's tabernacle, God's tent, and
also God's temple.

Later, Christ became mingled with His believers, and His
believers became His extension, His enlargement. Thus, the

church is God's home in the second step (Eph. 2:22). It is difficult to find a verse in Book One of the Psalms which speaks of
the city of God. The city of God signifies God's kingdom.
Christ as the tabernacle of God eventually became a kingdom. Christ cannot be a king without a "dom." When the
tabernacle becomes enlarged it becomes the temple, and
the temple is the church (1 Cor. 3:16). The church is also the
kingdom (Matt. 16:18-19; Rom. 14:17), the King with the
"dom." The kingdom is signified in the Psalms by the city.

Zion was a peak of the mountain range on which the city
of Jerusalem was built. Jerusalem was built on a mountain
range, that mountain range had a high peak, and on top of
that high peak was the temple. That high peak was called
Zion. On Zion a temple was built, and the temple was God's
house. Around that temple was the city of Jerusalem. Jerusalem as the city signifies God's kingdom. In Book Two the
psalmist begins to speak about the city. Thus, we have the
enjoyment of God in His house and in His city.

The universal God is located in His house, His dwelling
place. God's house is both Christ as God's tabernacle and
temple and the church as the enlargement of Christ, the
enlarged temple. On the one hand, God in Christ is our home,
our dwelling place (Psa. 90:1), and on the other hand, we
as the church are His home, His dwelling place. All the unbelieving sinners need to realize that because they are
homeless, God is also homeless. When we believe in the Lord
Jesus, we come back home. When we get into this home, into
Christ, God is also home in us. When I was younger, we
preached the gospel by telling the unbelievers that they
were homeless, not having any rest. Because they are restless, homeless, God is also homeless. But when we believe
in the Lord Jesus, we come back home. Then we are home,
and God is also home. We are no longer restless and neither is
God.

Many believed in the Lord through this kind of preaching.
We should not just tell people that they are sinners and
that Jesus died for them. Many people have heard this kind
of word, and they are not open to receive it. They would be
open, however, to realize that as human beings they are

homeless apart from God. In Book Two of the Psalms, God is home. We enjoy God in His home. This means that we enjoy God in Christ and in the church. Ephesians 3:21 says that God is glorified in Christ and in the church. God is glorified in His house and in His city, in Christ and in the church.

The psalmists enjoyed God through the suffering, exalted, and reigning Christ. Such a Christ is the way for us sinners to enter into God. Now we enjoy God as our God in Christ as the home and in the church as the city. Our enjoyment of God is through a stairway, and this stairway is Christ—the suffering One, the exalted One, and the reigning One. In Book Two of the Psalms, Christ's suffering, Christ's being exalted, and Christ's reigning are stressed.

II. PSALMS 42—49, 84, 85, 87, AND 88
BEING THE HOLY WRITINGS OF THE SONS OF KORAH

Psalms 42—49, 84, 85, 87, and 88 are the holy writings of the sons of Korah. Korah was the leader of the rebellion against Moses and God (Num. 16:1-3). After about four hundred seventy years, Samuel the prophet, Heman the singer, and some other psalmists came out of Korah the rebel's descendants at the time of David (1 Chron. 6:31-39). Even the descendants of a leading rebel became the godly writers of psalms, praising God in their holy writings as a record existing for generations. What a grace this was!

It is marvelous that the descendants of Korah wrote something that became a part of the Holy Bible. Their holy writings have become a record existing for generations. They were also faithful to tell people that they were the sons of Korah, the one who rebelled against God. This shows us that all the psalms were written based upon the infinite grace of God. The sons of Korah were the descendants, the sons, of that great sinner and rebel, Korah, yet they became holy people writing psalms to praise God. Today we are like the sons of Korah. In a sense, we are still poor sinners and rebels, yet we poor sinners can be those who are speakers of the holy Word!

III. PANTING AFTER GOD

The crucial point of Psalms 42—44 is the psalmist's panting after God.

A. After Being Stripped by God

The psalmist was panting after God at a time when he and his people had been stripped and defeated by the neighboring nations.

B. As the Hart Panting after the Streams of Water

He panted after God as the hart pants after the streams of water (Psa. 42:1-2).

C. Under the Adversaries' Reproaching and Oppression

The psalmist was also under the adversaries' reproaching and oppression (42:3, 9b-10). Psalm 42:3 says, "My tears have been my food / Day and night, / While they say to me all day long, / Where is your God?"

D. Recalling the Glorious and Pleasant Past in the Leading of the Festal Multitude to Enjoy God in His House with His People

On the one hand, the psalmist was panting after God. On the other hand, he was recalling the glorious and pleasant past in the leading of the festal multitude to enjoy God in His house with His people. Psalm 42:4 says, "These things I remember, / And I pour out my soul within me: / That I passed through with the throng; / I led them to the house of God / With the voice of a joyous shout and praise, / The festal multitude."

This is a very pleasant recounting of the past. But I would like us to consider whether or not this was the right thing to do. In the psalmist's captivity, he was panting after God. But at least in his thought, in his consideration, he left the panting after God and went to something else—the recounting of his past. How good that was, how glorious that was, and how pleasant that was! He remembered how wonderful it was when he was leading a multitude to ascend to the peak of Zion to enjoy God with God's people by feasting together with God.

This was a pleasant picture from the past, but should he have recounted his past in this way while he was panting after God? Actually, this was a departure from his panting after God. He should have remained in the state of panting after God. We may be having a time with the Lord in which we are panting after God, but then some consideration within us will take us away from our panting after God. We might remember how wonderful and pleasant the church life was many years ago. This consideration and remembrance of our past distracts us from enjoying the Lord.

Psalm 42:4 is a good verse, but it shows that there is a mixture within the sentiment of the writer of this psalm. There should be no mixture. Instead, there should be only panting after God and singing "Hallelujah! Praise the Lord!" Our considerations and thinking should not take us away from the panting after God. We should not be distracted from God to the treasuring of our past. Because the psalmist departed from his panting after God, the thoughts constituting his sentiment were expressed.

E. Encouraged by the Hope in God for the Salvation of His Countenance

Verse 5 says, "Why are you bowed down, O my soul? / And why are you disquieted within me? / Hope in God, for I will yet praise Him / For the salvation of His countenance." The psalmist was encouraged by the hope in God for the salvation of His countenance. The psalmist encouraged his soul, himself. He told his soul not to be cast down but to hope in God. He said that he would still praise God for the salvation of His countenance.

At that time the psalmist had been stripped of almost everything. He had lost his home and was in captivity. What could he enjoy? He could enjoy the countenance of God. He lost his home, his country, and he had been stripped of his earthly enjoyment. Now he was in captivity, but he could enjoy God's presence, God's countenance. God's countenance became his enjoyment in his captivity. However, while he was enjoying God's presence by panting after God, he became distracted by different thoughts. We are also like this. In our time with the Lord, we may be panting after Him, but then we are taken away from God by distracting thoughts.

F. Remembering God from a Distance

The psalmist remembered God from a distance—from the land of the Jordan and the Hermons, from Mount Mizar, quite far from Zion and Jerusalem, where God's house and city were. Psalm 42:6 says, "O my God, my soul is bowed down within me; / Therefore I remember You / From the land of the Jordan and the Hermons, / From Mount Mizar." This indicates that the psalmist was away from his home, from his country, from his nation. He remembered the Lord not from the door of the temple or from the gate of Jerusalem but from far away. This is because he was in captivity. This was during the time when the people of Israel, including those serving in the temple, had been defeated and captured by their invading enemies. This psalmist was such a serving one. The sons of Korah were Levites. Korah was a leader of the Levites who served the temple (Num. 16:8-10). The invaders defeated Israel and captured the people. Thus, the psalmist here was in a far away country.

G. Recognizing God's Sovereignty in Their Environment

Psalm 42:7-9a shows that the psalmist recognized God's sovereignty in his environment. Verse 7 says, "Deep calls unto deep / At the sound of Your water spouts; / All Your waves and Your billows / Pass over me." Some versions render "water spouts" as "waterfalls." This poetic expression describes the sufferings through which the psalmist passed.

Verse 8 says, "By day Jehovah commands / His lovingkindness, / And by night His song is with me, / A prayer to the God of my life." Of course, while he was passing through such a deep suffering, all the psalmist could do was to pray. In the day he enjoyed God's lovingkindness; in the night he enjoyed Jehovah's song being with him, a prayer to the God of his life.

Verses 9 and 10 say, "I say to God my rock, / Why have You forgotten me? / Why do I go mourning / Because of the oppression of the enemy? / As with a shattering in my bones, / My adversaries reproach me, / While they say to me all day long, / Where is your God?" His adversaries asked him where his God was since he was in captivity.

All of these thoughts came in to distract the psalmist from panting after God. Here we see the mixed expressions of the sentiment of the writer. When he was writing such a psalm, all kinds of distracting thoughts came to his mind, distracting him from panting after God and from the salvation of God's countenance. In verse 11 he said, "Why are you bowed down, O my soul? / And why are you disquieted within me? / Hope in God; for I will yet praise Him, / The salvation of my countenance and my God."

H. The Mixed Expressions
of the Psalmists' Sentiment
in Their Enjoyment of God
in His House and City

While the psalmist was enjoying God in His house and His city, a lot of things came into his thoughts to distract him. That constituted a kind of sentiment, which he poured out in his expressions. Psalm 43:1-2 shows us the mixed expressions of the psalmist's sentiment in his enjoyment of God in His house and city.

To pant after God and to thirst for God are marvelous, wonderful, and good. In this we should remain, but we lack control. Thoughts come in as darts to distract us. These thoughts constitute our sentiment, which we utter in expressions. Mixed expressions such as these are the contents of many of the psalms.

I. Asking God to Give Them Light and Truth
That Will Lead Them and Bring Them
to God's Holy Mountain

The psalmist asked God to give him light and truth that

would lead him and bring him to God's holy mountain and to His tabernacles that he might go to the altar of God, to the God of his exultation's rejoicing (43:3-4). This means that he was away from the holy mountain and from the temple. He asked God to send forth light and truth. When we have light and truth, we have the way, but at that time the people of Israel did not have a way to get out of their captivity. They did not have the way, the leading, to get back to Mount Zion, the holy mountain, so that they could return to God's house.

The psalmists who wrote Psalms 42—44 were really lovers of God. They were panting after God, thirsting for God, and desiring to go back to Jerusalem, to get to Mount Zion to reach the altar. Then they could enter into the temple to meet the God of their exultation's rejoicing. This is why they prayed that God would give them the light and the truth that they might know how to get out of their captivity and get back to God's dwelling place.

J. The Mixed Expressions of the Psalmists' Sentiment in Their Enjoyment of God in His House and City

Psalm 44 shows us the mixed expressions of the psalmists' sentiment in their enjoyment of God in His house and city.

1. Treasuring the Past

In verses 1-8 the psalmists were treasuring their forefathers' past history. Verse 1 says, "O God, we have heard with our ears; / Our fathers have recounted it to us, / The work You did in their days, / In the days of old." Their treasuring the past was a distraction as a part of their mixed sentiment.

2. Sighing for the Present

In addition to treasuring the past, the psalmists were sighing for the present (Psa. 44:9-26). Psalm 44:9 says, "Nevertheless You have rejected us and humiliated us, / And You have not gone forth with our armies." This verse begins with the word *nevertheless*. The psalmists were saying that even though God was so good and kind to their forefathers, He had rejected them now. Thus, they blamed God.

Verse 17 says, "All this has come upon us; but we have not forgotten You, / Nor have we been false to Your covenant." The psalmists maintained that even though all these bad things such as their defeat and captivity had come upon them, they had not forgotten God nor had they been false to His covenant. Was this true? In the Old Testament, especially in the Prophets, God told His people frequently that they had forsaken Him (Jer. 2:13) and had broken His covenant (Jer. 11:10; Hosea 6:7). Thus, it was false for the psalmists to say that they had not forgotten God or been false to His covenant.

Psalm 44:18 says, "Our heart has not turned back, / Nor have our steps slipped from Your way." God said in the Prophets that the people of Israel turned their hearts away from Him. Whose word is right—God's word or the psalmists'? In the Prophets God also said clearly that the people of Israel had left His way. In spite of this, the seeking psalmists argued with God in this way. This shows us that we should not think that every psalm is so wonderful. Again we need to realize that in the Psalms there are both the human concept and the divine concept.

We can see again that the psalmists' panting after God was disturbed, and their thirsting for God was taken away by all these different thoughts. The psalmists spoke of how good God was to their forefathers, but of how bad He was to them. They told God that even though He had rejected them, they had not rejected Him. They were vindicating themselves, but where was their panting after God and their thirsting for God? They were gone. All of us have had similar experiences. Often we may have been panting after God, but then we became distracted by many thoughts. Often we are distracted from panting after God, from enjoying God.

I hope that we are being helped to understand how to study the book of Psalms. Verses 1-2 and 5 of Psalm 42 are very good because they are according to the divine concept. Verses 1 and 2 speak of panting after God and thirsting for God, and verse 5 speaks of the salvation of God's countenance.

Like the psalmists, we may have lost everything, having been stripped of everything, yet we have not lost God. Even though we may have rejected Him, we have not lost Him. His presence is with us, and that presence is His countenance. His countenance is our salvation.

LIFE-STUDY OF THE PSALMS

THE PSALMISTS' INTENSIFIED ENJOYMENT OF GOD IN HIS HOUSE AND CITY THROUGH THE SUFFERING, EXALTED, AND REIGNING CHRIST

(2)

PRAISING CHRIST AS THE KING

(1)

Scripture Reading: Psa. 45:1-8

In this message we will begin to consider Psalm 45, the highest and the greatest of the one hundred fifty psalms. To enter into the significance of such a psalm is not easy. All seventeen verses of Psalm 45 are quite common, but the way this psalm presents Christ is very peculiar.

The title of this psalm tells us that it is a song of love. The word *love* in the title refers not to a father's love for his son but to the love between a male and a female. This is indicated by the fact that the Hebrew word for love here is in the feminine gender. Thus, the love in Psalm 45 is a feminine love.

In order to understand this psalm, we need to turn to the particular book in the Bible which is concerned with love—the Song of Songs. Psalm 45 is a psalm of love, and Song of Songs is a book of love. In that book the word love is used in both the masculine and the feminine gender. According to the English translation of Song of Songs, the Lord Jesus is called "the Beloved"; however, the Hebrew word is simply the word for love in the masculine gender. Likewise, when the Lord calls His seeker "My love," the Hebrew word for love is in the feminine gender. Moreover, Psalm 45:2a says, "You are fairer than the sons of men." This is similar to Song of Songs 5:10, where the seeker speaks of her beloved as "the chiefest among ten thousand." This is a further indication that Song of Songs helps us to understand Psalm 45.

In one of the life-study messages on Hosea 11—14, we pointed out that throughout Hosea Israel is depicted as the wife of Jehovah. However, when God's everlasting love is touched, Israel is called God's son (Hosea 11:1), indicating that Israel has the Father's life. God's everlasting love is not a love in affection, like the love of a husband toward a wife, but a love in life, like the love of a father toward a son. Love in affection does not transform, but love in life transforms people. It is in the Father's love, the love in life, that Israel is transformed. A husband who loves his wife in affection may spoil her, but a father who loves his son in life never spoils his son. Rather, a father's love in life perfects his son.

I am not suggesting that Christ's love for us as virgins, as those who are females in relation to Him (2 Cor. 11:2), is a love that can spoil us. According to the biblical truth, Christ's love does not spoil His believers. Nominal Christians, false Christians, do not know Christ's love. Genuine Christians, those who have a heart for the Lord, enjoy Christ's love, but they may enjoy it according to their own concept or feeling. As a result they are spoiled not by Christ's love itself but by their wrong application of Christ's love. For instance, if you speak to them concerning the kingdom truth, dispensational punishment, and the casting of certain believers into the outer darkness (Matt. 22:13; 25:30), they may say, "You are teaching heresy. Jesus loves me. He is not cruel, and He would not put me into outer darkness. As long as Jesus loves me, everything is all right." This indicates that even genuine believers have been spoiled by their mistaken application of the love of Christ.

Such believers need to consider the book of Hebrews. Hebrews is a book not on Christ's love but on the kingdom. Regarding the kingdom, Hebrews gives us five warnings, and each of these warnings concerns either reward or punishment. Furthermore, in Hebrews we have two kinds of words. The first is the good word of God (6:5), the word of the beginning of Christ (v. 1), which is the milk the believers taste when they believe in the Lord (5:13). The second kind of word is the word of righteousness (v. 13), which is solid food (v. 14), embodying the thought of God's justice and righteousness in His dispensational and governmental dealings with His people. In Hebrews 12:5 through 7 we have such a word of righteousness. "You have completely forgotten the exhortation which reasons with you as with sons, 'My son, do not regard lightly the discipline of the Lord, nor faint when reproved by Him; for whom the Lord loves He disciplines, and He scourges every son whom He receives.' It is for discipline that you endure; God deals with you as with sons." Today many believers do not want to hear such a word of righteousness. Instead, they prefer sugar-coated messages.

Psalm 45 is not on the Father's love; that is, it is not on love in life but on love in affection. This is why this psalm is called a song of love.

In this message we will cover the first eight verses of this psalm. These verses are on the praise of Christ as the King from four directions: His fairness, His victory, His kingdom, and His virtues. First, the psalmist praises the King in His fairness (v. 2a), in His handsomeness. Christ is truly fair; He is really handsome.

Christ's fairness, however, is balanced by His victory (vv. 3-5). Many husbands who love their wives have fairness, but they do not have victory. Instead, they have defeat after defeat. Thus, they are not balanced. But Christ, having both fairness and victory, is balanced. Yes, He loves us, but, as the four Gospels reveal, He also exercises His victory with its requirements. Because of His victory, He has high requirements.

We see Christ's victory and His requirements not only in the Gospel of Matthew but even in the Gospel of John. For example, in John 15, a chapter which speaks about abiding in Christ, the Lord Jesus tells us that if we do not bear fruit, we will be cut off and lose the enjoyment of Christ (vv. 2, 6). Whereas all believers love Matthew 1:21 and 23, they may not appreciate 5:20, a verse which says that unless our righteousness surpasses that of the scribes and Pharisees, we will by no means enter into the kingdom of the heavens. Likewise, today's believers may not pay attention to the parable for faithfulness in Matthew 25:14-30. Verse 30 says, "Cast out the useless slave into the outer darkness. In that place there will be the weeping and the gnashing of teeth." The point here is that Christ's fairness is balanced by His victory with its requirements. Hence, in Psalm 45 fairness and victory are a pair.

A second pair in this psalm involves Christ's kingdom (vv. 6-7) and His virtues (v. 8). The kingdom is higher than the victory. Christ's kingdom is the issue of His victory. If there were no victory, there would be no kingdom. Victory produces the kingdom. Because Christ has won the victory, the kingdom belongs to Him. The matter of His kingdom, however, is balanced by the sweetness of His virtues. Therefore, in the praise of Christ as the King in Psalm 45, there are two balanced pairs: fairness and victory, kingdom and virtues.

Let us now go on to consider this psalm in more detail.

I. A SONG OF LOVE
ACCORDING TO THE MELODY OF LILIES

The superscription of this psalm calls it "a Song of Love," and this love is feminine. It is the love between us and the Lord. This love makes us His love. This means that if we are those who love the Lord, we eventually become His love, His favorite. Just as He is our love, so we become His love.

The subject of this psalm is love, and the tune, the melody, is called "lilies." Here both love and lilies refer to the saints. Every lover of the Lord Jesus is feminine and is also a lily. A lily denotes a pure, simple, single life of trusting in God. Our love for the Lord Jesus should be a love full of affection. We should not only have a life of purity and simplicity as signified by the lily, but we should always have an affectionate feeling toward the Lord. According to Psalm 45, we all need to have a pure life with an affectionate love for the Lord.

John Nelson Darby, who lived to be eighty-four and never married, had such a love full of affection. One night in his old age, he was staying alone in a hotel, and at bedtime he said, "Lord, I still love You." When I read about this, I was deeply touched, desiring to have such an affectionate love for the Lord Jesus. Now I can testify that, as an elderly person, I love Him much more than I did when I was young. Recently I had a time of intimate, affectionate prayer to the Lord regarding a certain matter, and in my prayer I told Him, "Lord Jesus, I love You." As I was praying, I fell in love with the Lord Jesus once again.

II. A PSALM OVERFLOWING
WITH A GOOD MATTER CONCERNING THE KING
BY THE TONGUE AS THE PEN OF A READY WRITER

Verse 1 says, "My heart overflows with a good matter; / I speak what I have composed concerning the King. / My tongue is the pen of a ready writer." This verse says that the psalmist's heart overflows; we may also say the psalm overflows. The two are actually the same thing.

For the psalmist's tongue to be the pen of a ready writer means that the psalmist does not need to write a draft of what will be spoken concerning the King. Real love for the King makes a draft unnecessary. Regarding many things we may need to write a draft, but to write a draft of what we want to say to someone we love would be altogether mechanical; it would not be real. If we have an affectionate love for the Lord Jesus, we will have the tongue of a ready writer. Instead of needing to write a draft, we will be ready to write our love and our praise.

III. PRAISING THE KING IN HIS FAIRNESS

In verse 2 the psalmist praises the King (signifying Christ) in His fairness. When the Lord Jesus comes to us, He comes first in the aspect of His fairness. This is why, when we preach the gospel, we need to preach mainly Christ's fairness, telling others how good and loving Christ is. We may say that this kind of gospel preaching is a "hook" with a tasty "bait." Everyone who believes in the Lord Jesus and loves Him has been "hooked" by Him. Blessed are they who have been hooked by Christ! As one who has been hooked by the Lord, I often say to Him, "Lord Jesus, You have caught me. You have captured me. If I had not been captured by You, I would be a different person living a different life."

Now the One who has come to us in His fairness, the One who has caught us and who loves us, wants us to love Him in return. We need to love Him and even become His love. This is the issue of Christ's showing us His fairness and of our enjoyment of Christ in His fairness. It is impossible for us to speak in full concerning Christ's fairness.

A. Fairer than the Sons of Men

According to verse 2a, as the King Christ is fairer than the sons of men.

B. Grace Being Poured upon His Lips

Verse 2b says, "Grace is poured upon Your lips." This indicates that grace continually proceeds out of His mouth. Concerning this, Luke 4:22 tells us that the people marveled at the words of grace proceeding out of the mouth of the Lord Jesus.

C. God Having Blessed Him Forever

In Psalm 45:2c the psalmist continues the praise of the King, saying, "Therefore God has blessed You forever." Because the man Jesus is fair, sweet, and full of grace, God has been moved to bless Him forever. Thus, Romans 9:5 speaks of Christ as "God blessed forever."

IV. PRAISING THE KING IN HIS VICTORY

In Psalm 45:3-5 we have the psalmist's praising the King in His victory. Adam and all his descendants, including us, have been defeated. Only Christ is the Victor. The Gospels reveal that He has overcome everything and has gained the victory.

A. As the Mighty One
Girding His Sword upon His Thigh
in His Majesty and Splendor

Verse 3 says, "Gird Your sword upon Your thigh, O mighty One, / In Your majesty and Your splendor." In the eyes of

Satan and of all the fallen angels, Christ is the mighty One who has girded His sword upon His thigh, the One with majesty and splendor. Both His majesty and His splendor are signs of His victory.

B. In His Splendor Riding On Victoriously Because of Truth, Meekness, and Righteousness

Verse 4a continues, "And in Your splendor ride on victoriously / Because of truth and meekness and righteousness." Splendor is the expression of glory. While Christ was on earth, the only time He showed His splendor was when He was transfigured on the mountain (Matt. 17:1-2). But after His resurrection and ascension, He showed Himself in His splendor and majesty to Paul (Acts 26:13-15) and to John (Rev. 1:9-20).

C. His Right Hand Performing Awesome Deeds

Psalm 45:4b says, "Let Your right hand teach You awesome deeds." Here we understand the word *teach* to mean perform. Christ has performed many awesome deeds, including His crucifixion, resurrection, and ascension. The most awesome deed performed by Christ was His crucifixion. Christ's crucifixion was a great event that threatened Satan, the demons, and the fallen angels, the powers of darkness in the air. The cross of Christ is the most awesome thing in the universe. Whereas we appreciate the cross, Satan flees from it.

The Lord Jesus did many awesome things during His life and ministry on earth. Actually, everything He did was awesome. For example, His boldness in rejecting His natural relationship with His mother was awesome (Matt. 12:46-50). Likewise, His way of dealing with Peter in Matthew 17:24-27 was awesome. Peter spoke presumptuously concerning Christ's paying the temple tax, which was equal to a half-shekel (vv. 24-25a). After Peter did this, the Lord corrected him. Eventually, as part of His correction of Peter, He said to him, "Go to the sea and cast a hook, and take the first fish that comes up. And when you open its mouth, you will find a stater [equal to one shekel]; take that and give it to them for

Me and you" (v. 27). Because Christ is the Creator, He could do such an awesome thing. Everything the Lord Jesus does, whether great or small, is awesome.

D. His Arrows Being Sharp in the Heart of His Enemies

Psalm 45:5 goes on to say that the King's arrows are sharp and that the peoples fall under Him. His arrows are in the heart of His enemies.

V. PRAISING THE KING IN HIS KINGDOM

In verses 6 and 7 the psalmist praises the King in His kingdom. We have pointed out that the kingdom is the issue of the victory. Hence, before one can be a king, he must first be a victor. According to the ancient custom, the person who was victorious over the enemies became the king.

A. As God His Throne Being Forever and Ever

As God Christ's throne is forever and ever (v. 6a; Heb. 1:8a).

B. The Scepter of His Kingdom Being Upright

"The scepter of uprightness is the scepter of Your kingdom" (Psa. 45:6b). The scepter signifies authority. The authority of many of today's high officials is not upright, but Christ's authority is altogether upright.

C. Loving Righteousness and Hating Wickedness

As the King Christ has loved righteousness and hated wickedness (v. 7a; Heb. 1:9a). The more righteous we are, the more authority we have. However, the more we are involved with wickedness, the more we lose our authority.

D. God, His God, Having Anointed Him with the Oil of Gladness above His Companions

Psalm 45:7b continues, "Therefore God, Your God, has anointed You / With the oil of gladness above Your companions." The oil of gladness signifies the Spirit of God, and the companions signify the believers of Christ. God the Father has anointed Christ with the Holy Spirit above all His companions, above all His believers. This indicates that Christ's authority and kingdom are altogether a spiritual matter. He has been anointed for the purpose of the kingdom. Christ's authority, throne, scepter, and everything related to the kingdom are under the anointing of the Spirit and therefore are spiritual.

VI. PRAISING THE KING
IN THE SWEETNESS OF HIS VIRTUES

In verse 8 the psalmist praises the King in the sweetness of His virtues. Regarding Christ's virtues, 1 Peter 2:9 speaks of telling out "the virtues of Him who has called you out of darkness into His marvelous light." When we preach the gospel, we tell others what Christ has done for us and what He is doing for us today. To preach the gospel is actually to tell forth the many virtues of Christ, including His love, kindness, and forgiveness.

Christ's virtues are the expression of the divine attributes. For instance, with God the Father the divine love is an attribute of the Godhead. This attribute is in the divine life. As Christ lives out the divine life, He lives out the divine attribute of love. In Christ's living there is the virtue of love, and this virtue is the expression of the divine attribute of love. As we preach the gospel, we should tell others about the attributes of God expressed in the virtues of Christ.

A. All His Garments Smelling
of Myrrh and Aloes and of Cassia

Psalm 45:8a says of Christ the King, "All Your garments smell of myrrh and aloes, of cassia." A person's garments signify the virtues of that person, because the way we dress is an expression of the kind of person we are and indicates our attitude and demeanor. For this reason, we can know something about a person by the way he dresses. Actually, as human beings we are under two kinds of covering—our clothing and dwelling place, both of which express what kind of person we are. Here in Psalm 45 garments signify Christ's virtues; myrrh and aloes signify the sweetness of

Christ's death; and cassia signifies the fragrance of Christ's resurrection.

B. From Palaces of Ivory
Harpstrings Having Made Him Glad

Verse 8b says, "From palaces of ivory harpstrings have made You glad." In this verse palaces signify local churches; ivory signifies the resurrection life of Christ (John 19:36); and harpstrings signify praises. The local churches, which are beautiful in the eyes of the Lord and which are His expression, are built with the resurrection life of Christ, and from the local churches are the praises that make Him glad. As we praise the Lord, we need to appreciate what He is in His virtues and what He has done to produce the church to be His expression. In a very real sense, Christ's garments, His virtues, have produced the church as His expression, and both His garments and the church are full of sweetness. May we all learn to praise Him more, especially at the Lord's table.

LIFE-STUDY OF THE PSALMS

THE PSALMISTS' INTENSIFIED ENJOYMENT OF GOD IN HIS HOUSE AND CITY THROUGH THE SUFFERING, EXALTED, AND REIGNING CHRIST

(3)

PRAISING CHRIST AS THE KING

(2)

Scripture Reading: Psa. 45:9-17

Psalm 45 can be considered the sixth station in the unveiling of Christ in the Psalms. The first station is Psalm 2; the second is Psalm 8; the third is Psalm 16; the fourth is Psalms 22—24; and the fifth is Psalm 40. In this message on Psalm 45 we will consider verses 9 through 17. Before we come to these verses, however, I would like to say a word concerning the Bible and the way to understand it.

The Bible is a very particular, special, strange, and wonderful book. Because the Bible is such a book, it cannot be understood by the natural human mind. If we try to understand the Bible according to our natural mind, we will not have the proper understanding. Of course, in order to understand the Bible, we must exercise our mind. However, we should exercise not the natural mind but the renewed, enlightened mind. If we would understand the Bible, we must have a mind that is renewed and enlightened, that is, a mind whose understanding is under the divine light. Therefore, when we study the Bible, we should pray that the Lord will renew our mind and enlighten it.

If we do not have a renewed and enlightened mind, we will have trouble when studying Psalm 45, especially verses 9 through 15, which are about praising the king in the praising

of the queen with the daughters of kings and with the virgins.
We may be bothered by the fact that this king has so many
women with him. The Bible teaches us that a man should
have only one wife, and in the New Testament Paul tells us
that an elder should be "the husband of one wife" (1 Tim. 3:2).
But the king in Psalm 45 seems to be like a heathen king who
has a great many wives and concubines. As we will see, what
we have in this psalm is a matter not of ethics but of typology,
and to understand this type we need a renewed, enlightened
mind.

Regarding the interpretation of the Bible, especially the
book of Revelation, there are two schools. According to the
first school, the book of Revelation should be understood
literally. Those who follow this school say the New Jerusalem
is a physical city. According to the second school, Revelation
should be understood symbolically, since some items of its
content are revealed by "signs" (1:1b). Those who follow this
school say that as the golden lampstands are symbols of the
churches, so the New Jerusalem is also a symbol, a sign.

The Bible contains many symbols and types. We may
regard these symbols and types as pictures or "photographs."
The reason for the photographs in the Bible is that the Bible
unveils many heavenly, spiritual things, and these things are
invisible and mysterious. The photographs in the Bible help
us to understand such things.

An example of a biblical symbol or photograph is the tree
of life in Genesis 2 and 3. What is the tree of life? In the
Bible the tree of life is not actually a literal tree. Rather, the
tree of life is a symbol of God as the source and reality
of life. This means that the tree of life is a symbol of God as
life.

Other symbols in the Old Testament are types of the
church. The first of these types is Eve, the wife of Adam (Gen.
2:18-23). From Ephesians 5 we know that the relationship
between husband and wife portrays the great mystery—
Christ and the church. Without the picture of Eve as the
counterpart, increase, and enlargement of Adam, we would
not realize that the church is the counterpart, increase, and

enlargement of Christ. Thus, we need the type of Eve to symbolize what the church is to Christ.

The Old Testament also uses the tabernacle and the temple as symbols to unveil another aspect of the church. Eve, the tabernacle, and the temple are all photographs of the church. The church is not only Christ's counterpart, symbolized by Eve, but also God's house, God's dwelling place, symbolized first by the tabernacle and then by the temple. If we did not have these two symbols, we would not understand many of the details concerning the church being God's dwelling place. From this we see that the biblical way is to use symbols to portray spiritual things, and we need to keep this in mind as we come to Psalm 45.

Psalm 45 was written in praise of King Solomon, who was a symbol, a type, of Christ with a wife composed of many "daughters," of many believers. If God had no need of a king to symbolize Christ in this way, Solomon would not have been created. The Bible clearly reveals that God's intention is that a man have only one wife, yet Solomon had hundreds of wives (1 Kings 11:1, 3). As far as Psalm 45 is concerned, we should understand this not ethically but typically. Ethically, Solomon should not have had many wives. Typically speaking, however, there was the need for a man with hundreds of wives so that God would have a particular type of the church composed of many believers from many nations. Solomon with his wives is a type of Christ with His corporate wife, a wife composed of believers from every tribe, tongue, people, and nation (Rev. 5:9).

Solomon did not follow God's regulation about having only one wife, and many readers of the Bible would condemn him for this. Nevertheless, in Psalm 45, written in praise of Solomon, Solomon is a type of Christ as the One with a corporate wife. If we would understand this, we need a mind that is renewed and enlightened with spiritual understanding. This is the reason I have pointed out that we should not come to this psalm with our natural mind. The natural mind is of no avail in understanding Psalm 45.

If we are enlightened and renewed, we will realize that Psalm 45 is lovable. First, in verses 2 through 7, this psalm praises the king, Solomon, in his fairness, in his victory, in his kingdom, and in the sweetness of his virtues. After this, the psalmist continues by praising the king in the praising of his queen. The queen is not alone but is accompanied by the daughters of kings (v. 9) and by the virgins, her friends (v. 14). If we view this as a type, we will see that the king typifies Christ, that the queen typifies the church, and that those around the queen typify the believers. In type, this queen is not a single, individual person—she is corporate. The believers are the constituents, the components, of this corporate queen. Actually, the believers are both the constituents of the queen and the honorable and beautiful women.

The situation is the same in Revelation 19:7 and 9a. Verse 7 says, "Let us rejoice and exult, and let us give the glory to Him, for the marriage of the Lamb has come, and His wife has made herself ready." This verse speaks of the wife of the Lamb. However, verse 9a says, "Blessed are they who are called to the marriage dinner of the Lamb." This verse speaks of those who are invited to the Lamb's marriage dinner. When I was young I was troubled by this, believing that the wife is the church but not understanding much about the overcomers. Actually, the wife, the bride of Christ, here is not the church but the overcomers. Then who are the invited ones, the guests? The guests also are the overcomers. This means that, on the one hand, the overcomers are the bride and that, on the other hand, they are the guests. We may say that the bride is composed of the guests. First the overcomers are the corporate bride, and then they are also the guests. In Psalm 45 the bride of Christ is typified by the queen, and His overcoming guests are typified by the honorable women around the queen. The bride of Christ, therefore, is actually the group of overcomers. We need to have this understanding as we study Psalm 45.

In this psalm we see the praise to Solomon as a type of Christ, the King appointed by God to rule over His people and over the entire universe. The praise here is marvelous. It praises Christ not only concerning the things that are of Him directly—His fairness, victory, majesty, kingdom, and sweetness—but also concerning the things that are of Him indirectly through His church and His overcomers. Since the overcomers are Christ's members, whatever is of them directly is of Him indirectly and is His glory. Thus, the fairness of Christ in this psalm is of two layers: the first layer, the layer that is of Himself directly, and the second layer, the layer that is of His Body, His members, directly and of Him indirectly.

With such an understanding as a foundation, we come now to verses 9 through 17 of Psalm 45.

VII. PRAISING THE KING
IN THE PRAISING OF THE QUEEN
WITH THE DAUGHTERS OF KINGS
AMONG THE KING'S MOST HONORABLE WOMEN
AND THE VIRGINS, THE QUEEN'S COMPANIONS

In verses 9 through 15 we have the praising of the king in the praising of the queen with the daughters of kings among the king's most honorable women and the virgins, the queen's companions.

A. The Daughters of Kings
Being among the King's Most Honorable Women

Verse 9a says, "The daughters of kings are among your most prized [honorable]." The daughters of the kings signify the believers of Christ in their royalty, and the king's most honorable (or, glorious) women signify the believers of Christ in their honor and majesty. Not only does the king have honor and majesty, but the queen and the women around her also have honor and majesty. This is a type, a picture, of the church with the believers.

In the New Testament we have a clear word concerning the church and the believers. Paul exhorted us to behave in a way that matches our status. For instance, in Ephesians 4:1 he beseeches us to walk worthily of the calling with which we were called. However, Paul's word of exhortation cannot compare with the revelation regarding our status as believers given in the type in Psalm 45. Do you realize that, as a believer, you are one of "the daughters of kings"? We all, males and females, are daughters of kings because we have been born of the King and thus are of the royal family. We need to realize that Psalm 45 speaks about us. If we have this realization, we will say, "Lord, I am one of the daughters of the King, one of the honorable women. I have royalty, honor, and majesty. I am not an ordinary person." This is our status as believers.

If we are conscious of our royal status, our behavior will be changed and our character will be uplifted. We will not sell ourselves cheaply and we will not fight or quarrel with others, but will behave ourselves more honorably. Then, as a husband and wife, will we argue, behaving like "scorpions"? If we realize that we are royal people, our behavior will surely be affected by our understanding of the mysterious, spiritual, and heavenly things, the things which are related to the invisible scene in the universe.

In Psalm 45 we have some features of the spiritual scene that are not found in the New Testament. This is why we need the types, the symbols. I wish to emphasize the fact that in this psalm we have a strange and wonderful type of Christ—the type of a man with hundreds of wives. Remember, this symbol is a matter not of ethics but of typology. With respect to typology, there was the need for Solomon and his many wives. For this reason, God created Solomon and appointed him to be the king above all the kings. God even created the princesses who were to come from Egypt and other nations to be Solomon's wives. God did all this so that in the Bible there would be this particular type of the church composed of the believers to be the corporate wife of Christ.

From this Old Testament type we see that the believers are Christ's counterpart. In one sense, He is the King and we are the queen, His wife. In another sense, we are the components of the queen. These components are signified by the many virgins, the queen's companions. Since in verse 14 the words "virgins" and "friends" are in apposition, they refer to the same persons. According to the type, this signifies that the queen here is not an individual; rather, she is corporate, and all her companions are her components, with whom she is constituted and composed to be the wife of Christ the King.

The proper way to understand Psalm 45 is to understand it according to typology. If we understand the type, we have the key to understanding the entire psalm. However, apart from understanding the type, we have no way to understand this psalm, and the more we read it, the more we will be led into a "forest."

Understanding Psalm 45 according to typology, we see that the King is Christ. Christ has only one queen, a corporate queen composed of the overcomers. The components of this queen are believers, but these believers are not the defeated ones. If they were defeated ones and not overcoming ones, they would not be honorable or majestic. I hope that we all will be among the overcomers and thus be components of the bride of Christ.

B. The Queen Standing
at the King's Right Hand in the Gold of Ophir

Verse 9b says, "The queen stands at your right hand in the gold of Ophir." The queen signifies the church, and her being covered with gold signifies the church's appearing in the divine nature. This gold that covers her is Christ. In 1 Corinthians 1:30 we are told that God has made Christ to be righteousness to us for our justification, for us to be justified by God. As our righteousness, Christ is our covering. This covering is altogether divine. Christ is pure gold, "the gold of Ophir." This is the first layer of our covering.

C. The Daughter Hearing and Seeing
and Forgetting Her People
and Her Father's House,
and the King Desiring Her Beauty

Verse 10 goes on to say, "Hear, O daughter, and see; and incline your ear; / And forget your people and your father's house." The daughter is the queen, who signifies the church, and her father's house signifies the natural relationships of the church. This word about the daughter's forgetting her people and her father's house corresponds to the Lord's word about denying the natural relationships (Matt. 10:37; Luke 14:26) and caring for the church. Throughout the centuries, many believers have been persecuted by their family.

Psalm 45:11a continues, "Thus the king will desire your beauty." The queen's beauty here signifies the virtues of Christ expressed through the church. The beauty of the church, her beauty in the presence of Christ, is Christ's virtues lived out of us.

D. Worshipping the Lord

"Because he is your lord, / Worship him" (v. 11b). This signifies that as the Lord of the church Christ is worthy not only of her love but also of her worship.

E. The Daughter of Tyre Coming with a Gift, and the Rich among the People Entreating Her Favor

"The daughter of Tyre will come with a gift; / The rich among the people will entreat your favor" (v. 12). Tyre, a seaport, was a flourishing, commercial center known for its riches. Here the daughter of Tyre signifies the people of the flourishing world. The rich among the people signify the high class. The rich have great wealth, but they do not have what this verse calls "favor." The favor they entreat of the queen signifies the grace of God enjoyed by the church. The grace of God which we have in the church is the real favor. As indicated by this verse, the rich will come to the church to obtain the grace of God.

F. The King's Daughter Being All Glorious within the Royal Abode

Verse 13a says, "The king's daughter is all glorious within the royal abode." The king's daughter is the queen signifying the church, and her being all glorious within the royal abode signifies the glorious church taking Christ as her royal abode.

The word "abode" here refers to the church's taking Christ as her abode. First we, the believers of Christ, take Christ as our abode, and then we become His abode. This means that the abode becomes the abode. Christ becomes an abode when we take Him as our abode, abiding in Him, and thus become His abode in Him. Concerning this, the Lord Jesus said, "Abide in Me and I in you" (John 15:4a). This indicates that if we take Him as our abode, we become His abode. In this way the abode becomes the abode.

This abode is a matter of experiencing Christ through the church. Christ, as the Son, is an abode to the Father and the Spirit, and His being such an abode involves the coinherence among the three of the Divine Trinity—the Father, the Son, and the Spirit. But when we believe in Christ, we enter into Him and take Him as our abode. Then, being in Him as our abode, we, the church, become His abode.

G. Her Garment Being of Woven Work Inwrought with Gold

"Her garment is a woven work inwrought with gold" (Psa. 45:13b). This signifies that the Christ who has been dealt with through death and resurrection is the righteousness of the church to meet the righteous requirement of God for her to be justified before God. Thus "woven work inwrought with gold" again refers to the first layer of her covering—Christ as our righteousness through whom we are justified—signified by the gold of Ophir.

H. She Being Led to the King in Embroidered Clothing

"She will be led to the king in embroidered clothing" (v. 14a). This embroidered clothing, another garment, the second layer of her covering, signifies that the church will be led to Christ at their marriage clothed with the righteousnesses of the saints to meet the requirement of Christ for their marriage.

Regarding this, Revelation 19:8 says, "It was given to her [the overcomers as the Lamb's wife] that she should be clothed in fine linen, bright and clean; for the fine linen is the righteousnesses of the saints." The word "righteousnesses" refers to Christ as our subjective righteousness, Christ lived out of us. The righteousness (Christ) that we received for our salvation (1 Cor. 1:30) is objective and enables us to meet the requirement of the righteous God, whereas the righteousnesses of the overcoming believers are subjective (Phil. 3:9) and enable them to meet the requirement of the overcoming Christ. If we would have these righteousnesses, we must have Christ Himself lived out of us to be our subjective righteousnesses. Thus, the queen in Psalm 45 has two garments. The first garment, the gold of Ophir, the woven work inwrought with gold, corresponds to Christ as our objective righteousness, which is for our salvation. The second garment, the embroidered clothing, corresponds to Christ as our subjective righteousnesses, which are for our victory.

I. The Virgins behind Her, Her Friends, Being Led to the King

Psalm 45:14b says, "The virgins behind her, her friends, / Will be led to you." This signifies that the overcoming saints will be invited to the marriage dinner of Christ (Rev. 19:9).

J. The Virgins Being Led with Rejoicing and Exultation and Entering the King's Palace

"They will be led with rejoicing and exultation; / They will enter the king's palace" (Psa. 45:15). This signifies that the overcoming saints will enter, with rejoicing and exultation, the New Jerusalem as Christ's palace (Rev. 3:12).

As we read this psalm, we need to pay attention to the crucial points concerning Christ and the church. One crucial point is the matter of the abode and the palace. First we have the abode and then the palace. When Christ becomes our abode, we become His abode—a mutual abode. Because Christ is the King and we are the queen, eventually this mutual abode becomes the palace, which signifies the New Jerusalem.

What is the New Jerusalem? In brief, the New Jerusalem is the redeeming God wrought into the believers and mingled with them to be one entity. The church today is such an entity, for, like the New Jerusalem, the church is actually the redeeming God wrought into the believers and mingled with them to be a single entity. Today the church is a miniature of the coming New Jerusalem. In eternity in the new heaven and new earth, the New Jerusalem will be the consummation of the church. Therefore, both the church and the New Jerusalem are the Triune God Himself wrought into us and mingled with us to be one entity. This entity is a mutual abode; it is both our dwelling place and God's dwelling place.

In the New Jerusalem, a mutual abode, God will dwell with His redeemed people for eternity.

VIII. PRAISING THE KING
IN THE PRAISING OF HIS SONS

Thus far in Psalm 45 we have seen the praising of Christ in Himself and the praising of Christ in the praising of His church, of His redeemed. Now, in verses 16 and 17, we have the praising of the king in the praising of his sons, his descendants. Here, the sons of the king signify the members of Christ. On the one hand, as believers, we are the members of Christ; on the other hand, we are the sons, the descendants, of Christ.

A. The King's Sons Being
in the Palace of His Fathers,
and the King Making Them Princes
in All the Earth

"In the place of your fathers will be your sons; / You will make them princes in all the earth" (v. 16). Here "fathers" signifies Christ's forefathers in the flesh, and "sons" signifies the overcomers of Christ. The word "princes" signifies the overcomers of Christ reigning with Christ over the nations.

No one can solve the problems of today's world. Only Christ the King can solve these problems. When Christ reigns on earth, the overcomers will be His helpers in the kingship, His co-kings. The sons of Christ, the overcomers, will be the princes reigning with Christ over the nations.

We need to see not only the beauty of Christ that is in Christ Himself and the beauty of Christ that is in the church but also the beauty of Christ that is in all His descendants, all His members, as the princes. If we see Christ's beauty in these three ways, we will have a complete view, the full picture, of His beauty.

B. His Name Being Remembered
in All Generations, and the Peoples
Praising Him Forever and Ever

Finally, in verse 17 the psalmist says, "I will cause your

name to be remembered in all generations; / Therefore the peoples will praise you forever and ever." This reveals that Christ's name will be remembered in all generations through the overcoming saints and that Christ will be praised by the nations through His overcoming and co-reigning saints.

LIFE-STUDY OF THE PSALMS

MESSAGE TWENTY-TWO

THE PSALMISTS' INTENSIFIED ENJOYMENT OF GOD IN HIS HOUSE AND CITY THROUGH THE SUFFERING, EXALTED, AND REIGNING CHRIST

(4)

PRAISING GOD IN HIS GREATNESS AND EXALTATION PARTICULARLY IN HIS CITY

Scripture Reading: Psa. 46—48

In our study of the Bible, we need to learn to ask questions of the Lord, and we should do this as we come now to Psalms 46—48. We should ask why these three psalms are placed immediately after Psalm 45, a psalm praising king Solomon (typifying Christ) with his queen (typifying the church). If you were the compiler of the Psalms, would you have put these psalms right after Psalm 45?

Psalm 46 does not seem to be a continuation of Psalm 45. However, there is definitely a continuation here. Psalm 45 is on the king, and Psalm 46 is on the city. Surely the king has much to do with the city. If a king did not have a city, what kind of king would he be? A king must have a city. The king in Psalm 45 typifies Christ, but what is the city mentioned in Psalm 46? This city is Jerusalem.

In the previous message we pointed out that in studying the Bible, we need an enlightened and renewed mind. When we study a psalm such as Psalm 45, we should not have any trust in our natural understanding or our natural concept. Instead of relying on our natural mind, we need to exercise our renewed and enlightened mind.

In addition, if we would understand the Bible, we also need to know the spiritual, divine, and heavenly significance of the things in the Bible and the significance of the things concerning Christ. As we study Psalm 45, for instance, we must find out the spiritual significance of the king, the queen, the daughters, and the sons. Likewise, as we study Psalm 46, we must find out the spiritual significance of the city.

The Bible was written not only in letters, and it not only contains many types, but it is a book filled with matters that have a spiritual significance. Consider the first two chapters of Genesis. If we read Genesis 1 and 2 only according to the letters without caring for the spiritual significance, we will not understand these chapters. As we study chapter one, we need to learn the significance of the heavens, the earth, the light, the land emerging from the water, the vegetable life, the animal life, the human life, the divine life, and the matters of image and dominion. If we know the significance of the items in Genesis 1, we will see that man was created according to God's kind to bear God's image and to represent Him.

As we go on to Genesis 2, we see that the man created by God is tripartite. He has a body, made from the dust of the ground; he has a spirit, the issue of the breath of God; and he has a soul (v. 7). The man thus formed by God was put in a garden in Eden and placed before two trees—the tree of life and the tree of the knowledge of good and evil. This chapter also speaks of the river that went out of Eden and of gold, bdellium, and onyx stone. Furthermore, in Genesis 2 we are told that God took a rib out of the man and used it to make a woman. All these things have a spiritual significance, and we need to know this spiritual significance.

The city in Psalm 46 has a spiritual, divine, and heavenly significance. In the Bible as a whole and in this psalm in particular, a city signifies a kingdom. The primary city in the Bible is Jerusalem, and a city that stands in opposition to Jerusalem is Babylon. If we would understand the Bible, we need to understand the significance of both Jerusalem and Babylon.

The Psalms are full of matters that have a spiritual, divine, and heavenly significance. The first matter of significance is the law in Psalm 1. Although the law was exalted according to the human concept of the psalmist, the Spirit came in to correct the psalmist and, in Psalm 2, to turn him from the law to Christ. Psalm 2 is the first station of the unveiling of Christ in the Psalms. Other stations are Psalm 8, Psalm 16, Psalms 22—24, Psalm 40, and Psalm 45.

Through Christ and by Christ we experience the house of God, another matter of spiritual significance in the Psalms. The house of God signifies the church. According to Psalm 23, as we experience Christ in His shepherding, we are brought into the house of God to dwell there forever. The house of God is also emphasized in Psalm 27 and again in Psalm 36. In Psalm 27:4 the psalmist aspires to dwell in the house of Jehovah all the days of his life. In Psalm 36:8 the psalmist speaks of the fatness (signifying the abundance) of God's house, where there is the fountain of life and where we see light in God's light.

In Psalm 31 we have a word concerning the city, and in Psalm 24, a word concerning the mountain, which implies the city. Psalm 31:21 says, "Blessed be Jehovah, / For He displayed His lovingkindness wondrously / To me in a fortified city." Psalm 24:3 speaks about the mountain of Jehovah. In Matthew 5:14b the Lord Jesus says, "It is impossible for a city situated upon a mountain to be hidden." This indicates that, according to the Bible, the mountain is for the city. Book One of the Psalms has turned the psalmists from the law to Christ, and Christ has brought them to the enjoyment of God in His house and city.

In my opinion, Psalm 45 is the greatest and highest psalm concerning Christ. In this psalm Christ, typified by Solomon, is unveiled and praised as the King. Immediately afterward, Psalm 46 goes on to speak not of the house but of the city. The house is a place of dwelling, but a city is a kingdom for ruling. As the One unveiled as the King in Psalm 45, Christ needs a city in which to rule and reign, and we see this city in Psalm 46. We may enjoy Christ as the King, and this King reigns in the city, which is His kingdom. If we are clear regarding this, we may now consider, from Psalms 46—48, the matter of praising God in His greatness and exaltation, particularly in His city.

I. A RIVER GLADDENING THE CITY OF GOD

Psalm 46 speaks concerning a river gladdening the city of God.

A. God Being Our Refuge, Strength, and Help

God is our refuge, strength, and a help in distress; He is most readily found (v. 1). God is all this to us in the city. Therefore, even though the earth changes and the mountains slip into the heart of the sea, we will not fear (v. 2). In verse 3 the psalmist says, "Let the waters of the sea roar and foam; / Let the mountains shake at its swelling."

B. There Being a River Whose Streams Gladden the City of God, the Holy Place of the Tabernacle of the Most High

"There is a river whose streams gladden the city of God, / The holy place of the tabernacles of the Most High" (v. 4). This river signifies the flowing of the Triune God as life to us, as mentioned in Revelation 22. The streams of this river gladden the city of God, which is the holy place of the tabernacles of the Most High.

C. God Being in the Midst of the City to Be Our High Retreat

God is in the midst of the city to be our high retreat (Psa. 46:7b, 11b). The city will not be moved; God helps her at the dawn of morning (v. 5b). In verses 6 and 7 the psalmist says, "The nations rage; the kingdoms are moved. / He utters His voice; the earth melts. / Jehovah of hosts is with us; / The God of Jacob is our high retreat." In the city we enjoy God as our place of retreat.

D. God Making Desolations on Earth

God has made desolations on earth, and He makes wars cease unto the ends of the earth (vv. 8-9). Throughout the centuries, God has made many desolations on earth. For example, He made Hitler a desolation.

E. God Being Exalted
among the Nations on Earth

"Be still and know that I am God. / I will be exalted among the nations; I will be exalted on earth" (v. 10). This is a word to the nations. Today the nations are raging, but one day God, who rules and reigns in the city, will command them to be still and know that He is God.

II. A GREAT KING OVER ALL THE EARTH

In Psalm 47 the psalmist speaks concerning God as a great King over all the earth.

A. The Peoples Clapping Their Hands
and Shouting to God
with the Voice of a Triumphant Sound

In verse 1 the peoples are told to clap their hands and shout to God with the voice of a triumphant sound. For Jehovah Most High is awesome; He is a great King over all the earth (v. 2).

B. God Subduing Peoples under Israel
and Choosing an Inheritance for Them

Jehovah subdues peoples under Israel and nations under their feet. He also has chosen an inheritance for them as the excellency (glory) of Jacob, whom He loved (vv. 3-4).

C. God Arising amidst Shouting
at the Sound of a Trumpet

"God arises amidst shouting; / Jehovah, at the sound of a trumpet" (v. 5). When we shout, God arises. If we do not shout, God may not arise.

D. Singing Psalms to Our King

Next, the psalmist charges us to sing psalms to God our King. He is the King of all the earth, reigning over the nations and sitting upon His holy throne (vv. 6-8).

E. Those Who Are Noble among the Peoples Being Gathered with the People of the God of Abraham

Verse 9 goes on to say that those who are noble among the peoples have been gathered with the people of the God of Abraham. The shields of the earth belong to God; He is greatly exalted.

III. THE CITY OF THE GREAT KING

Psalm 48 is about the city of the great King.

A. Jehovah Being Great and Much to Be Praised in the City of Our God, in His Holy Mountain

"Great is Jehovah, / And much to be praised / In the city of our God, / In His holy mountain" (v. 1). In this verse "city of our God" and "His holy mountain" are in apposition. This indicates that the city is the mountain and that the mountain is the city.

B. Mount Zion Being Beautiful in Elevation

Mount Zion, the sides of the north, the city of the great King, is beautiful in elevation. It is the joy of the whole earth (v. 2).

Verse 3 says, "God has made Himself known / In her palaces as a high retreat." The city signifies the church, the universal church, but the palaces in the city signify the local churches. God has made Himself known in the palaces, in the local churches. Thus, if we want to know God, we need to come to the local churches, which are a high retreat. First, God Himself is a retreat, and then the local churches become a retreat. The local churches today are a retreat. If you need a retreat, come to the local churches.

C. The Kings, Having Assembled Themselves to Pass by the City Together, Seeing It and Being Astounded and Dismayed

"Behold, the kings have assembled themselves; / They passed by together. / They saw; therefore they were astounded. /

They were dismayed; they hurried off in alarm" (vv. 4-5). The kings here are the enemies, who are astounded and dismayed at seeing the city and who hurry off in alarm. They are seized by trembling and writhing, like that of a woman in labor (v. 6).

D. God Establishing the City Forever

"As we have heard, / So we have seen / In the city of Jehovah of hosts, / In the city of our God. / God will establish it forever" (v. 8). God will establish the city forever.

E. Considering God's Lovingkindness in the Midst of His Temple

The psalmist continues by saying that we consider God's lovingkindness in the midst of His temple. As His name is, so is His praise unto the ends of the earth (vv. 9-10). "Let Mount Zion rejoice; / Let the daughters of Judah [the people of Judah] exult / Because of Your judgments" (v. 11).

F. God Being Our God Forever and Being Our Guide Even unto Death

"Walk about Zion, and go around her; / Count her towers. / Consider carefully her bulwarks; / Pass between her palaces; / That you may recount it to the generation following" (vv. 12-13). Towers and bulwarks are for fighting the enemies to protect the city, and palaces are for the king's dwelling. All these indicate the functions of the church. We should walk around the church, count her "towers," consider carefully her "bulwarks," and pass between her "palaces" that we may recount it to the following generation.

"For this God is our God forever and ever. / He will guide us even unto death" (v. 14). Here we see that God is our guide, even our tour guide. Our human life is a tour, and we are tourists who do not know where to go or how to get to our destination. We need a guide, and our guide is God Himself. He will continue to guide us until we die and go to Paradise.

Where do we experience God's being our guide? He is our guide in the church, both in the universal church, the Body of Christ, and in the local churches. We do not know what our next step should be, but He is directing our steps. We do not know where to go, but He is guiding us, the tourists, on our tour of human life. Since God will continue to guide us even unto death, there is no need for us to worry. Instead, we should simply enjoy His presence, guidance, and direction.

God's guidance is an aspect of the enjoyment of God in the city. This enjoyment of God is through Christ, in Christ, and with Christ, and it is in the church and in the local churches—in the universal church as the Body of Christ and in the local churches as the expressions of the Body.

In Psalms 46—48 God is our refuge, our retreat, and our guide. The God whom we enjoy through Christ, in Christ, and with Christ in the church and the local churches is our refuge, retreat, and guide. Have you experienced and enjoyed Him in this way? At present, our experience may be limited, but we thank the Lord for the new "shoots" and "branches" of such an experience of God in Christ that are springing forth. May we all learn to enjoy God in Christ in the church and in the local churches.

Thus far in our life-study, we have covered forty-eight psalms. In which psalm do you intend to linger? Will you stay in Psalm 1 or go to enjoy Christ in Psalm 2, Psalm 8, Psalm 16, and Psalms 22—24? The Christ we enjoy in Psalm 23 is the Shepherd, the One who is shepherding us into the house of God, the local church. Eventually, when we are built up, strengthened, and enlarged, the church becomes the city, the kingdom of God, where the King rules and reigns.

The Psalms indicate that we first need to experience Christ. Then Christ will lead us to the local church to enjoy God. As the house, the church is God's home, the place of His dwelling. As the city, the church is God's kingdom, the place of His ruling. When the church, the house, is enlarged it becomes the city—the kingdom for God's ruling and reigning. In the church as the house, we enjoy God in the aspect of His dwelling. In the church as the city, we enjoy God in the aspect of His ruling and reigning. This is the enjoyment of God in Christ in the church and in the churches.

LIFE-STUDY OF THE PSALMS

MESSAGE TWENTY-THREE

THREE CATEGORIES OF PERSONS
REGARDING THE ENJOYMENT OF GOD IN CHRIST

Scripture Reading: Psa. 49—51

In studying the Psalms, we need to pay attention to the sequence of the psalms and also to how the psalms are arranged in groups. We have seen that Psalm 45 is a psalm concerning the king and that Psalms 46—48 are a group of psalms concerning the city of the king, Jerusalem. In this message we will consider another group of three psalms—Psalms 49—51.

Psalms 49—51 cover three categories of persons regarding the enjoyment of God in Christ. The first category (Psa. 49) consists of those who trust in their wealth (that is, in anything other than Christ). In the second category (Psa. 50) are those who call upon the Lord according to His covenant. The third category (Psa. 51) is a single person, King David, repenting, confessing his sins to God, and asking God for His purging. Those in the first category have no share in the enjoyment of God in Christ; those in the second category participate in the enjoyment of God; and the one in the third category has a full portion of the enjoyment of God in Christ. We need to ask ourselves where we are. Are we in Psalm 49, Psalm 50, or Psalm 51? If we want to have the full enjoyment of God in Christ, we must be like the one in Psalm 51, the one who thoroughly repented and confessed his sins to God.

I. THOSE TRUSTING IN THEIR WEALTH

Psalm 49 is about those who trust in their wealth (anything other than Christ). According to the Lord's word, in this age wealth, which is mammon, represents the entire world (Matt. 6:24). Some people think that money can do anything; they believe that as long as they have money, they do not need anything else. Instead of trusting in God, they trust in money. They are the ones in Psalm 49.

The word in Psalm 49 should be a warning to us. To trust in money—to trust in anything other than Christ—is to be in Psalm 49. Things such as our education or car may be a kind of wealth, or treasure, to us. If we trust in such things, we have no share in the enjoyment of God in Christ.

A. A Word of Wisdom

Psalm 49 is a word of wisdom, the meditation of understanding (vv. 1-5). In verse 3 the psalmist says, "My mouth will speak wisdom, / And the meditation of my heart will be that of understanding." The Hebrew word translated "meditation" may also be rendered "utterance."

To love money is to be foolish. A person who is lacking in money may be very sober, clear, and full of understanding. However, a person who has a great deal of money is likely to be foolish and use his money to do foolish things. Likewise, those who are greedy and covetous also are foolish. Such persons do not have the wisdom and understanding found in Psalm 49.

B. Unable to Redeem Their Brothers

Those who trust in their wealth are unable to redeem their brothers, needless to say themselves (vv. 6-9).

C. Appointed to Die and Perish

The ones who trust in their wealth are appointed to die and perish (vv. 10-14). They will leave their wealth to others (vv. 16-20). The psalmist, on the contrary, has the assurance that God will redeem his soul from the power of Sheol, for God will receive him (v. 15).

Those who trust in their wealth are not only foolish and senseless (v. 10) but are also likened to animals, even to beasts. Verse 12 says, "But man in honor does not remain; / He is like the beasts that perish." Verse 20, the last verse of the psalm, concludes, "A man in honor but without understanding / Is like the beasts that perish." Like the beasts, the foolish ones who trust in their wealth are appointed to die and to perish.

D. Not Trusting in Christ
for Their Redemption

Those who trust in their wealth do not trust in Christ for their redemption. The worst thing a person can do is not to trust in Christ. To trust in Christ simply means to believe in Him. It is most foolish not to believe in Christ.

E. Having No Share
in the Enjoyment of God
in His House and in His City

Finally, the ones who trust in their wealth have no share in the enjoyment of God in His house and in His city. Because they are outside of Christ, they are excluded from the enjoyment of God in His house, the church, and in His city, the kingdom.

II. THOSE CALLING UPON THE LORD
ACCORDING TO HIS COVENANT

In Psalm 50 we have the second category of persons regarding the enjoyment of God in Christ—those who call upon the Lord according to His covenant. To call upon the Lord, saying, "O Lord Jesus," makes a very real difference in our situation.

According to this psalm, we need to call upon the Lord according to His covenant. The Bible is the book of a covenant, the book of a testament. A covenant may be compared to the title deed to a house. To give someone the title deed to a house is actually to "covenant" the house to that person. In the Bible, a book of covenant, God has covenanted Himself to us, and now we need to call upon the Lord according to this covenant. We should say, "O Lord, You have covenanted Yourself to me. According to Your covenant, You are now my possession, my portion, and my enjoyment." This is to call upon the Lord according to His covenant.

A. As the Saints of God,
Who Have Made
a Covenant with God by Sacrifice

In this psalm, those who call upon the Lord according to His covenant are the saints of God who have made a covenant with God by sacrifice. They have been charged by the righteous God, who is Judge, to offer Him a sacrifice of thanksgiving and to call upon Him in the day of trouble that they may participate in His deliverance, His salvation (vv. 1-15, 23). To make a covenant with God by sacrifice is to make a covenant by Christ as our Mediator, as the "middleman" between us and God. If we pray to God in the name of the Lord Jesus, this means that we pray to God by Christ as our sacrifice.

In ancient times the people of Israel offered different kinds of offerings to God, such as the burnt offering, the meal offering, the sin offering, the trespass offering, and the peace offering. Of all these offerings, the one that was the most touching to the hearts of the people was the peace offering. Because the peace offering touched the heart of the one who offered it, it became a thanksgiving offering. One could offer to God a burnt offering, a meal offering, a sin offering, or a trespass offering without much affection. This means that one could offer such an offering without his heart being touched. However, whenever a person, being thankful to God, offered a thanksgiving offering to God, that person's heart was touched.

Psalm 50 tells us that some of the saints of God were offering burnt offerings and other kinds of offerings (vv. 8-13), but, because they were lacking in affection, they would not offer the thanksgiving offering. Thus the psalmist, speaking for God, indicated that what God wants is not the burnt offering but the thanksgiving offering. In verse 14a the psalmist says, "Offer to God a sacrifice of thanksgiving." Here the psalmist seemed to be saying, "God does not want your burnt offering. God wants you to offer Him your thanksgiving offering, an offering that is touching to both you and God, an offering full of affection."

We need to consider this in the light of our experience with the Lord. Many of us have prayed in this way: "O God the Father, I am a sinner. The Lord Jesus Christ is my burnt offering, sin offering, and trespass offering." This is a prayer without affection, without tender feeling. This indicates that we can offer certain offerings without being touched in our heart. Suppose, however, that after passing through a time of trouble, you pray, "O God the Father, I would like to offer to You my thanksgiving." Such a prayer touches your heart, fills you with affection, and causes you and God to become intimate.

Which experience is better—to offer the burnt offering, the meal offering, the sin offering, and the trespass offering, or to offer the thanksgiving offering? Surely the experience of offering the thanksgiving offering is better. We may offer Christ as the other kinds of offerings without being deeply touched. But when we are thankful to God and offer to Him a prayer of thanksgiving, we may be deeply touched. This is what God wants. We should not contact Him without being touched in our heart. Rather, our contact with God needs to be full of affection and tender feeling.

In verses 16 through 22 we have God's warning to the wicked, who are not included in the category of those who call upon the Lord according to His covenant.

B. Redeemed by God in Christ

Those who call upon the Lord according to His covenant are those who have been redeemed by God in Christ, typified by the sacrifices.

C. Enjoying God in His Shining Forth
out of His House in Zion, the Perfection of Beauty

Verse 2 says, "Out of Zion, the perfection of beauty, / God shines forth." Just as the shining of the sun is a dispensing of the sun's goodness, so the shining forth of God out of His house is a dispensing of His goodness. Under such a shining, such a dispensing, we enjoy God in Christ.

This is the second category of persons regarding the enjoyment of God in Christ. I believe that most of us are in this category.

III. A PERSON REPENTING,
CONFESSING HIS SINS TO GOD,
AND ASKING GOD FOR HIS PURGING

In Psalm 51 we have the third category—a person repenting, confessing his sins to God, and asking God for His purging. In the life of each one of us, there needs to be a period of time, perhaps lasting for several days, in which we thoroughly repent, confess our sins to God, and plead with Him to deal with our sins and with our sinful nature. Furthermore, day by day we need to repent and confess.

A. David, after Committing His Great Sin and Being Rebuked by the Prophet Nathan

The title of Psalm 51 is significant: "A Psalm of David, when Nathan the prophet came to him, after he had gone in to Bath-sheba" (2 Sam. 11:1—12:14). This indicates that this psalm was composed after David's great sin in murdering Uriah and robbing him of his wife Bath-sheba and then being rebuked by the prophet Nathan.

B. Repenting and Confessing His Sins to God

In verses 3 through 5 and 17 David repented and confessed his sins to God.

C. Begging God

1. To Blot Out His Transgressions, Wash Him Thoroughly from His Iniquity, Cleanse Him from His Sin, and Purge His Sin with Hyssop

David begged God to blot out his transgressions, wash him thoroughly from his iniquity, cleanse him from his sin, and purge his sin with hyssop (vv. 1-2, 7, 9). The verbs used by David—"blot out," "wash," "cleanse," and "purge"—indicate that his repentance and confession were thorough and that his asking for forgiveness was genuine.

In contrast, suppose someone would pray, saying, "God, I know that You are merciful. No matter how many sins I have committed, I know that You will forgive me." This kind of confession does not mean anything. Like David, we need to stay in the presence of God, confessing that we were born in sin and pleading with Him to wash us and cleanse us, to blot out our transgressions, and to purge our sin. To pray in this way indicates that we have no trust in ourselves. Realizing that we are sinful and that God is holy, we trust only in Him. Also, we realize that we need Christ to be our Mediator and our sacrifice.

In verse 7a David prayed, "Purge my sin with hyssop, and I will be clean." Hyssop typifies Christ in His humble and humiliated human nature (1 Kings 4:33a; Exo. 12:22a). In Psalm 51:7a hyssop implies Christ as the Mediator and the sacrifice.

2. To Create in Him a Clean Heart and Renew a Steadfast Spirit within Him

In verse 10 David prayed, "Create in me a clean heart, O God, / And renew a steadfast spirit within me." The Hebrew word for "clean" here may also be translated "pure." David begged God not only to forgive him and purge him but also to renew him.

By sinning we become old, but after we are forgiven by God we may be renewed. Thus, after we enjoy God's forgiveness, we need to ask Him for His renewing. We need to pray that He will give us a pure heart and a steadfast spirit.

3. To Not Cast Him from His Presence and Not Take the Spirit of His Holiness Away from Him

In verse 11 David continued, "Do not cast me from Your presence, / And do not take the Spirit of Your holiness away from me." We need a new heart and a steadfast spirit, and we also need God's presence. If we lose God's presence, we lose everything. God's presence is actually the Spirit. When the Spirit is away, God's presence also is gone.

4. To Restore to Him the Gladness of His Salvation and Sustain Him with a Willing Spirit

In verse 8a David prayed, "Let me hear gladness and joy,"

and in verse 12 he asked, "Restore to me the gladness of Your salvation, / And sustain me with a willing spirit." Here we see a connection between gladness and willingness of spirit. When we are happy, we also have a willing spirit. This is the overcoming life. A defeated person, on the contrary, is unhappy and does not have a willing spirit. If such a defeated one confesses his sin and asks God for His forgiveness, he will have the gladness of God's salvation and will also have a willing spirit. It is by the gladness of God's salvation that a willing spirit is sustained within us.

5. To Deliver Him from the Guilt of Bloodshed

Finally, in verses 14 and 15 David begged God to deliver him from the guilt of bloodshed that his tongue may ring forth His righteousness and his mouth may declare His praise.

D. Participating in the Enjoyment of God in His House and in His City through the Offerings on the Altar

"Do good in Your good pleasure unto Zion; / Build the walls of Jerusalem. / Then You will delight in the sacrifices of righteousness, / In burnt offerings and whole burnt offerings; / Then they will offer sacrifices of bullocks upon Your altar" (vv. 18-19). This signifies the participation in the enjoyment of God in the local church as God's house and in the church as God's city through the all-inclusive Christ as the offerings. If we are those who repent, confess our sins, and ask God for His purging, we will have the enjoyment of God in Christ in His house, the local church, and in His city, the universal church. This is related to God's favoring of the local churches and the building up of the universal church. May this be our practical experience day by day.